Cinema Futures

Film Culture in Transition

Thomas Elsaesser: General Editor

Double Trouble
Chiem van Houweninge on Writing and Filming
Thomas Elsaesser, Robert Kievit and Jan Simons (eds.)

Writing for the Medium: Television in Transition
Thomas Elsaesser, Jan Simons and Lucette Bronk (eds.)

Between Stage and Screen
Ingmar Bergman Directs
Egil Törnqvist

The Film Spectator: From Sign to Mind
Warren Buckland (ed.)

Film and the First World War
Karel Dibbets and Bert Hogenkamp (eds.)

A Second Life
German Cinema's First Decades
Thomas Elsaesser (ed.)

Fassbinder's Germany
History Identity Subject
Thomas Elsaesser

Cinema Futures: Cain, Abel or Cable?

The Screen Arts in the Digital Age

edited by

Thomas Elsaesser and Kay Hoffmann (EIKK)

AMSTERDAM UNIVERSITY PRESS

This publication has been made possible thanks to a financial contribution
by Cinematheek Haags Filmhuis, The Hague

Cinematheek HAAGS FILMHUIS

and the editorial and financial support of the European Institute for Cinema
Culture (EIKK), Karlsruhe

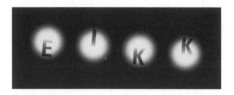

Cover illustrations: Front: Promotion still IMAX 3D. Photo John Madere.
Back: Images of Louis Lumière's WORKERS LEAVING THE FACTORY (1895).
Coll. Haus des Dokumentarfilms, Stuttgart
Cover design: Korpershoek Ontwerpen, Amsterdam
Typesetting: JAPES, Jaap Prummel, Amsterdam

ISBN 90 5356 282 6 (hardcover)
ISBN 90 5356 312 1 (paperback)

Table of contents

Preface

Thomas Elsaesser and Kay Hoffmann

In the late 1960s, cinema was pronounced dead. Television, like a biblical Cain, had slain his brother Abel, bewitching the mass audience and provoking an exodus – East of Eden – from the movie houses to the living rooms. Some thirty years later, a remarkable reversal: rarely has the cinema been more popular, as inner-city multiplexes record rising attendances, and more film festivals are held in Europe alone than there are days in the year. Nonetheless, rarely has the European cinema's future seemed more uncertain. Of all films shown on commercial screens 70-80% come from Hollywood, launched with publicity campaigns costing more than the total budget of most European films. Television, the independent cinema's chief financier for the past decades, cannot match these investments, nor can it compete, even if it wanted to, with the barrage of special effects, the roller coaster rides of ever more spectacular sensations, or rival with the blockbusters that double also as video-games. The New Media, virtual images, the relentless 'digitization' of reality, it is argued, are responsible for the global concentration of production, which in turn leads to the global uniformity of the products. Just as Cain and Abel were about to bury their differences, along comes Cable to 'resolve' them both into mere snowstorms of pixels.

Beyond the hyperbole and the metaphors, *Cinema Futures: Cain, Abel or Cable?* presents a more careful, but also more forceful argument about the pitfalls of predictions made when new technologies appear. The computer has replaced the manual typewriter but it did not do away with the keyboard. Television did not swallow radio, just as it did not replace the cinema. Yet each new technological medium changes the place of the others in society and profoundly affects not only their function, but the way we think about their history. What do such precedents as cinema and television tell us about the future of the screen arts in the digitial age, and in particular, about the future of 'the experience' of cinema, as it redefines itself across private media consumption in the home – thanks to television, video-games or the internet – and in public, next to shopping malls, theme parks, tourist sites and other entertainment complexes?

Examining the dynamics of convergence and divergence among the audiovisual media from such a broader vision of technological change, the authors in this collection are, it seems to us, realistic in their estimate of the future of the cinema's distinctive aesthetic identity, and robustly optimistic that the different social needs which audiences bring to both the public and domestic media will ensure their distinctiveness, opening up new cultural spaces and chances for new creative input. Special attention is, of course, given to the questions of 'digital cinema' and 'interactive narratives'. The chief contributors include filmmaker Edgar Reitz, screenwriter Mick Eaton, media historians Siegfried Zielinski and Brian Winston, media theorist Lev Manovich, avant-garde filmmaker Grahame Weinbren, television theorist John Ellis, film historian Pierre Sorlin, as well as producers, critics, academics and journalists from Switzerland, The Netherlands, Germany and Italy. Their views make for a volume of many voices, rich in information and case studies, useful to media students and film scholars, as well as anyone interested in better understanding the momentous changes transforming our worlds of sound and image.

Cinema Futures: Cain, Abel or Cable? is a collaborative effort in more senses than one. The idea first arose after an international symposium organized by Rien Hagen and GertJan Kuiper at the Cinematheek Haags Filmhuis, The Hague in 1993. They deserve our warmest thanks for making available the transcript of papers. In EIKK, the European Institute for Cinema Culture in Karlsruhe (Germany), an enthusiastic partner was found, with its staff contributing both materially and intellectually. Special thanks go to its deputy director, Professor Lothar Spree. Finally, the Department of Film and Television at the University of Amsterdam was generous in allowing one of the editors time off in order to complete the volume.

Our chief thanks, of course, go to the contributors, their quick response to our requests, their patience and, finally, their expertise. Among the other names whose help and support we gratefully acknowledge, special mention should be made of Sofie Bosma, Warren Buckland, Anne-Marie Duguet, GertJan Kuiper, Patricia Pisters, Joachim Polzer, Jan Simons, Femke Wolting. The translations are by Sofie Bosma, Catherine Brickwood, David Hudson, Françoise Pyszora and Daniela Sohst.

Permission to reprint previously published material has been kindly given by Ars Electronica, Linz; Verlag der Autoren, Frankfurt; Heise Verlag, Munich; The Soros Foundation, Moscow.

Amsterdam, January 1998

Cinema Futures: Convergence, Divergence, Difference

Thomas Elsaesser

The media are no longer competing with each other, they exist side by side. [...] The history of art of the last 180 years has shown that the spectrum has extended itself without a single medium having become obsolete. Television did not kill off the cinema. Both are vying with each other, but the prediction that we'll all have 2 x 2 meter screens in our living rooms which would do away with the cinema has not come true, at least not yet. Likewise, computer graphics will not necessarily make draftsmanship redundant. It would be a very silly idea of progress indeed to assume that the new media replace the old media. In this discussion around the old and the new I always maintain that you need the historical perspective, in order to have a yardstick for what is happening today and tomorrow.

(Heinrich Klotz, in Florian Rötzer, ed., *Digitaler Schein* (Frankfurt: Suhrkamp, 1991, p. 361)

Must There Be Convergence?

Among the changes the computer and the telephone have brought to areas of life previously unaffected, the innovations in sound and moving image technology are probably not the most decisive.[1] Yet, as the 'information revolution' rolls on, transforming the way we communicate, work and entertain ourselves, 'deregulated' television and the internet have become the most visible indices, at once reflecting and embodying shifts in consciousness, and greatly aiding the impression of an increasingly 'mediated' or even 'mediatized' reality. In the process, television's older 'brother', the cinema seems to have been overshadowed, if not altogether eclipsed as a subject of public concern or debate. And yet, cinema has always been also a metaphor for much that extends beyond individual films and movie theatres. André Bazin called it the ancient dream of mankind for its double, its mirror: the creation of an imaginary self alongside the physical self, and a way of preserving that other self – the 'Mummy Complex'.[2] In its relatively brief history of a hundred years, the cinema has thus become more than the sum of the films made for public projection, but it is also less than the sum of the fantasies the culture projects into the moving image. Trying to seize this something-both-more-and-less of cinema at the threshold of the 'digital age' is one of the purposes of this book, and the task of this introduction.

How does the cinema, for instance, maintain its place as a prime attraction? Can it hold its ground among the public spaces and private occasions where cinema, television and digital media are competing with each other for audiences? Is there such a thing as 'digital cinema', and how innovative can the cinema in this respect be as an art form or a technology of sound and image reproduction? Before one can answer such questions, there is a more fundamental one. Do cinema, television, video and digital media belong together at all? When one compares them, on what basis and by which criteria? If there is a family resemblance, what are the bonds keeping them together as well as the feuds that keep them apart? This was the theme of a conference, held in The Hague in November 1993, under the title *Cain and Abel?*, and several of the essays below were first presented there.[3] The question mark suggested that there were doubts whether the relation between cinema and television – for this was the focus of the Hague meeting – could be thematized under such a metaphoric title, borrowing the biblical story of the rival brothers, of whom one ended up slaying the other.

Yet the two names are not just followed by a question mark; they should also be in quotation marks, since the reference is itself borrowed from Jean-Luc Godard. Chalked on a blackboard by his fictional alter-ego, Paul (Jacques Dutronc) in SAUVE QUI PEUT...: LA VIE (1980), the slogan 'vidéo et cinéma = Cain et Abel' is itself part of a dialogue Paul has with the writer/filmmaker Marguerite Duras. Godard, we might infer, was at the time reflecting on what turned out to be a crucial move in his work, namely to confront cinema (the photographic image and montage) with video (magnetic tape, synthesizer sound and electronic editing). The director's motives were many, and included the economic necessity of a 'marginal' and avant-garde artist to appropriate for himself the cheapest and most compact audiovisual technology available, in order to remain at once a working film-producer and 'independent'.

The technological and economic horizon which Godard's move alludes to is crucial to the media kinships discussed, irrespective whether they turn out to be dominated by sibling rivalry, generational succession, incest or parricide (all suggestions made in the papers presented). In the non-metaphoric realm, the forces of convergence and 'synergy' are economic and demographic, determined by multi-national company policy and the quest for global audiences. Since the early years of this century, the audiovisual media have (apart from military uses) always developed primarily as mass-produced commodities in a sector of the economy – the leisure, culture and information industries – which has seen quite exponential growth after World War II, with an accelerated pace of change during the past twenty years. Convergence in this sense is entirely under the sign of capitalist concentration, merger and cartelization: the result are the mega-media-empires of the 1990s: Time-Warner and Ted Turner's CNN, Rupert Murdoch's News International and Fox Television, or European media

1) *Imprint and trace of the real? Film as a photographic medium, materially related to the represented: Louis Lumière's* WORKERS LEAVING THE FACTORY *(1895).*

2) *Different media converging, merging and superimposed: Photographers recording a fashion show, reproduced as a video image in a big screen movie: A production still from* NOTEBOOK OF CLOTHES AND CITIES *(1989) by Wim Wenders.*

giants like Bertelsmann, Silvio Berlusconi and Leo Kirch. In short, what is holding the audio-visual, print and electronic media together is first of all their common social base: the mass-market consumer, targeted by a huge and still hugely expanding service industry.

Not all the implications of 'late capitalism', this 'untranscendable horizon'[4] also of our thinking about the media are quite that obvious. Consider the technologies of image generation and sound production, or of their distribution and delivery. These have all undergone such major upheavals that any sort of kinship or family resemblance from cinema to television to digital media looks like arranged marriages made not in heaven but beamed from a satellite-infested sky. Even apart from their basic technologies, the media just named differ widely in their institutional histories, their legal frameworks and social practice: the cinema came from serial photography, and depended on advances in cellulose production, as well as perfecting the transport mechanism of the sewing machine. Demographically, it grafted itself on the music hall and vaudeville houses, and aesthetically on the magic lantern and the stereoscope as popular entertainment. Television depended on the technology of the cathode-ray tube, it shares most of its institutional history with radio, and took quite some time to decide whether it was 'armchair theatre', an electric variety programme, or an instrument of state-controlled political consensus-building. Video is technically an extension of the audio-tape, itself a wartime invention, while the internet, as we know, exploits the combination of the computer and the telephone: developed by the US military, it became a mass-medium thanks to university scientists and research scholars, and its institutional forms are hotly contested between law-makers, business interests and defenders of global, if not millennial egalitarianism. Multi-media, virtual reality, telepresence and digital sound have their own serendipitous and leap-frogging histories, so that it requires some feat of the synthesizing imagination to conceive of them as belonging together, let alone, as sharing a common evolutionary ladder. And yet, such is the impact of this 'information revolution' that we now tend to think them 'naturally' linked.

Video is the starkest example of a seemingly total reversal from a distinct technology with the potential for a unique aesthetics, to an almost wholly commercial, standardized social function. Think of how the video camera and the video tape, their versatility and low cost, was to have made everyone an artist-producer, or open up television to 'the people' by giving 'access to all' and thus create an alternative public sphere.[5] In the end, what has remained of these political programmes and emancipatory dreams are the domestic video recorders on stand-by for the football game, the pre-recorded video casettes for the adult movies, rented for the weekend or kept

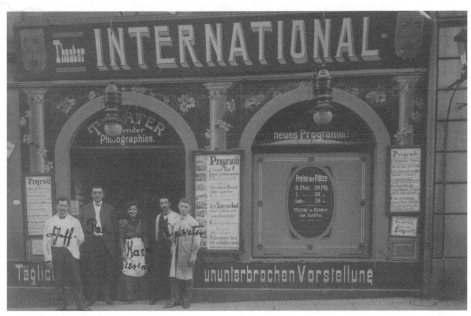

3) The conversion of shop-front cinemas to Nickelodeons, quickly taking hold in the early years of the century, announced permanent screenings of 'living photographs', as well as promoting an international image – even in Germany.

4) Video stores started in the 1980s also as small shops. Soon, they too may become anachronisms, as the concentration on blockbusters makes specialized outlets obsolete: the 'New York Video-Point' in Stuttgart.

in the sideboard next to the camcorder family videos from weddings, holidays, births and anniversaries.

Responsible for this clutter of electronic gadgets and software around home entertainment is 'digitization', that is, the technology that converts the analogue image, sound or text into a uniform signal of digits and bits which it stores and transmits electro-magnetically or optically. Indifferent to the nature of the source, the electronic signal only 'rematerializes' at the point of reception, once it has passed through the dedicated interfaces of screen, monitor or amplifier. Industrial concentration appears to mirror technological convergence, as the digital revolution creates media-empires and homogenizes the 'content' or 'products' these have to offer. But we need to be extremely sceptical about such an argument: the digital in this account functions more like a 'symbolic flag-pole'[6] around which media gurus, politicians and pundits can rally. Not only does it risk confusing cause and effect, it also conflates several very distinct processes. As the filmmaker George Lucas (who ought to know) famously phrased it: 'Digital is like saying: are you going to use a Panavision or an Arriflex [camera]? Are you going to write with a pen or on your little laptop? I mean, it doesn't change anything.'[7] Digitization is in fact a contradictory factor: there is no denying that in the film industries it is significantly altering the relation between production and post-production, input and output. But it has not by itself changed the way films are made, nor how viewers understand them. Neither, however, is digitization quite as neutral: to stay in Lucas' vocabulary, it could be argued that it has replaced the camera by the pen. Yet instead of handling like a pen, it works like a brush, but instead of using paint, the digital signal is more like electronic putty. At the same time, to blame this putty for the death of our notion of what is real or true is a claim greatly exaggerated.

In order to understand what the new media mean for the cinema as it enters its second century, we have to take the longer view. Each medium not only has its own history, it also requires its own technological and cultural 'archaeology'. We need to ask, for instance, what the cinema's early years teach us about media transitions generally, what 'pertinent facts' we have selected or omitted to construct its history, or conversely, what 'dead-ends' may reveal themselves as having been 'ahead of their time'.[8] In this respect, quite a few apparently peripheral technologies and their cultural contexts played a more central part in early cinema than the history books tell us, and perhaps this history ought more correctly be rewritten as an archaeology of cinema's possible futures. For one need not dig very deep to notice that filmmaking practice at the turn of the century was often informed by ways of thinking, by techniques of representation or traditions of image-making that cast a more enigmatic light on *why* the 'pioneers' did *what* they did, and therefore tell us that we may understand their legacy in very different ways. The essay on 'Louis Lumière – the cinema's first virtualist?' tries to track down some of the perhaps too hastily discarded questions to which this godfather of cinematic realism might have intended his films to be the answer.

Similarly, Lev Manovich's essays on the archaeology of the computer screen and the history of representational technologies argue that virtual reality and virtual presence are nothing new. He, too, notes that the early period of film history, before the classical paradigm, already had a very good idea of what an immersive visual environment might look and feel like, while the history of maps, architectural drawing, X-rays and the radar screen give us a very cogent pre-history of simulation, interactivity and telepresence.

These genealogies and proto-histories only underscore the media's distinctiveness, a fact often recognized, and valorized as such, not only by artists. The promised diversity also led to practical experiments, even in the case of television, often judged the most 'second-hand' among the mass-media, considering its debt to radio, journalism, the performing arts. Vito Zagarrio's essay makes a good case for an archaeology of the many other kinds of television we nearly had or might have had, during the 1940s and 1950s. Others have written elsewhere about the pioneers of television in different countries: Anne-Marie Dugay, for instance, has helped rediscover Jean-Christophe Averty in France, who is often referred to as the 'Méliès of Television'.[9]

These multiple histories or parallel universes of television never quite intersect with that of video-art which is a far better documented world, from the moment Nam Jun Paik picked up the first portable video-recorder at the Sony laboratory around 1963.[10] By entering the gallery spaces, video-art guaranteed itself recognition and legitimacy, and thus also a history, its critical discourses secured by the presence of a Bill Viola, Gary Hill or Lynn Hershman, original artists and distinctly innovative, whose interventions and body of work have written video into modern art up to this day, alongside pop, happenings, as well as contemporary painting, sculpture and installations. But this is perhaps a double-edged achievement: having made its pact with the gallery, performance spaces and installation art, video stayed aloof from the mainstream, keeping a cautious truce with the art market and museum culture (which often enough tried to exclude them), while fighting shy of the entertainment supermarket of popular culture (which, familiar with the basic technology in the form of the camcorder, might have enjoyed its often ingenious and witty exhibits). The fine art label was both its strength, preserving a genuinely experimental dimension, and its weakness, in that video now has to redefine its own place, faced with what is arguably an entirely different configuration, as digital art and the CD-ROM enter the museum in the form of art-work *and* commodity, and permanent collections look like becoming 'real-time' extensions of the museum shop.

What happened to each medium's specificity in its 'modernist' or avant-garde phase, is therefore only one side of the story. For finally, those who proclaim a convergence among the visual and electronic media are not simply wrong. If too quick a reference to digitization obfuscates the issues rather than explains them, the pressures of convergence are still there, displaying a logic which may pre-date digitization as well as side-step it, but nonetheless emanates from changes in the nature of the public and the markets through which this public becomes visible, which include (the commercial advantages and technical possibilities opened up by) digitization. Even though the audio-visual media today reach not only millions of people, but reach them in very different life situations and social environments, this has not in itself either destroyed or fostered diversity. The proverbial 'market forces' did ensure that those media exposed to the mainstream had to bury their differences, so to speak. Irrespective of their histories or archaeologies, they have had to make common cause and develop along lines that also articulated their mutual interdependence. As some of the essays collected here show, the outcome is still controversial and far from self-evident. This is true of the relations between cinema and television, no less than in the case of video, split so drastically between the camcorder at home and the video installation in the museum. But if we add to cinema and video the computer, animation and graphics, we can also note a curious melding of the very old and the brand-new; skills of draftsmanship and techniques of modelling dating back a century or more are being 'rediscovered', making some unlikely candidates enter into different kinds of alliances. New ideas and services are generated across genres and even 'species' boundaries, as in the case of toy manufacturers offering virtual reality concepts to both Disney and the US military.[11] Which brings us back to the kinship wars of Cain and Abel, or at any rate, their metaphoric progeny in the digital age.

The End of Divergence?
Godard specifically contrasted cinema and video. And in this sense, the French-Swiss director's subsequent development – avoiding the fratricidal act by opting for cinema *and* video – is only logical, in that he succeeded in practically reinventing (a certain vision of) cinema across his bold, unusual

and unconventional use of video (and its electronic companion, sound) in films like PASSION, PRÉNOM CARMEN or HÉLAS POUR MOI.[12]

For most other filmmakers, the choice was between either cinema or television, a battle that dominated the debate about the future of cinema from the 1950s to the mid-1970s. Bucking the generally hostile trend, such classical filmmakers as Jean Renoir (LE TESTAMENT DU DR. CORDELIER, 1959) and Roberto Rossellini (LA PRISE DU POUVOIR PAR LOUIS XIV, 1966) threw themselves into the new medium, discovering ways of expanding their own work.[13] Ingmar Bergman was scathing about television in the 1960s, but went on to do some of his finest work, such as *Scenes from a Marriage* for television in the 1970s, conceding that television had made a certain kind of cinema (including his own speciality, the chamber-play) look terribly old-fashioned. A more typical reaction, especially on the part of the film industry, was to regard film and television as implacable enemies: 'not a single meter of film for television' used to be the slogan in the 1960s, for instance, of German film producers and cinema owners, fearing for their audiences, inexorably drifting away to television. In the decades that followed, heated arguments about screen size and picture quality, rapt attention and distracted viewing, about tv-dinners and the tyranny of the remote control, about 'amphibious' films and talking-heads drama have been put forward and quietly put aside.[14]

Since the 1980s, the relationship has, at least in Europe, reversed itself completely from the days of directors dismissing the small screen. Hardly a single feature film has been made in the last twenty years without television directly financing it, co-producing it or putting down an advance on the rights.[15] Even the US film industry reckons some 60% of its earnings via pay-tv, cable networks, broadcast television or the sale of pre-recorded videos, while most terrestrial television companies rely for a substantial part of their daily output on the extensive film libraries bought from Hollywood studios in the 1960s, or acquired by media retailers like Leo Kirch. Flops at the box-office can break even on cable television or in the videotheques, and many film companies now specialize in making 'through-to-video' films.[16]

There is thus no doubt that television has profoundly affected the cinema, in both obvious and more subtle ways. Conversely, big budget films, with star attraction and spectacular action scenes are the jewels in the crown of all mainstream television programming. In order to maintain its appeal to audiences as well as for cultural prestige, television relies heavily on the accumulated cultural capital of film history, nowhere more so than in the United States itself, while in the rest of the world film history is equated with Hollywood. In this respect, television shows off with goods it cannot itself afford to manufacture, while recycling what has become economically unprofitable in the film industry's primary market, the theatrical circuits. On the other hand, the fact that television needs to fill airtime and fill it with material both cheap to its programmers and known to its audiences, has given a second life to large tracts of an otherwise 'sunken' continent of cinema history, some of it having become part of the 'classic' repertoire with a firm place in film culture. Yet not everything is taken up by television, with the result that much has also dropped out of sight and mind altogether, making our collective visual memory a very selective one. This is especially true of European (art) cinema and documentaries.

Such a double-edged process of devaluation and revaluation, repetition and obscurity has many manifestations, not least a way of showing up in the 'real world'. It is in the nature of television's cultural logic that it claims the cinema as the past it would like to imagine was once its own, while film fantasies are what it dreams about as tv-heaven. But it is also part of the film industry's economic logic that it tries to profit from television's need to 'dream' the cinema, borrowing its genres, stories, locations and associations. What odd recognition effects this 'dream-logic' can at times produce is charted in the paper on *Fantasy Island* and the Warner Studio Tour.

The crossovers in the cinema-tv symbiosis can also run the other way, considering how far the cinema, in the last twenty-five years, has adopted one of television's most defining characteristics: episodic story-telling and open-ended narration in a series format. The serial format was first used in films of the 1910s and 1920s, in order to boost star personalities, but its structural function of building loyal audiences is more consistently exploited by television, hooking the viewer to the day-time soaps and prime time series with an intricate weaving of unfinished storylines. It is the open or ambiguous ending that mainstream Hollywood cinema since the 1980s has in turn copied, when following a box office success with sequels and even prequels, especially where characters and plots seem to be coming from the early history of television, as with STAR WARS, INDIANA JONES or BACK TO THE FUTURE. When switching back-and-forth between television programme and cinema film, which is the case of a cult classic like *Star Trek*, the impact on popular culture, via fanzines, conventions and the internet, clearly exceeds the series' presence on television, creating a spill-over effect into pop paraphernalia that has become the norm for blockbusters like BATMAN or television series like *The X-Files*.

The play of similarity and difference can, however, also be more subtle, as Pierre Sorlin shows in his essay comparing the frequency and function of the close-up in cinema and television. Noting that its comparative rarity in the 'classical' feature film stands in inverse relation to its visual impact and dramaturgical importance, Sorlin speculates on the significance of the fact that it is infinitely more common in television, but there serves a quite different purpose, not least of 'hailing' the spectator and 'refocusing' his/her distracted attention – the latter a problem quite alien to the director of a cinema film, counting on the more or less undivided concentration of his audience. What Sorlin's reflections about film aesthetics in the age of television also seem to point to is the fact that the European cinema's near-total dependence on television for funding, for primary distribution as well as for its cultural survival might imply that European art-cinema will have to engage more directly and more vigorously with Europe's very diverse popular cultures, as they have established themselves during the 1970s and 1980s, so that a filmmaker like Almodovar is at once distinctly Castilian (or 'Madrilenean'), but partakes as well in his country's (necessarily hybridized and internationalized) television culture, on which he has yet another perspective, that of a gay subculture using popular media clichés for comic or ironic self-representations. These have secured his films a like-minded, international public.

Several other essays also review the cinema *vs* television or cinema *and* television debate, not least to indicate where certain positions have become obsolete. John Ellis moves beyond the comparison of screen size or such tv-barbarisms as panned and scanned cinemascope films, to put the emphasis on the distinct ways film and television appeal to a public, and thereby create different kinds of public spaces, related to the screening conditions typical of each medium. Mick Eaton speaks primarily as a screenwriter, working at the interface of both media. He shows how in Britain, the single play has been television's attempt to grapple with the difficulties that professionals encounter when making films which they know to be destined for television as well as the cinema. Institutional constraints finely balance national differences, leading to frustrations but also to creative solutions, since to write visual drama is the crucial exigency in both modes.

This echoes Conrad Schoeffter's plea not to be blinded by appearances into thinking the differences between drama for the big screen and for television to be greater than they are. In 'Scanning the horizon: a film is a film is a film' he argues that both cinema and television know laws of drama. A good documentary on television has to obey certain rules that are not so dissimilar to the dramatic rules of big Hollywood productions. In this respect, the two modes, whether or not as media they are moving towards convergence, do share deep-structures at the level of 'syntax' or cognitive schemata.

If these essays suggest it might be an exaggeration to claim that cinema and television have 'resolved' their differences, they concur that the two have nonetheless found a way of cohabiting. The French critic Serge Daney once called film and television 'the old couple', arguing that in crucial matters of film style, such as travellings, off-screen space and continuity editing the cinema had been overrun by the telephoto zoom, by images without edges or frames ('the erogenous zones of cinema'), while television editing, rather than putting together a puzzle, is always busy breaking things up to make a puzzle. For him, the cinema has reinvented itself *after* television, but like couples who have been together for a long time, they are beginning to resemble each other – too much, for Daney's taste.[17]

Using an ecological metaphor, one might say that the two media behave more like parasite and host than siblings. With the classical feature film the rich nutrient from which the television viewer feeds, and television sustaining and supporting much European feature filmmaking, each lives off the other, even though it is not always clear who benefits most from the arrangement. Some might argue that the kinship metaphor does still apply, but to a family stained by incest and self-abuse. The example of *Star Trek*, of studio-tours and theme parks, but also of fashion, sub-cultures and lifestyles is a reminder of the well-aired but still murky subject of marketing and merchandizing, where the two media are indeed obliged not only to play in tandem, but to be part of wider networks and 'synergies' which (in the all-important youth market, for instance) bind movies and television into the music business and print media, and the audio-visual sector as a whole into the complex of leisure, tourism and entertainment industries. At this point, the picture gets too intricate for the dualism of the biblical reference or the family metaphor to be of much use, in the face of so many harsh commercial realities.

Generally, we assume that the emergence of the mass market has been bad for art, a brake on innovation, a muzzle for creativity. Yet this is at best a half-truth. The 'technological' argument suggests in fact also the reverse: the audio-visual industries have experienced such an innovatory boost because money could be made, because a huge market was ready and eager for such often highly innovative products and services as the walkman, the CD player, the video-game or the pre-recorded video cassette for rent or sale. The twin forces of convergence and diversity discussed above, when seen from the point of view of this consumer demand turn out to be also a stimulus to growth, to creativity and to the deployment of talent, albeit talent which may at first seem at odds with traditional notions of creativity and art.

Siegfried Zielinski's paper, for instance, shows how the principle of niche-marketing and flexible response production principles may in fact be adopted by film- and video-makers. His example comes from the work of German director Alexander Kluge who, after a lifetime as a filmmaker, has been prepared to exploit a loophole within commercial television, in order to create that counter-public sphere once talked about as the goal of access-television. Zielinski concedes that this is élite television, but squeezed between late night 'Men Only' magazines, and paid for by a Japanese advertising agency, it is guerilla television, nonetheless, and represents Kluge's whispered but audible protest against what he calls the 'industrialization' of consciousness, and the 'privatisation' of public opinion.

Documentary Truth – The Digital Age's First Casualty?

Alexander Kluge is a pre-eminent example of a director operating on what used to be called 'the margins' of fiction and documentary, fact and invented incident, the 'personal' documentary and the interventionist reportage. This strategy has become so dominant, however, that to speak of it as 'the margins' is clearly problematic. It has obliged makers and critics to look once more at the various practices of documentary, less from the (untenable) assumption that the real and the represented can ever be the same, but in order to define the traditional forms of documentary either within the more encompassing category of 'visual ethnography' or from the vantage point of the digital image. Martin Emele thinks it would be too facile to blame digitization for the loss of 'the original', while Kay Hoffmann's 'Documentary and the Digital' cites a well-publicised incident from 1996, when a German freelance reporter successfully sold staged news reports to television companies. It gives rise to more general reflections on the problems confronting both law-makers and programme-makers when – if only for economic reasons – the digital television image will be the (technical) standard and therefore also (so some fear) the standard of truth. Yet in the theoretical part of their argument both Hoffmann and Emele underscore that images have always been 'representations', and from their essays a nuanced but far from pessimistic case about the state of documentary emerges, emphasizing the gains in argumentative force that come with new techniques of visualization.

Such a perspective also alters our view of the history of documentary film. Exemplary in this respect is Brian Winston's new look at one of the most enduring genres that film and television are said to have in common – the socially committed documentary. Gathering information and evidence for a counter-public sphere in the 1960s, the underground movement, cinéma vérité and television fly-on-the-wall documentary all contributed to documentary occupying the moral and political high ground. But as Winston points out, contrary to orthodox film histories, the function of documentary films for cinema audiences has always been highly problematic, nowhere more so than with the Grierson school of documentary, the genre's

touchstone of responsible reporting. Showing how marginal – and politically ambiguous – a place such documentaries with a social brief inhabited
in the cinema, Winston exposes as complacent myth the view that television
is responsible for making documentaries disappear from movie theatres: on
the contrary, even the Grierson ethic always implied the sort of consensus
that only the regulated state television apparatus could be expected to provide.

Stan Lapinski and René van Uffelen, in their witty commentary 'From
Butterflies and Bees to ROGER AND ME' offer some complementary reflections about the documentary's brief history on the big screen in Europe.
Shortly after the war, a nature film could win a prize at the Cannes festival: a
notion that would stretch credibility today, were it not that documentarists
are increasingly producing (and audiences are appreciating) intriguingly
hybrid forms, spanning from the 'fake' documentary to the 'faction' film,
and including invisible narration as different as that of the 'participant observer', the 'found footage' compiler, and the outright faker: all utilizing at
once documentary methods, narrative or para-narrative forms, yet designed for the cinema experience, and aimed at the big screen audience
(even, at times, finding it).

From these essays, few of which depend on digitization for their examples and argumentation, it would seem that the case of documentary is a
pre-eminent example of an audio-visual practice that raises issues of ontology and epistemology, irrespective of the changes digitization might bring
to the already highly problematic status of the image as truth, evidence or
document. One other point worth stressing in this context, because it is also
attributed to digitization, is the position of the image as commodity. An often expressed worry concerns the increasingly 'privatized' nature of recorded images: the fact that most of them are 'owned' by large commercial
archives or communication corporations. It is feared that their accelerated
circulation in digitized form threatens to turn a common audio-visual heritage into merchandise, consumable, tradeable and expendable like any
other commodity. Access to information is indeed likely to be almost as
much of a political issue in the decades to come as how to manage the information overload will be an 'ecological' issue. But what exactly is taken as
proven when asserting that something has become a 'commodity'? It is true
that the commodity form disguises the mode of production (in the media,
usually highly paid, because highly skilled and specialized) and the ownership of the means of production (the multi-national media empires or more
rarely an individual like Bill Gates). The commodity does indeed 'eye' the
consumer, seducing him/her with its fake aura and fetishistic presence – a
phenomenon that cultural critics from T.W. Adorno to Walter Benjamin and

Jean Baudrillard have exhaustively analyzed.[18] But what this fetishism, by disguising the history and material conditions of its existence, also exhibits the more clearly are the 'symbolic' values the commodity partakes in, as sounds and images become icons of culture, addressing the viewer not only as buyer but as 'subject', in the play of recognition and desire, of mirroring and identification. The debate about the truth of the image and its commodity status are therefore ultimately two sides of the same coin: the nexus of image-sign-meaning into which the audio-visual media bind us.

This is the more relevant when one recalls what stands behind the media convergence brought about by the economic pressures of penetrating consumer culture. The drive to exploit new technologies within the mass-market generally leads to 'successful' commodities only where these shape themselves around symbolic as well as practical needs: I shop, therefore I signify. Even if such pressures lead to standardization of product and the monopoly of a small number of producers, it does not by itself preclude diversity manifesting itself elsewhere. Digitization may give the illusion that one single device can take on all the distinct entertainment needs in sound and image reproduction. But developments among the brand leaders of the electronics industry paradoxically point also in the opposite direction, namely towards diversification of production, greater flexibility in the assembly-line process and in product design, leading to customized goods and specialized services for smaller segments of the market, be these in response to regional or local differences, or in order to cater for a privileged or niche clientele.[19] As already alluded to, a kind of 'post-Fordism' has become as common in the visual media as it is in the Japanese-pioneered 'just-in-time' restocking process for car manufacture or the knitwear retail business, led by Benetton's famous direct feedback ordering and distribution system.

But is diversity and individual choice what the 'customer' of cinema wants? Could it be that the cinema is distinguished from other mass-market products not only by the fact that one pays for an experience rather than a material object, and thus for a particular kind of 'subjectivation' and 'address', but also by the fact that watching a film is also a gesture of sharing and participation, and thus a negotiated choice and a social act? Located in time and space, 'going to the cinema' is a practice that can mean many things, depending on a number of material conditions, embedding it in 'contexts' that may seem to have little to do with film as commodity or film as art object and self-contained visual text.

160   GRAUMAN'S CHINESE THEATRE, HOLLYWOOD, CALIFORNIA

5) Classical movie palaces from the 1920s and 1930s like Grauman's Chinese Theater in Los Angeles created a world of their own. In the 1980s, they were seen as the dinosaurs of the movie-business.

The Dictate of the Digital: Cain, Abel, Cable

These contexts are explored in the third section, where the 'digital' in the future of the cinema is at once central and peripheral. What the contributions suggest is that neither the economic nor the technical horizon of cinema is sufficient in itself for understanding the newness of the 'new media', nor do they give us the reasons why at least the American cinema's fortunes have revived so dramatically since the 1980s. Even if one foregoes an all too convenient cultural pessimism regarding Hollywood supremacy, the popularity of movies as mass entertainments reflects complex and even ambivalent developments in contemporary societies, of which the fact that the experience of subjectivity is penetrated by the commodity form is unquestionably one.[20] But however much the shock and speed of change tempt one to extrapolate undreamed of futures, or to give in to the new media's breathless hyperbole, one may do well to remember Bertolt Brecht's sarcastic remarks about radio from 1927. It was, he said, an 'invention [...] that society had not ordered':

6) *Yet like the prehistoric monsters, large cinemas are staging a come-back: Modern multi-plex theaters like the Cinedom in Cologne cross-breed the traditional theater culture with new sound and image technology.*

> Now that it is here, no-one bothers about the results; people stick to the 'possibilities'. The results of radio may be pitiful, but its potential stays 'unlimited'. Ergo, it is assumed that radio must be a 'good thing'.[21]

Are the digital media an innovation we have not ordered, and for which artists and filmmakers are now, even a little desperately, trying to invent uses and excuses? Several essays in the present collection are written by filmmakers, each one setting out to intervene both in the debate about digital media and in their practical developments. Grahame Weinbren, Martin Emele and Edgar Reitz all describe past or ongoing projects, while the essays by Lev Manovich, Ed Tan and Kay Hoffmann also reflect on the more general implications. They are in no doubt about the 'potential' of digital media, in archaeology or telecommunications, in interactive filmmaking, installation art, or simply in providing new delivery systems for that old favourite, the live action feature film. But they are also far from 'hyping' this potential.

Rather than summarize their arguments, I have chosen to enter the fray with an essay that follows through a number of points made above and, in the other essays I have contributed to the collection, to probe, from the perspective of university film studies, what else might be at stake when speaking of 'digital cinema'. Is it what the cinema's inventors had always wanted it to be? Is it a contradiction in terms? And if the digital will not change the cinema, is it at least a chance to comprehend it better? In order to be able to speak on my own behalf, and not as editor of the work of others, I have put these thoughts down as an argument in which the digital features as a 'tool' not for making movies in a new way, but for thinking about them in new ways. Concentrating on a few features of contemporary cinema that strike me as at once obvious and rather enigmatic, I want to treat the digital as a possible 'vanishing point', which it implicitly is in the collection as a whole. Hopefully, the different voices that follow convey a clear enough message of what especially the cinema might have in store, after television and in the digital age: what, in other words, are the cultural rather than technical conditions of a 'family reunion', a change of guard and generational shift, where all the terms, determinations and identities seem to be sliding, in fact are as slippery as the pun that Mick Eaton first gave us: 'Cable' squeezed out of 'Cain and Abel.' The point, however, is not how Cain and Abel continue on cable, but just as much how Cain or Abel live on *in* Cable, live on *as* Cable.

Towards an Archaeology of the Computer Screen

Lev Manovich

A Screen

Contemporary human-computer interfaces appear to offer radical new possibilities for art and communication.[1] Virtual reality (VR) allows us to travel through non-existent three-dimensional spaces. A computer monitor connected to a network becomes a window through which we can be present in a place thousands of miles away. Finally, with the help of a mouse or a video camera, a computer is transformed into an intelligent being capable of engaging us in a dialogue.

VR, interactivity and telepresence are made possible by the recent technology of a digital computer. However, they are made real by a much, much older technology – the screen. It is by looking at a screen – a flat, rectangular surface positioned at some distance from the eyes – that the user experiences the illusion of navigating through virtual spaces, of being physically present somewhere else or of being hailed by the computer itself. If computers have become a common presence in our culture only in the last decade, the screen, on the other hand, has been used to present visual information for centuries – from Renaissance painting to twentieth-century cinema.

Today, coupled with a computer, the screen is rapidly becoming the main means of accessing any kind of information, be it still images, moving images or text. We are already using it to read the daily newspaper, to watch movies, to communicate with co-workers, relatives and friends, and, most importantly, to work (the screens of airline agents, data entry clerks, secretaries, engineers, doctors, pilots, etc.; the screens of ATM machines, supermarket checkouts, automobile control panels, and, of course, the screens of computers.) We may debate whether our society is a society of spectacle or of simulation, but, undoubtedly, it is the society of a screen. What are the different stages of the screen's history? What are the relationships between the physical space where the viewer is located, his/her body, and the screen space? What are the ways in which computer displays both continue and challenge the tradition of a screen?

A Screen's Genealogy

Let us start with the definition of a screen. Visual culture of the modern period, from painting to cinema, is characterized by an intriguing phenomenon: the existence of another virtual space, another three-dimensional world enclosed by a frame and situated inside our normal space. The frame separates two absolutely different spaces that somehow coexist. This phenomenon is what defines the screen in the most general sense, or, as I will call it, the 'classical screen'.

What are the properties of a classical screen? It is a flat, rectangular surface. It is intended for frontal viewing (as opposed to, for instance, a panorama). It exists in our normal space, the space of our body, and acts as a window into another space. This other space, the space of representation, typically has a different scale from the scale of our normal space. Defined in this way, a screen describes equally well a Renaissance painting (recall Alberti) and a modern computer display. Even proportions have not changed in five centuries, they are similar for a typical fifteenth-century painting, a film screen and a computer screen. (In this respect it is not accidental that the very names of the two main formats of computer displays point to two genres of painting: a horizontal format is referred to as 'landscape mode' while the vertical format is referred to as 'portrait mode'.)

A hundred years ago a new type of screen became popular, which I will call the 'dynamic screen'. This new type retains all the properties of a classical screen while adding something new: it can display an image changing over time. This is the screen of cinema, television, video. The dynamic screen also brings with it a certain relationship between the image and the spectator – a certain viewing regime, so to speak. This relationship is already implicit in the classical screen but now it fully surfaces. A screen's image strives for complete illusion and visual plenitude while the viewer is asked to suspend disbelief and to identify with the image. Although the screen in reality is only a window of limited dimensions positioned inside the physical space of the viewer, the latter is supposed to completely concentrate on what is seen in this window, focusing attention on the representation and disregarding the physical space outside. This viewing regime is made possible by the fact that, be it a painting, movie screen or television screen, the singular image completely fills the screen. This is why we are so annoyed in a movie theater when the projected image does not precisely coincide with the screen's boundaries: it disrupts the illusion, making us conscious of what exists outside the representation.[2]

Rather than being a neutral medium of presenting information, the screen is aggressive. It functions to filter, to screen out, to take over, rendering non-existent whatever is outside its frame. And although, of course, the degree of this filtering varies between cinema viewing (where the viewer is asked to completely merge with the screen's space) and television viewing (where the screen is smaller, lights are on, conversation between viewers is allowed, and the act of viewing is often integrated with other daily activities), overall, this viewing regime remains stable – until recently. This stability has been challenged by the arrival of the computer screen. On the one hand, rather than showing a single image, a computer screen typically displays a number of coexisting windows. (Indeed, the coexistence of a number of overlapping windows has become a fundamental principle of modern computer interface since the introduction of the first Macintosh computer in 1984.) No single window completely dominates the viewer's attention. In this sense the possibility of simultaneously observing a few images which coexist within one screen can be compared with the phenomenon of zapping – the quick switching of television channels that allows the viewer to follow more than program.[3] In both instances, the viewer no longer concentrates on a single image. (Some television sets now enable a second channel to be watched within a smaller window positioned in a corner of the main screen. Perhaps future TV sets will adopt the window metaphor of a computer.) A window interface has more to do with modern graphic design, which treats a page as a collection of different but equally important blocks of data (text, images, graphic elements), than with cinema.

On the other hand, with VR, the screen disappears altogether. VR typically uses a head-mounted display whose images completely fill the viewer's visual field. No longer is the viewer looking forward at a rectangular, flat surface located at a certain distance and which acts as a window into another space. Now s/he is fully situated within this other space. Or, more precisely, we can say that the two spaces, the real, physical space and the virtual simulated space, coincide. The virtual space, previously confined to a painting or a movie screen, now completely encompasses the real space. Frontality, rectangular surface, difference in scale are all gone. The screen has vanished.

Both situations (window interface and VR) disrupt the viewing regime which characterizes the historical period of the dynamic screen. This regime, based on the identification of the viewer with a screen image, reaches its culmination in the cinema which goes to the extreme to enable this identification (the bigness of the screen, the darkness of the surrounding space) while still relying on a screen (a rectangular flat surface). Thus, just as we celebrate a hundred years of cinema in 1995, we should also celebrate – and mourn – the era of the dynamic screen which began with cinema and is ending now. And it is this disappearance of the screen – its splitting into many windows in window interface, its complete take over of the visual field in VR – that allows us today to recognize it as a cultural category and begin to trace its history.

The origins of the cinema's screen are well known. We can trace its emergence to the popular spectacles and entertainment of the eighteenth and nineteenth centuries: magic lantern shows, phantasmagoria, eidophysikon, panorama, diorama, zoopraxiscope shows, and so on. The public was ready for cinema and when it finally appeared it was a huge public event. Not by accident the 'invention' of cinema was claimed by at least a dozen individuals from a half-dozen countries.[4]

The origin of the computer screen is a different story. It appears in the middle of this century but it does not become a public presence until much later; and its history has not yet been written. Both of these facts are related to the context in which it emerged: as with all the other elements of modern human-computer interface, the computer screen was developed by the military. Its history has to do not with public entertainment but with military surveillance. The history of modern surveillance technologies begins at least with photography. From the advent of photography there existed an interest in using it for aerial surveillance. Félix Tournachon Nadar, one of the most eminent photographers of the nineteenth century, succeeded in exposing a photographic plate at 262 feet over Bièvre, France in 1858. He was soon approached by the French Army to attempt photo reconnaissance but rejected the offer. In 1882, unmanned photo balloons were already in the air; a little later, they were joined by photo rockets both in France and in Germany. The only innovation of World War I was to combine aerial cameras with a superior flying platform – the airplane.[5]

Radar became the next major surveillance technology. Massively employed in World War II, it provided important advantages over photography. Previously, military commanders had to wait until the pilots returned from surveillance missions and the film was developed. The inevitable delay between the time of the surveillance and the delivery of the finished image limited its usefulness because by the time the photograph was produced, enemy positions could have changed. However, with radar, as imaging became instantaneous, this delay was eliminated. The effectiveness of radar had to do with a new means of displaying an image – a new type of screen.

Consider the imaging technologies of photography and film. The photographic image is a permanent imprint corresponding to a single referent (whatever was in front of the lens when the photograph was taken) and to a limited time of observation (the time of exposure). Film is based on the same principle. A film sequence, composed of a number of still images, represents the sum of referents and the sum of exposure times of these individual images. In either case, the image is fixed once and for all. Therefore the screen can only show past events.

With radar, we see for the first time the mass employment (television is founded on the same principle but its mass employment comes later) of a fundamentally new type of screen, the screen which gradually comes to dominate modern visual culture – video monitor, computer screen, instrument display. What is new about such a screen is that its image can change in real time, reflecting changes in the referent, be it the position of an object in space (radar), any alteration in visible reality (live video) or changing data in the computer's memory (computer screen). The image can be continually updated in real time. This is the third (after classic and dynamic) type of a screen – the screen of real time. The radar screen changes, tracking the referent. But while it appears that the element of time delay, always present in the technologies of military surveillance, is eliminated, in fact, time enters the real-time screen in a new way. In older, photographic technologies, all parts of an image are exposed simultaneously. Whereas now the image is produced through sequential scanning: circular in the case of radar, horizontal in the case of television. Therefore, the different parts of the image correspond to different moments in time. In this respect, a radar image is more similar to an audio record since consecutive moments in time become circular tracks on a surface.[6]

What this means is that the image, in a traditional sense, no longer exists! And it is only by habit that we still refer to what we see on the real-time screen as 'images'. It is only because the scanning is fast enough and because, sometimes, the referent remains static, that we see what looks like a static image. Yet, such an image is no longer the norm, but the exception of a more general, new kind of representation for which we do not have a term yet. The principles and technology of radar were worked out independently by scientists in the United States, England, France and Germany during the 1930s. But, after the beginning of the War only the U.S. had the necessary resources to continue radar development. In 1940, at MIT, a team of scientists was gathered to work in the Radiation Laboratory or the 'Rad Lab', as it came to be called. The purpose of the lab was radar research and production. By 1943, the 'Rad Lab' occupied 115 acres of floor space; it had the largest telephone switchboard in Cambridge and employed 4,000 people.[7]

Next to photography, radar provided a superior way to gather information about enemy locations. In fact, it provided too much information, more information than one person could deal with. Historical footage from the early days of the war shows a central command room with a large, table-size map of Britain.[8] Small pieces of cardboard in the form of planes are positioned on the map to show the locations of actual German bombers. A few senior officers scrutinize the map. Meanwhile, women in army uniforms constantly change the location of the cardboard pieces by moving them with long sticks as information is transmitted from dozens of radar stations.[9]

Was there a more effective way to process and display information gathered by radar? The computer screen, as well as all of the other key principles and technologies of modern human-computer interface – interactive control, algorithms for 3-D wireframe graphics, bit-mapped graphics – were developed as a way of solving this problem.

The research again took place at MIT. The Radiation Laboratory was dismantled after the end of the War, but soon the Air Force created another secret laboratory in its place – Lincoln Laboratory. The purpose of Lincoln Laboratory was to work on human factors and new display technologies for SAGE – 'Semi-Automatic Ground Environment', a command center to control the U.S. air defenses established in the mid-1950s.[10] Paul Edwards writes that SAGE's job 'was to link together radar installations around the USA's perimeter, analyze and interpret their signals, and direct manned interceptor jets toward the incoming bee. It was to be a total system, one whose 'human components' were fully integrated into the mechanized circuit of detection, decision and response.'[11] Why was SAGE created and why did it require a computer screen? In the 1950s the American military thought that when the Soviet Union attacked the U.S., it would send a large number of bombers simultaneously. Therefore, it seemed necessary to create a center which could receive information from all U.S. radar stations, track the large number of enemy bombers and coordinate the counterattack. A computer screen and the other components of the modern human-computer interface owe their existence to this particular military doctrine.

The earlier version of the center was called the Cape Cod network since it received information from the radars situated along the coast of New England. The center was operating right out of the Barta Building situated on the MIT campus. Each of 82 Air Force officers monitored his own computer display which showed the outlines of the New England Coast and the locations of key radars. Whenever an officer noticed a dot indicating a moving plane, he would tell the computer to follow the plane. To do this the officer simply had to touch the dot with the special 'light pen'.[12] Thus, the SAGE system contained all of the main elements of the modern human-computer interface. The light pen, designed in 1949, can be considered a precursor of the contemporary mouse. More importantly, at SAGE the screen came to be used not only to display information in real time (as in radar and television) but also to give commands to the computer. Rather than acting solely as a means to display an image of reality, the screen became the vehicle for directly affecting reality.

Using the technology developed for SAGE, Lincoln researchers created a number of computer graphics programs that relied on the screen as a means to input and output information from a computer. They included programs

7) As action and suspense drama, media wars are hard to beat. Yet it is increasinly obvious how 'authentic' war footage has always relied on image manipulation and has served propaganda purposes: Sissy Spacek getting too close for comfort in VIOLETS ARE BLUE *(1986).*

8) Visual communication is vital in warlike conflicts, even when James Bond is fighting the 'bad guys'. Modern screen technology and the military complex are often hard to tell apart: Bond's opponent in MOONRAKER *(1979).*

to display brain waves (1957), simulate planet and gravitational activity (1960), as well as to create 2-D drawings (1958).[13] The single most well known of these became a program called Sketchpad. Designed in 1962 by Ivan Sutherland, a graduate student supervised by Claude Shannon, it widely publicized the idea of interactive computer graphics. With Sketchpad, a human operator could create graphics directly on computer screen by touching the screen with a light pen. Sketchpad exemplified a new paradigm of interacting with computers: by changing something on the screen, the operator changed something in the computer's memory. The real-time screen became interactive.

This, in short, is the history of the birth of the computer screen.[14] But even before a computer screen became widely used, a new paradigm emerged – the simulation of an interactive three-dimensional environment without a screen. In 1966, Ivan Sutherland and his colleagues began research on the prototype of VR. The work was co-sponsored by ARPA (Advanced Research Projects Agency) and the Office of Naval Research.[15] 'The fundamental idea behind the three-dimensional display is to present the user with a perspective image which changes as he moves', wrote Sutherland in 1968.[16] The computer tracked the position of the viewer's head and adjusted the perspective of the computer graphic image accordingly. The display itself consisted of two six-inch-long monitors which were mounted next to the temples. They projected an image which appeared superimposed over the viewer's field of vision. The screen disappeared. It completely took over the visual field.

The Screen and the Body

I have presented one possible genealogy of the modern computer screen. In my genealogy, the computer screen represents an interactive type, a subtype of the real-time type, which is a subtype of the dynamic type, which is a subtype of the classical type. My discussion of these types relied on two ideas. First, the idea of temporality: the classical screen displays a static, permanent image; the dynamic screen displays a moving image of the past and finally, the real-time screen shows the present. Second, the relationship between the space of the viewer and the space of the representation (I defined the screen as a window into the space of representation which itself exists in our normal space).

Let us now look at the screen's history from another angle – the relationship between the screen and the body of the viewer. This is how Roland Barthes described the screen in 'Diderot, Brecht, Eisenstein', written in 1973:

Representation is not defined directly by imitation: even if one gets rid of notions of the "real," of the "vraisemblable," of the "copy," there will still be representation for as long as a subject (author, reader, spectator or voyeur) casts his gaze towards a horizon on which he cuts out a base of a triangle, his eye (or his mind) forming the apex. The "Organon of Representation" (which is today becoming possible to write because there are intimations of something else) will have as its dual foundation the sovereignty of the act of cutting out [découpage] and the unity of the subject of action... The scene, the picture, the shot, the cut-out rectangle, here we have the very condition that allows us to conceive theater, painting, cinema, literature, all those arts, that is, other than music and which could be called dioptric arts.[17]

For Barthes, the screen becomes the all-encompassing concept which covers the functioning of even non-visual representation (literature), even though he does make an appeal to a particular visual model of linear perspective. At any rate, his concept encompasses all types of representational apparatuses I have discussed: painting, film, television, radar and computer display. In each of these, reality is cut by the rectangle of a screen: 'a pure cut-out segment with clearly defined edges, irreversible and incorruptible; everything that surrounds it is banished into nothingness, remains unnamed, while everything that it admits within its field is promoted into essence, into light, into view.'[18] This act of cutting reality into a sign and nothingness simultaneously doubles the viewing subject who now exists in two spaces: the familiar physical space of his/her real body and the virtual space of an image within the screen. This split comes to the surface with VR, but it already exists with painting and other dioptric arts.

What is the price the subject pays for the mastery of the world, focused and unified by the screen?

THE DRAUGHTSMAN'S CONTRACT, a 1981 film by Peter Greenaway, concerns an architectural draughtsman hired to produce a set of drawings of a country house. The draughtsman employs a simple drawing tool consisting of a square grid. Throughout the film, we repeatedly see the draughtsman's face through the grid which looks like prison bars. It is as if the subject who attempts to catch the world, to immobilize it, to fix it within the representational apparatus (here, perspectival drawing), is trapped by this apparatus himself. The subject is imprisoned. I take this image as a metaphor for what appears to be a general tendency of the Western screen-based representational apparatus. In this tradition, the body must be fixed in space if the viewer is to see the image at all. From Renaissance monocular perspective to modern cinema, from Kepler's camera obscura to nineteenth century camera lucida, the body had to remain still.

The imprisonment of the body takes place on both the conceptual and literal levels; both kinds of imprisonment already appear with the first screen apparatus, Alberti's perspectival window. According to many interpreters of linear perspective, it presents the world as seen by a singular eye, static, unblinking and fixated. As described by Norman Bryson, perspective 'followed the logic of the Gaze rather than the Glance, thus producing a visual take that was eternalized, reduced to one "point of view" and disembodied.'[19] Bryson argues that 'the gaze of the painter arrests the flux of phenomena, contemplates the visual field from a vantage-point outside the mobility of duration, in an eternal moment of disclosed presence.'[20] Correspondingly, the world, as seen by this immobile, static and atemporal Gaze, which belongs more to a statue than to a living body, becomes equally immobile, reified, fixated, cold and dead. Writing about Dürer's famous print of a draftsman drawing a nude through a screen of perspectival threads, Martin Jay notes that 'a reifying male look' turns 'its targets into stone'; consequently, the marmoreal nude is drained of its capacity to arouse desire.[21] Similarly, John Berger compares Alberti's window to 'a safe let into a wall, a safe into which the visible has been deposited.'[22] And in THE DRAUGHTS-MAN'S CONTRACT, time and again, the draughtsman tries to eliminate all motion, any sign of life from the scenes he is rendering.

With perspectival machines, the imprisonment of the subject also happens in a literal sense. From the onset of the adaptation of perspective, artists and draftsmen have attempted to aid the laborious manual process of creating perspectival images and, between the sixteenth and nineteenth centuries, various 'perspectival machines' were constructed.[23] By the first decades of the sixteenth century, Dürer described a number of such machines.[24] Many varieties were invented, but regardless of the type, the artist had to remain immobile throughout the process of drawing.

Along with perspectival machines, a whole range of optical apparatuses was in use, particularly for depicting landscapes and conducting topographical surveys. The most popular optical apparatus was the camera obscura.[25] Camera obscura literally means 'dark chamber'. It was founded on the premise that if the rays of light from an object or a scene pass through a small aperture, they will cross and re-emerge on the other side to form an image on a screen. In order for the image to become visible, however, 'it is necessary that the screen be placed in a chamber in which light levels are considerably lower than those around the object.'[26] Thus, in one of the earliest depictions of the camera obscura, in Kircher's *Ars magna Lucis et umbrae* (Rome, 1649), we see the subject enjoying the image inside a tiny room, oblivious to the fact that he had to imprison himself inside this 'dark chamber' in order to see the image on the screen.

Later, smaller tent-type camera obscura became popular – a movable prison, so to speak. It consisted of a small tent mounted on a tripod, with a revolving reflector and lens at its apex. Having positioned himself inside the tent which provided the necessary darkness, the draftsman would then spend hours meticulously tracing the image projected by the lens. Early photography continued the trend toward the imprisonment of the subject and the object of representation. During photography's first decades, the exposure times were quite long. The daguerreotype process, for instance, required exposures of 4 to 7 minutes in the sun and from 12 to 60 minutes in diffused light. So, similar to the drawings produced with the help of camera obscura, which depicted reality as static and immobile, early photographs represented the world as stable, eternal, unshakable. And when photography ventured to represent the living, such as the human subject, s/he had to be immobilized. Thus, portrait studios universally employed various clamps to assure the steadiness of the sitter throughout the lengthy time of exposure. Reminiscent of torture instruments, the iron clamps firmly held the subject in place, the subject who voluntarily became the prisoner of the machine in order to see her/his own image.[27]

Toward the end of the nineteenth century, the petrified world of the photographic image was shattered by the dynamic screen of the cinema. In "The Work of Art in the Age of Mechanical Reproduction", Walter Benjamin expressed his fascination with the new mobility of the visible: 'Our taverns and our metropolitan streets, our offices and furnished rooms, our railroad stations and our factories appeared to have us locked up hopelessly. When came the film and burst this prison-world asunder by the dynamite of the tenth of a second, so that now, in the midst of its far-flung ruins and debris, we calmly and adventurously go traveling.'[28]

The cinema screen enabled audiences to take a journey through different spaces without leaving their seats; in the words of Anne Friedberg, it created 'a mobilized virtual gaze.'[29] However, the cost of this virtual mobility was a new, institutionalized immobility of the spectator. All around the world large prisons were constructed which could hold hundreds of prisoners – movie houses. The prisoners could neither talk to each other nor move from seat to seat. While they were taken on virtual journeys, their bodies had to remain still in the darkness of the collective camera obscuras.

The formation of this viewing regime took place in parallel with the shift from what film theorists call 'primitive' to 'classical' film language.[30] An important part of the shift, which took place in the 1910s, was the new functioning of the virtual space represented on the screen. During the 'primitive' period, the space of the film theater and the screen space were clearly separated much like those of theater or vaudeville. The viewers were free to interact, come and go, and maintain a psychological distance from the cinematic diegesis. In contrast, classical film addressed each viewer as a separate individual and positioned her/him inside the diegetic space. As noted by a contemporary in 1913, 'they [spectators] should be put in the position of being a "knot hole in the fence" at every stage in the play.'[31] If 'primitive cinema keeps the spectator looking across a void in a separate space,'[32] the spectator is now placed at the best viewpoint of each shot, inside the virtual space.

This situation is usually conceptualized in terms of the spectator's identification with the camera eye. The body of the spectator remains in the seat while her/his eye is coupled with a mobile camera. However, it is also possible to conceptualize this differently. We can imagine that the camera does not, in fact, move at all, that it remains stationary, coinciding with the spectator's eyes. Instead, it is the virtual space as a whole that changes its position with each shot. Using the contemporary vocabulary of computer graphics, we can say that this virtual space is rotated, scaled and zoomed to always give the spectator the best viewpoint. Like a striptease, the space slowly disrobes itself, turning, presenting itself from different sides, teasing, stepping forward and retracting, always leaving something unrevealed, so the spectator will wait for the next shot ... the endless seductive dance. All the spectator has to do is remain immobile.

Film theorists have taken this immobility to be the essential feature of the institution of cinema. Friedberg wrote: 'As everyone from Baudry (who compares cinematic spectation to the prisoners in Plato's cave) to Musser points out, the cinema relies on the immobility of the spectator, seated in an auditorium.'[33] Jean-Louis Baudry has probably more than anyone put the emphasis on immobility as the foundation of cinematic illusion. Baudry quoted Plato: 'In this underground chamber they have been from childhood, chained by the leg and also by the neck, so that they cannot move and can only see what is in front of them, because the chains will not let them turn their heads.'[34] This immobility and confinement, according to Baudry, enables prisoners/spectators to mistake representations for their perceptions, regressing back to childhood when the two were indistinguishable. Thus, rather than a historical accident, according to Baudry's psychoanalytic explanation, the immobility of the spectator is the essential condition of cinematic pleasure. Alberti's window, Dürer's perspectival machines, camera obscura, photography, cinema – in all of these screen-based apparatuses, the subject had to remain immobile. In fact, as Friedberg perceptively points out, the progressive mobilization of the image in modernity was accompanied by the progressive imprisonment of the viewer: 'as the "mobility" of the gaze became more "virtual" – as techniques were developed to paint (and then to photograph) realistic images, as mobility was implied by changes in lighting (and then cinematography) – the observer became more immobile, passive, ready to receive the constructions of a virtual reality placed in front of his or her unmoving body.'[35]

What happens to this tradition with the arrival of a screen-less representational apparatus — VR? On the one hand, VR does constitute a fundamental break with this tradition. It establishes a radically new type of relationship between the body of a viewer and an image. In contrast to cinema, where the mobile camera moves independent of the immobile spectator, now the spectator has to actually move around the physical space in order to experience the movement in virtual space. The effect is as though the camera is mounted on user's head. So, in order to look up in virtual space, one has to look up in physical space; in order to 'virtually' step forward one has to actually step forward and so on.[36] The spectator is no longer chained, immobilized, anesthetized by the apparatus which serves him the ready-made images; now s/he has to work, to speak, in order to see.

At the same time, VR imprisons the body to an unprecedented extent before. This can be seen clearly with the earliest VR system designed by Sutherland and his colleagues in the 1960s to which I have already referred. According to Howard Rheingold's history of VR, 'Sutherland was the first to propose mounting small computer screens in binocular glasses – far from an easy hardware task in the early 1960s – and thus immerse the user's point of view inside the computer graphic world.'[37] Rheingold further wrote: 'In order to change the appearance of the computer-generated graphics when the user moves, some kind of gaze-tracking tool is needed. Because the direction of the user's gaze was most economically and accurately measured at that time by means of a mechanical apparatus, and because the HMD [head-mounted display] itself was so heavy, the users of Sutherland's early HMD systems found their head locked into machinery suspended from the ceiling. The user put his or her head into a metal contraption that was known as the "Sword of Damocles" display.'[38]

A pair of tubes connected the display to tracks in the ceiling, 'thus making the user a captive of the machine in a physical sense'.[39] The user was able to turn around and rotate her/his head in any direction but s/he could not move away from the machine more than a few steps. Like today's computer mouse, the body was tied to the computer. In fact, the body was reduced to nothing else – and nothing more – than a giant mouse, or more precisely, a giant joystick. Instead of moving a mouse, the user had to turn her/his own body. Another comparison which comes to mind is the apparatus built in the late nineteenth century by Etienne-Jules Marey to measure the frequency of the wing movements of a bird. The bird was connected to the measuring equipment by wires which were long enough to enable it to flap its wings in midair but not to fly anywhere.[40]

The parodox of VR that requires the viewer to physically move in order to see an image (as opposed to remaining immobile) and at the same time physically ties her/him to a machine is interestingly dramatized in a 'cybersex' scene in Hollywood's LAWNMOWER MAN. In the scene, the protagonists, a man and a woman, are situated in the same room, each fastened to a separate circular frame which allows the body to freely rotate 360 degrees in all directions. During 'cybersex' the camera cuts back and forth between the virtual space (i.e., what the protagonists see and experience) and the physical space. In the virtual world represented with psychedelic computer graphics, their bodies melt and morph together disregarding all the laws of physics, while in the real world each of them simply rotates within his/her own frame.

The paradox reaches its extreme in one of the most long standing VR projects – the Super Cockpit developed by the U.S. Air Force in the 1980s.[41] Instead of using his own eyes to follow both the terrain outside of his plane and the dozens of instrument panels inside the cockpit, the pilot wears a head-mounted display that presents both kinds of information in a more efficient way. What follows is a description of the system from Air & Space magazine:

> When he climbed into his F-16C, the young fighter jock of 1998 simply plugged in his helmet and flipped down his visor to activate his Super Cockpit system. The virtual world he saw exactly mimicked the world outside. Salient terrain features were outlined and rendered in three dimensions by the two tiny cathode ray tubes focused at his personal viewing distance...His compass heading was displayed as a large band of numbers on the horizon line, his projected flight path a shimmering highway leading out toward infinity.[42]

If in most screen-based representations (painting, cinema, video) as well as in typical VR applications the physical and the virtual worlds have nothing to do with each other, here the virtual world is precisely synchronized to the physical one. The pilot positions himself in the virtual world in order to move through the physical one at a supersonic speed with his representational apparatus which is securely fastened to his body, more securely than ever before in the history of the screen.

* * *

In summary, on the one hand, VR continues the screen's tradition of viewer immobility by fastening the body to a machine, while on the other hand, it creates an unprecedented new condition, requiring the viewer to move. We may ask, in conclusion, whether this new condition is without an historical precedent or whether it fits within some other alternative tradition we so far have not noticed.

In Ancient Greece, communication was understood as an oral dialogue between people. It was also assumed that physical movement stimulated dialogue and the process of thinking. Aristotle and his pupils walked around while discussing philosophical problems. In the Middle Ages, a shift occured from a dialogue between subjects to communication between a subject and an information storage device, i.e. a book. A Medieval book chained to a table can be considered a precursor to the screen.

The screen, as I defined it (a flat rectangle that acts as a window into the virtual world), makes its appearance in the Renaissance with modern painting. Previously, frescoes and mosaics were inseparable from the architecture. In contrast, a painting is essentially mobile. Separate from a wall, it can be moved anywhere. But at the same time, an interesting reversal takes place. The interaction with a fresco or a mosaic, which can't be moved anywhere, does not assume immobility on the part of the spectator, while the mobile Renaissance painting does presuppose such immobility. Do frescoes, mosaics and wall paintings, which are all part of the architecture, represent this alternative tradition I am searching for, the tradition which encourages the movement of the viewer?

I began my discussion of the screen by emphasizing that a screen's frame separates two spaces, the physical and the virtual, which have different scales. Although this condition does not necessarily lead to the immobilization of the spectator, it does discourage any movement on her or his part: Why move when s/he can't enter the represented virtual space anyway? This was very well dramatized in *Alice in Wonderland* when Alice struggles to become just the right size in order to enter the other world.

The alternative tradition of which VR is a part can be found whenever the scale of a representation is the same as the scale of our human world so that the two spaces are continuous. This is the tradition of simulation rather than that of representation bound up to a screen. One example is mosaics, frescoes and wall paintings which create an illusionary space that starts behind the surface. The nineteenth century, with its obsession with naturalism, pushes this trend to the extreme with the wax museum and the dioramas of natural history museums. Another example is a sculpture on a human scale (for instance, Auguste Rodin's 'The Burghers of Calais'). We think of such sculptures as part of post-Renaissance humanism which puts the human at the center of the universe, when in fact, they are aliens, black holes within our world into another parallel universe, the petrified universe of marble or stone, which exists in parallel to our own world ...

VR continues this tradition of simulation. However, it introduces one important difference. Previously, the simulation depicted a fake space which was continuous with and extended from the normal space. For instance, a wall painting created a pseudo landscape which appeared to begin at the wall. In VR, either there is no connection between the two spaces (for instance, I am in a physical room while the virtual space is one of an underwater landscape) or, on the contrary, the two completly coincide (i.e., the Super Cockpit project). In either case, the actual physical reality is disregarded, dismissed, abandoned.

In this respect, nineteenth-century panorama can be thought of as a transitional form from classical simulations (wall paintings, human size sculpture, diorama) toward VR. Like VR, panorama creates a 360 degree space. The viewers are situated in the center of this space and they are encouraged to move around the central viewing area in order to see different parts of the panorama.[43] But in contrast to wall paintings and mosaics which, after all, acted as decorations of a real space, the physical space of action, now this physical space is subordinate to the virtual space. In other words, the central viewing area is conceived as a continuation of fake space (rather than vice versa as before), and this is why it is empty. It is empty so that we can pretend that it continues the battlefield, or a view of Paris or whatever else the panorama represents. From here we are one step away from VR where the physical space is totally disregarded and all the 'real' actions take place in virtual space. The screen disappeared because what was behind it simply took over.

And what about the immobilization of the body in VR which connects it to the screen tradition? Dramatic as it is, this immobilization probably represents the last act in the long history of the body's imprisonment. All around us are the signs of increasing mobility and the miniaturization of communication devices – cellular telephones and modems, pagers and laptops. Eventually VR apparatus will be reduced to a chip implanted in a retina and connected by cellular transmission to the Net. From that moment on, we will carry our prisons with us – not in order to blissfully confuse representations and perceptions (as in cinema), but to always 'be in touch', always connected, always 'plugged-in'. The retina and the screen will merge.

This futuristic scenario may never become a reality. For now, we clearly live in the society of a screen. The screens are everywhere: the screens of airline agents, data entry clerks, secretaries, engineers, doctors, pilots, etc.; the screens of ATM machines, supermarket checkouts, automobile control panels, and, of course, the screens of computers. Dynamic, real-time and inter-active, a screen is still a screen. Interactivity, simulation, and telepresence: like centuries ago, we are still looking at a flat rectangular surface, existing in the space of our body and acting as a window into another space. What-ever new era we may be entering today, we still have not left the era of the screen.

Louis Lumière – the Cinema's First Virtualist?

Thomas Elsaesser

The Spirit of St. Louis

At a conference in Paris in March 1995, called 'Le cinéma: vers son deuxième siècle'[1], the well-known critic Jean Douchet seized the opportunity to ride an attack against the contemporary cinema: 'One hundred years after the birth of the cinema, we are witnessing a revival of the famous – historically inaccurate but symbolically correct – dispute between Georges Méliès and Louis Lumière. The shift towards virtual reality is a shift from one type of thinking to another, a shift in purpose which modifies, disturbs, perhaps even perverts man's relation to what is real.'[2] Douchet went on to specify that with it the cinema championed by André Bazin and *Cahiers du cinéma*, and practiced by 'Lumièrists' as diverse as Robert Flaherty and Frederick Wiseman, Nicholas Ray and Satyajit Ray, Jean Renoir and Roberto Rossellini, Jacques Rivette and Jean Marie Straub will soon be no more: 'All good films, we used to say in the 1960s, when the cover of *Cahiers du cinéma* was still yellow, are documentaries, [...] and filmmakers deserved to be called 'great' precisely because of their near obsessive focus on capturing reality and respecting it, respectfully embarking on the way of knowledge. [Today, on the other hand], cinema has given up the purpose and the thinking behind individual shots, in favour of images – rootless, textureless images – designed to violently impress by constantly inflating their spectacular qualities.'[3]

One can agree or disagree with Douchet's sense that imaging and image-making has become a more rootless business than it was a hundred years ago and still doubt that citing Louis Lumière as his crown witness is justified. Could the occasion of the centenary not have equally well been the moment of defending Lumière also against some of the Lumièristes themselves? The Lumière brothers, justly famous for their spirit of exploratation and enterprising independence, encourage one to ask what precisely their *cinématographe* and the films they made for it tell us not only about the double legacy of their invention – the 'documentary' as well as 'fictional' paths taken by cinema, but also what they might have made of the 'new images' that so upset Douchet and a great many other cinephiles. Or to turn the question around: what contradictions, paradoxes and dilemmas are we left with, when we align the Lumières with a notion of 'documentary' they probably would not have recognized?

For what exactly were we commemorating when in 1995 and 1996 the 'birth' of the cinema was being celebrated? I do not mean to allude merely to the many parallel devices, the near-simultaneous appearance of the cinema in different countries, or the exact sequence of events that led to the famous show at the Grand Café. In this respect, the centenary has unearthed a great many new facts and given some lucidly corrective accounts of the rival contenders. Rather, I wonder if one can speak of birth at all, with its associated notions of progress and destiny. It is a question that hides a number of further queries, such as whether there were some deeper – cultural, ideological, technological – reasons for its emergence, or what was it that the so-called inventors thought they were inventing, and was the cinema what the world had been expecting?[4] In other words, in what sense can an innovation like the cinema, so momentous to the twentieth century, be said to 'know itself' either then or now?

One of the most persistent assumptions – and perhaps the foundational gesture on which all histories of the cinema have been based – is that of the inevitability of cinema. Like a baton relay, or the pieces of a jigsaw puzzle, from Plato's parable of the cave and Balinese shadow-plays, from Leonardo's studies of water in motion to Alberti's treatise on the laws of perspective, from camera obscuras and mechanical drawing aids to magic lanterns, fog pictures and fantasmagorias, from dioramas and phenakistoscopes to thaumatropes and chronophotography, historians have been at pains to line up, indifferently, philosophical speculations, scientific experiments, aids to observation and drawing, as well as optical toys, in order to give the appearance of logic and cogency to the cinema's creation myth: the moment when on March 21st, 1895 the Lumière Brothers projected their first film WORKERS LEAVING THE FACTORY to an assembly of savants and amateur scientists, at the 'Société pour l'encouragement de l'industrie nationale' in Paris.

These pedigrees, with their flattering notions of progress are, of course, themselves deeply imbued with the spirit of the nineteenth century, and it is a useful starting point to remind oneself just how much the cinema straddles two centuries, the nineteenth and the twentieth. As far as its technology is concerned, but also in terms of its epistemology of realism ('the pencil of nature'), the *cinématographe* belongs squarely to the nineteenth century. Yet its social dimension, the way it participates in the modernity of urban living, technologically-driven communication, leisure time, travel, transport and consumption, it belongs to the twentieth century. Another way of putting it is to say that the cinema, far from being inevitable or having a manifest destiny, emerged directly out of a certain crisis of cultural self-definition – for instance, that which was intended to mediate and maintain a balance between science, technology, education and entertainment (a symptom for which, from the latter part of the nineteenth century onwards, the big world fairs of London, Paris and St. Louis presented themselves as solutions).[5]

Inevitability of an Invention or Archaeology of an Imagined Future?

One slightly heretical rationale for commemorating the centenary would be to argue that the cinema is an invention without origin because it is without inherent determinisms, be they of goal, function or use, thereby belatedly vindicating father Antoine Lumière's famous 'le cinéma – c'est une invention sans avenir'. Put less paradoxically, the cinema's origin is quite clearly a function of how we define what actually constitutes cinema, that is, what agencies, causalities and pedigrees we retroactively invoke to construct this history. Is it the magic lantern (of Athanasius Kircher and Christian Huyghens), serial photography which captures movement (Marey, Muybridge), is it images – whether painted or photographic – which, when mechanically transported, give the impression of continuous motion (Théâtre Emile Raynaud), the development of instant photography, the invention of the cellulose sheet on which light sensitive emulsion could be painted (George Eastman), the showing of moving images to a paying public (Edison), the projected image (George Demeny)? We can already see how such definitions depend on a number of variables that are not only matters of historical record, but inflected with a-priori assumptions, fed by hindsight and implying a choice of vantage point – even a declaration of interest – which alone makes such a 'history' either possible or meaningful.[6]

If considered as merely a new technology, the cinema's introduction is not just an accumulative process adding to an instrumentarium of 'tools'. Instead, it reconfigures the larger environment on which such a practice may have an impact. It changes the field, and even more so, it alters the very idea one can have of such a field, making apparent connexions which had always been there but never seemed to matter.

To take a relatively recent, but crucial example: the telephone has been in existence and use longer than the cinema, but only video, the electronic image and digitization have shown the complex filiations that have always existed between these apparently distinct technological systems: technically, economically, and in the ways their uses could be envisaged. There is evidence that the late nineteenth century did not expect the cinema:[7] rather, the imagination of the 1880s and 1890s was fired by an impatience for devices of simultaneity and instantaneity, which suggests an altogether different 'history': one that leads from serial photography via the phonograph to the polaroid, the video image, the VCR and the digital disk, while on the other,

9) Archaeologies of imagined futures, or what the 19th century century was waiting for: simultaneity and interactivity. Combining the telephone with a panoramic moving image for domestic consumption, this Punch cartoon from December 9th, 1878 was captioned: "The whole world into the home".

imposing itself as the incremental history of the telegraph, the wireless, the telephone, satellite-links and the computer.

If, for instance, one were to see the cinema not primarily under its aspect of representation and signification – the perspective of both 'classical' film theory and film history – but in the light of the social spaces it either transformed or helped bring into being, one might be obliged to count as primary evidence that elusive experience enacted a million times in all the afternoons or evenings spent at the movies. They belong as much to the 'history' of the cinema as the question whether moving images that are not registered on celluloid, but on video or digitized can still be the legitimate object of film history.

On the other hand, if instantaneity is granted status of determinant in the culture to which we owe the cinema, the telephone could also be seen as a relevant entry-point in another respect. For what makes the cinema socially remarkable and historically significant is not least the unconstrained but by no means unstructured time it buys. Thus, its use value has to do with articulating, modelling, and finally, 'wasting' time. The telephone, too, it could be said, with its phatic contact and interactivity gives its user the pleasures of simultaneity as well as those of ostentatiously 'wasting time'.

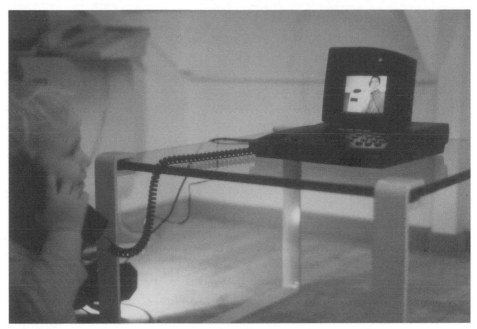

10) A little over a hundred years later, such voice-image interactive machines now exist and make use of the telephone-line. Dispensing with the large image, they are still dedicated to 'keeping the family in touch'.

This cultural need of wasting time, on the other hand, is itself a function of a modernity which thanks to the new technologies of transport and communication (the railways, the telephone and telegraph) had standardized and synchronized time to a point where leisure was in the first instance synonymous with escaping such time constraints. By a curious irony, however, chronophotography (or serial photography), one of the chief contenders for the role of cinema's necessary condition – making possible both the analysis and synthesis of movement – was devised precisely in order to break down time and motion, and analyse the labouring body. Eadweard Muybridge, for instance, used his chronophotographic studies to help rationalize the assembly line operations at the production sites of the steel industry of Philadelphia. The nineteenth century was also under pressure to administer and economically exploit time itself as a divisible and thus recombinable/assemblable entity. Human bodies had to be fitted around the standardized time of the factory production process, and synchronized with the motion of its machines. Thus underpinning the cinema is a technology – chronophotography – whose social and industrial application was one of the chief causes of the cultural malaise for which going to the movies appeared to bring relief: the cinema as the disease for which it pretended to be the cure![8]

These multiple entry-points to a history of the cinema want to illustrate that its 'origins' and early years are an eminently suitable path for thinking also about its 'future'. But they also oblige one to have recourse to what historians would probably qualify as counter-factual or 'virtual' history – one of the contexts my title tries to invoke. Such a counter-factual conception of history is not the opposite of 'real' history, of *wie es eigentlich gewesen ist* (though I shall come back to Leopold Ranke), but a view prepared to think into history all those histories that might have been, or might still be, the ghosts that shadow the living, and not unlike the cinema itself, populate it with all the 'undead': workers forever leaving the factory, the delegates forever arriving at Neuville-sur-Saône, and the baby forever being fed its breakfast porridge.

This may sound as if I am suggesting that we should 'master the past' by digitally 'remastering' old movie footage. Not at all. Rather, film history is, strictly speaking, inconceivable if we cannot find in it the appropriate space that recognizes cinema's place in our dreams as well as in our industries, but also its role in giving substance to all kinds of other possible universes and alternative histories which human beings have imagined and tried to make real. Think of the Holodeck of STAR TREK as part of film history, or as a German colleague of mine put it, think of the fact that cinema studies taught in the humanities has turned them from being 'Geisteswissenschaften' into 'Geisterwissenschaften'.

Taking account of the curious ontological status of the moving image, we can learn a good deal about the cinema from the apparent 'losers' of the first hour – pioneers such as William Paul and Louis Le Prince, Georges Demeny and Birt Acres, Max and Emil Skladanowsky and William Kennedy Dickson. Their stories are inestimable sources for understanding the assumptions, the values and imagined goals that animated those men (and they were invariably men: that, too, a 'historical fact'; the cinema, as an apparatus, has always been a sort of bachelor machine!).[9] What the metaphor of the 'invention' or the 'birth' of the cinema unfortunately tends to obscure is the fact that, a hundred years ago, camera, film strip and projector were at first seen as the technical continuation of already existing practices, which is to say, often as 'improvements' of that which was already known and in use, and not at all as the epistemic break for which we so often take the cinema when looking back. Interrogating the pioneers, we would be exploring not so much the 'eureka' moments of cinema, but the archaeology of all the possible futures of the cinema (as well as television and interactive media!), what it was envisaged to engender at the moment it was 'born', which means in effect to study all the image-making, image-consuming pasts the cinema was supposed to continue and improve on. For what did the cinema initially claim to be doing, other than proclaim itself as just these pasts' most logical extensions?[10]

This perspective is useful also for discussing Louis Lumière, out of a sense that especially the 'documentary' film can be grasped more justly in its history if it is not juxtaposed too radically to the narrative film, but also if we do not make of its early years a Golden Age, when reality was still real. At the same time, the relative neglect of documentary or actuality film in film histories, which from one point of view may appear as a grievous wrong that must be put right, emerges, from another point of view, as precisely its theoretical surplus value, perhaps allowing us to conceptualize film history differently, and with it, gain a less polemical or paranoid view of its future.

I want to single out a curious phenomenon, namely that just about all the so-called pioneers – Etienne-Jules Marey, Eadweard Muybridge, Thomas Edison and the Lumière brothers – seemed to think the cinema an invention of doubtful prospects. Marey, the scientist and 'father' of chronophotography had nothing but haughty disdain for anyone interested in reconstituting movement rather than analyzing it; he is said to have sacked his then assistant Georges Demeny for trying to beat the Lumières to the first functioning projection device. Louis Lumière would later say, dismissively: 'of my many inventions, the cinematograph was the one that cost me the least effort', and by 1902 he had apparently lost all interest in either making films or taking out copyright on them. Edison of all people had neglected to register the patents to his kinetoscope in Europe, thus allowing the Lumières and countless others to buy his machines, take them apart and – as one would now call it – reverse engineer them. Edison also did not think at first that projection would catch on, reckoning it made no sense to show the same film to hundreds of spectators when you could apply the vending machine or one-arm-bandit logic, and extract from people five cents at individual kinetoscopes, at any time of day, anywhere you choose to install them.

As historians with 20/20 hindsight vision, we tend to see in such judgments only the hollow irony of 'if only they had known'; the counter-factual historian, on the other hand, might pause and ponder these gestures of hesitation, of doubt and disconcertedness, trying to extract meaning from the very force behind the act of withholding approval or withdrawing interest.

Let There Be Louis Lumière

This gesture of hesitation is undoubtedly most perplexing in the case of Louis Lumière, not only because he was the most accomplished film director for almost a decade, but also because he is supposedly the name for a body of work forever associated with documentary, and the camera's ability to give access to unmediated reality. Lumière's diffidence, on the other hand, obliges us to locate an energy of friction between the *cinématographe* developed as an improved 'system of chronophotography' and the films Lumière took with it, or rather with the way these films came to be read and thus appropriated. Contemporary accounts make it clear that Lumière's films were regarded as 'animated' views of the subjects before his camera, brought to life as if by magic. As the Parisian journal *La Poste* was to write after the December 1895 performance at the Salon Indien: 'Picture a screen on which appears a photographic projection. So far, nothing new. But suddenly, the image starts to move and comes alive, the door of a factory opening to let out a flood of men and women workers, with bicycles, dogs running, carriages; all that is moving, swarming. It is life itself, it is movement taken from life.'[11]

Apart from the echo in this passage of the metaphor of flowing water, so typical for the aesthetics of nineteenth century salon painting, this evaluation is significant for another reason: it reminds us of what Tom Gunning has called the 'aesthetics of astonishment'.[12] By their contemporaries, the Lumières were perceived as magicians, not at all as realists. Rather than promoting the illusion of life, they emphasized the gap between one kind of representation, 'the view', and another, the 'animation' of the view. Nevertheless, it was for their realism, as we know, that the Lumière films entered both history and theory, which leaves us to resolve the inherent contradiction. Not least because we also have to account for why the films made especially by Louis Lumière have retained their extraordinary freshness and vividness, and have remained undisputed masterpieces of cinema by any subsequent standard.

What were the arguments supporting this assessment of Lumière as a cineaste of genius? We already heard Jean Douchet. But while in France, around the *Cahiers* school, an aesthetics of realism claimed Lumière as its godfather, in the United States, a revaluation of film aesthetics got underway that shaped our cinematic sensibility almost as decisively as the *Cahiers* school, and which a little later, towards the end of the 1960s, helped to change our view of early cinema, including a radical reinterpretation of the Lumière films. But contrary to the passage just quoted from *La Poste* or Douchet's views, what was noted was neither the realism nor the magic of the images, but the extreme artificiality of the Lumière films, their sophisticated mise-en-scène, the exactly calculated camera placements and the almost uncanny precision with which the technical and material limitations – the predetermined length of film, the fixed camera and the absence of editing – were made productive as a 'will to style' and a conscious principle of formal organization.

If the evidence of deliberation and planning now seems inescapable, we owe these insights not to film historians. It was the filmmakers and critics who were part of (or versed in) the works of the American and Canadian avant-garde of the 1960s who 'rediscovered' early cinema, albeit with formalist preoccupations and polemical intent. Thanks to Ken Jacobs and Stan Brackage, Standish Lawder and Noel Burch, Marshall Deutelbaum, Tom Gunning and Charles Musser, our eyes were sharpened for what is so extraordinary about many of the Lumière films (and by extension, those of Edwin Porter). Using canny defamiliarization strategies, their interpretations tried to establish an acceptance for a non-normative and non-narrative practice, and thus create a pedigree that amounted to an alternative history. And yet, by pointing out how early films (up to about 1907) fundamentally deviated from the classical film image (from 1917), they freed us from the presumptions of thinking of the films of the pioneers as either 'primitive' or as spontaneous home-movie making. The avant-garde's boldness to imagine that the development of the cinema could have been otherwise, its sheer perversity of reading for instance those well-known Lumière films, such as WORKERS LEAVING THE FACTORY, DEMOLITION OF A WALL, ARRIVAL OF A TRAIN and THE CARD PLAYERS in terms of their formal coherence and meta-cinematic structures, made these films strikingly modern, as if they had been shot by Paul Sharits, Hollis Frampton or Michael Snow. One recalls the story of the 'Author of Don Quixote', by Jorge Luis Borges, who does not accuse his hero, Pierre Menard, of having plagiarized Cervantes, but rather marvels at his bold stroke of genius and depth of literary understanding, shown by writing such a mock-epic *after* the works of Flaubert and Henry James, Proust and Joyce.

In this vein, I remember looking at BOAT LEAVING THE HARBOUR after reading an essay by the British filmmaker Dai Vaughan. An almost unbearable suspense overcame me, as I watched this heart-breaking drama unfold before my eyes: not whether the boat might ever reach the open sea, but whether it might make the frame edge top left. Here was a constructivist film of the purest kind, dedicated to the proposition that the frame edge equals space edge, thus ironically both foreclosing (illusionist) off-screen space and yet implying it by its negation.

Similarly, it was convincingly argued that Lumière's single shot, single-scene films taken with a static camera set-up, were not, as traditional film history has it, 'plotless' or 'the recording of unadjusted, unarranged, untampered reality,' but highly structured wholes 'reflecting a number of carefully chosen decisions about sequential narrative.'[13] By attending especially to the beginnings and the endings, the archivist-critic Marshall Deutelbaum was able to show that most Lumière films record actions and events in

11) In 1895 this train is supposed to have shocked spectators into panic reactions. But the Lumieres' ARRIVAL OF A TRAIN AT LA CIOTAT STATION *(1895) is a piece of staged outdoor theatre, with almost all the passengers members of the Lumiere household.*

12) Virtual trains arriving at virtual stations: computer simulation of a high speed locomotive used by the German Bundesbahn to train its engine drivers.

which the end either rejoins or inversely mirrors the beginning (opening and closing the factory gates in WORKERS LEAVING THE FACTORY) thus providing a very effective narrative closure. DEMOLITION OF A WALL, for instance, which as we know was traditionally shown both forward and backward, could be called the first visual-performative palindrome, and it often concluded the programme. Lumière's films also enact another favourite narrational form which became constitutive for the industrial documentary: the progress-as-process film,[14] such as the breaking up of a slab of coke, the firing of a canon, the demolition of a wall: in each case, the film's temporal and spatial organization foregrounds the causal or functional logic of the event itself, making the beginning of the action coincide with and reinforce the beginning of the film, each being the other's structuring metaphor.

Furthermore, one can say that scope and duration of the actions are signalled in the films themselves, providing a form of narrative suspense and anticipation which generates active spectatatorial involvement. In films like THE SACK RACE, or THE ARRIVAL OF THE DELEGATES, Deutelbaum discovered evidence of very complex 'structural uses of space,' a doubling of protagonists, repetition of action, movement within the frame, and 'arrangement in depth' which indicate a sophisticated formal sense inflecting the apparently artless presentation of 'simple content'.[15] Framing and camera-placing are chosen to highten closure, balance and symmetry. The films also respect the minimal requirements of any basic narrative, i.e. the triple 'beat' of equilibrium, disequilibrium, reestablishment of equilibrium, and this at several levels (formal, spectatorial, and in the subject matter), or they put in place a play of symmetry and a-symmetry which gives both action and location a uniquely adequate shape.

A very peculiar kind of suspense emerges, which, as indicated, derives from the knowledge not only of the nature and duration of the actions depicted, but the length of the film strip itself – 53 seconds – providing what in the classical narrative cinema is known as the deadline structure, but one in which the film as fictional event and as material object spectacularly converge. One could speak of a double frame: a temporal one, in which the action is set and must unfold, and a spatial one, beyond which the action cannot and must not stray. This is especially impressive in L'ARROSEUR ARROSÉ (the title itself containing the moment of mirroring and reversal), where the gardener has to drag the young culprit back into the frame before administering the forcefully graphic punishment. Equally astonishing is the use of depth of field and space in Lumière. Some of the films seem entirely conceived around exploiting this effect, as in the special, almost exaggerated sense of depth in ARRIVAL OF A TRAIN, which – at first a mere dot on the horizon – eventually overwhelms us with its size and proximity. David Lean's LAWRENCE OF ARABIA merely rendered homage to Lumière with his camels in the desert, and in his DR ZHIVAGO it is indeed a train which, in an apparently interminable scene, comes out of the depth of the Russian steppes.

It was Noel Burch, for instance, who pointed out how the Lumière films were in fact experiments in a particular kind of space, as in WORKERS LEAVING THE FACTORY, where the people moving past the camera greatly increase the sense of depth, of space not only expanding and existing past the frame (thus applying the complementary 'structural principle' from that at work in BOAT LEAVING THE HARBOUR), and obliging us to distinguish between 'off-screen' (imaginary space) and 'off-frame' (physical frame of the image). I recall here the metaphor used by the first reviewer of flowing water as the symbol of life itself. Because of the permanent movement into off-frame, the spectator implied in the Lumière films becomes the spectator par excellence of the cinema, immersed in the irreversibility of the Heraclitean river, as distinct from the 'materially unrestricted time of contemplation' that is available to the spectator of a painting or a still photography. Additionally, the frame itself, and the function of camera placement in centering the eye and at the same time containing movement, initiates a play of masking and doubling which makes the Lumière film its own mise-en-abyme, at some distance from any 'referential transparency' which traditionally is attributed to Lumière as the father of documentary.[16] WORKERS LEAVING THE FACTORY is of course also a supreme example of a multiplication of internal frames: the double doors, one big, one small, the opening of gates/workers out/closing of gates after the last one has left. Here, the two frames complement each other: the spatial one, established by the fixed camera position and the temporal one, given by the film length, forming together the set of constraints which already act as an aesthetic system (precisely, one which makes Louis Lumière the cinema's first film auteur, but also a proponent of an aesthetics of minimalism, and thus with a modernist's appeal).

What is of interest in such an analysis – and perhaps goes beyond the pleasures always derived from self-indulgently ingenious interpretations – is the realization that one may have to ask where the 'structural features' noticed by the avant-garde critics might have found their historical rationale, and how this historical rationale might have found in Louis Lumière its biographical embodiment.[17] It is evident that the success of the cinematograph – its technical superiority over the many similar machines – has to be thought of as different from, indeed distinct from the films themselves, and yet neither is conceivable without reflecting on the professional identity of the Lumières, namely as businessmen interested in promoting the use of their patented software, such as photographic plates (the famous *étiquette bleue*). It was the plates' increasingly widespread use in the domestic environment of the amateur photographer which necessitated the development of new product, so that the cinematograph can be seen as the new hardware the Lumières needed to expand the application of their branded software.

Where the avant-garde approach to the Lumière films is so interesting is that its analysis and interpretation, assumption and intent are self-consciously, and as I said, polemically counter-factual. A more traditionally film historical approach, for instance, would argue that the persistence of symmetry and a-symmetry, as indeed of the narrative mise-en-abymes, is less the advent of cubism or other avant-garde artistic movements, as Henri Langlois imagined for BABY'S BREAKFAST or THE CARD PLAYERS (when he called the Lumières the last of the impressionists), but more prosaically the fact that the Lumière films – as indeed most of the films made before 1906 – were part of a variety programme. If right at the end of WORKERS LEAVING THE FACTORY, one worker is seen going in the opposite direction, it is as if to say, there is no final closure: a 'formalist' point of balance and a-symmetry perhaps, but one which leads to the more specifically socio-historical conclusion that the Lumière films were meant to be seen over and over again, that they were built in order to be experienced as both 'closed' and 'open' at the same time, thus improving on, but also commenting on the loops of Edison's kinetoscope, now for a different entertainment space, that of the continuous performances of vaudeville.[18] This seems particularly evident in THE CARD PLAYERS. Utilizing a pictorial motif borrowed from Cézanne, the film, in its temporal articulation, is built like a perpetuum mobile whose source of infinitely renewable energy is the coin we see the player on the left first pocket and then put down once more on the table in the very last frames, signalling that a new round commences, and representing, as it were, the spectatorial position en-abyme, for s/he too is caught in the cinema as a *dispositif* or institution based on repetition, a repetition activated by the money paid at the box office. But the film's 'circularity' also reminds us of the nineteenth century's many optical toys, from the praxinoscope to the mutoscope, which only knew repetition and the loop as their narrative-kinetic attraction. In a more directly Borgesian vein, watching Lumière films like THE GOLDFISH BOWL, THE SWING, THE BACKYARD in the late sixties, *after* SLEEP, or EMPIRE STATE BUILDING, one could only marvel at Louis Lumière's wit in having understood Andy Warhol so concisely, and with such consummate economy.

The reference to Cezanne, to Cubism and the Impressionists reminds us that, apart from film history, art history, too, has begun to interest itself in early cinema, and in particular, in the special 'way of seeing' that photography and film have brought to the world of images. What art historians from Norman Bryson to Jonathan Crary have focused on is the gaze, the form of attention which the new medium implicitly or explicitly assumes in the observer.[19] There have also been attempts to distinguish between a 'realist' and a 'naturalist' gaze, the former scanning or 'touching' the image in view of its overall coherence and its material properties, which – when compared with the perspectivally centred gaze of Renaissance painting – opens up an intriguing tension (as explored in Alois Riegl's theories of haptic space, and the role his concept played, for instance, in theories of German Expressionism, both in painting and film).[20]

The naturalistic gaze, on the other hand, is directed more towards the penetration of an image, of an eye 'entering' a visual space, also in order to take it apart and permeate it analytically. This distinction, here sketched only very perfunctorily, might nonetheless offer important clues regarding the function of mechanical mimesis in the history of modern painting, literature and the plastic arts, in relation to which photography and the moving image are both more and less than simply rivals and antagonists. Although such reflections are no doubt of interest for film history, one may nevertheless conclude that for understanding the historical imaginary and conceptual premises animating the film pioneers, these 'artistic' parallels played a secondary role. True, Louis Lumière seems to have possessed a highly developed sensibility, which we without hesitation would qualify as 'aesthetic' or 'artistic'. But after what I have been arguing above, any interpretation which categorizes the Lumière films as belonging to either the realistic or the naturalistic gaze might arrive at too hasty a conclusion, even though the startling divergence in how the films have been interpreted over the past hundred years does cry out for just such an underlying, perhaps even categorical opposition.

Lumière's concept of cinematographic vision, however, can also be approached from another historicist perspective. Here one would go back to a tradition of seeing and viewing images which is no longer directly accessible to us, belonging as it does (or did until recently) squarely to the nineteenth century, and having left relatively few traces in our visual culture. This tradition developed around the practice of the photographic view, itself a manner of thinking about images and a way of looking, deriving from at least a century of the picturesque in the visual arts but also implying an act of visual possession, the latter enhanced by one of the views' most widespread variants, popular as parlour entertainment and a publicly consumed show, namely the stereoscope. The stereoscope had its heyday with the machines developed by Charles Wheatstone and David Brewster in the 1860s, and considerably boosted the trade from which the Lumières made their living, the photographic plate. In my scheme of counter-factual history, one could now add the 'dog that did not bark' theory of film history, where stereoscopy would have been, for almost a hundred years, the sort of clue partly missed when trying to reconstruct the pre-history of the cinema.[21]

Stereoscopy was revived in the 1890s in Germany with August Fuhrmann's *Kaiser Panoramas*, circular caroussels where up to 24 people could sit and look in turn at a slowly revolving stereoscopic slide show. Next to the magic lantern, it was the *Kaiser Panorama* which must be regarded as one of the most important precursors of publicly consumed image-shows in Europe. Without at least recalling in passing just how pervasive the fascination of and vogue for stereo-images once was (they were produced industrially in their hundreds of thousands), it may be difficult to understand the subtlety found in Louis Lumière's films. His stagings in depth, his use of off-screen space, the axis and angle of vision all seem to combine into a particular way of looking, and this may have its simplest explanation in the presence and persistence of stereoscopy, which would therefore provide the historical-materialist basis for the formalist obsessions that the avant-garde filmmaker and critics 'recognized' in the films.[22]

Study of the 'view' raises the question whether the advent of so-called 'classical' cinema of continuity editing and the mobile point of view narration made stereoscopic vision 'obsolete' by replacing its pleasures with other functional equivalents.[23] On the other hand, reference to stereoscopy might allow us to connect Louis Lumière's life-long preoccupation not only with three-dimensional seeing, but also with colour photography, ultrasound measuring devices and other, to us, rather eccentric pursuits (the Lumière Brothers took out some 150 patents).[24] It might also, more directly than we could have suspected, connect these interests with the present day, and contemporary work in image-recognition, machine intelligence and the ever more crucial use of optical and acoustic sensors, giving a third meaning to my subtitle, and ranging Lumière among the S-M practitioners of the cinematic apparatus: that is, science and medicine, sensoring and measurement, surveillance and military use....

It is the 'stereoscopic' dimension of Lumière's practice, characterized by at once excessive symmetry (if looked at from the vantage point of illusionism) and the symmetry of excess (if seen as the careful and deliberate multiplication of planes of action, focal points of attention and gradations in scale and distance) which distinguishes him from his immediate successors, while showing him very much in line with his scientific predecessors (for instance, Pierre Jules César Janssen had adapted Marey's photographic rifle for use in astronomy, taking stereoscopic images in order to calculate the distance of stars). Instead of constructing the image according to the laws of perspective and the single vanishing point (the markers of the classical image), Lumière seems to have chosen a different logic, one that splits perception, utilizes parallax vision, and one that presses the eye to see the image as a bi-level or even tri-level representation, at once flat and in depth, at once unified and divided, at once anamorphic and centred. His films, once viewed with this in mind, are quite remarkable for the way in which the eye is scanning the image; one also notices the multiplication of points of interest and attraction, while they force the eye out of the pictorially trained, monocular perspective.[25]

Apart from the already mentioned examples, such as WORKERS LEAVING THE FACTORY, or THE CARD PLAYERS, one could cite the extraordinary THE WASHERWOMEN, with its frontal staging and triple picture plane doubled by multiple action spaces, or the left-right division, doubled by a foreground-background division, in LE FAUX CUL-DE-JATTE/THE FAKE CRIPPLE which allows the policeman to be visible to us – as the beggar's impending nemesis – for a veritable eternity before he eventually accosts the unfortunate faker, forcing him to run and the policeman to give chase. A similar anamorphosis, this time not in space but in time, can be observed in CHARGEMENT D'UN WAGON DE TONNEAUX, in which a seemingly endless number of horses trot through the frame until we finally see what they are pulling: an enormous boiler drum of a steam-engine or a locomotive, symbolizing, as one contemporary critic shrewdly remarked, the patient toil of the nineteenth century in ushering in the twentieth century.[26]

Thus, it is surely not too counter-factual to conceive of the first moving pictures not only as exercises in animating or bringing to life what had hitherto been static and frozen (the effects that a Georges Méliès so much appreciated at the first Lumière showings, and from which he drew maximum effect in his own films), but as a kind of perversely improved version of the stereoscope, as an apparatus that could generate more effectively and more efficiently the impression of a new kind of space. Apparently three-dimensionally illusionist but actually structured so as to allow for entirely novel readings of the visual field and pictorial experience, this space committed Louis Lumière neither to the aesthetics of perspectival realism nor to the effects of illusionism, both of which were to determine the history of cinema in direct proportion – so one might now surmise – to his disaffection and lack of interest in the consequences of his own invention.[27]

The victory of illusionism in the cinema is thus, in a way, merely the trace of a positivist history behind which stand a number of virtual histories: those symbolized by Louis Lumière as the first master not of *the* cinema, but of all kinds of cinemas, possibly seeing into and seeing through the illusionism his *cinématographe* could – but need not – give rise to, and giving his own films the detail and precision he would expect of a scientist and an engineer, while following an agenda as idiosyncratic and personal as it proved to be pregnant in and for other histories.[28] Lumière's disaffection with and doubt about the cinema at the threshold of the twentieth century, we might say, has preserved him for the twenty-first century and for the complexities but also possibilities which the paradigm of the virtual is bound to bring in its train, as the cinema becomes not so much a virtual medium as the first medium of the culture of virtuality. And whether we regret this virtuality or see in it a new adventure of the human spirit, we can in either case salute Louis Lumière as one of its ancestors and begetters.

But – to return to my initial question: what would this salute mean? That we recognize, and therefore 'know' in what ways Lumière and his epoch had, as the German historian Leopold Ranke would say, their own 'immediate access to God the Almighty', or does it signal that we now know how to explain Louis Lumière to himself, giving his particular past its own truth – restore him to full knowledge, so to speak, which he could not have had without the historian? Let us assume instead that in Louis Lumière we call upon his ghost, his spectre, his virtual self, whom we summon, finally, only in order to help us better know ourselves.

Speed is the Mother of Cinema

Edgar Reitz

Much can be said about the contemporary situation of media, film, technology and about the aesthetic questions arising from them. With every year, it seems, how we relate to the world is increasingly determined by the pictures we come across in the media or those we produce ourselves.

When I was asked, some time ago, to make a selection of films for a conference on the future of film, I realized that at the beginning of my career as a filmmaker, which was 30 years ago, I was already closer to the answers than I am today. This seems very strange because in those days, at the beginning of the 1960s, nobody could foresee which of the utopian ideas then in circulation would one day become technically realizable. In fact, we were still living fully in the mechanical age and everything we understood by progress was still closely connected with mechanical thinking. Furthermore, the world of physics – or what was then of current interest in this field, nuclear physics – promised mankind incredible progress in energy production etc., yet it also represented a basic image of threat. There was a sceptical, pessimistic attitude towards physics and the world of technology. As young filmmakers of that time, we grew up in that split world.

However, there was another very important aspect. As children of the Nazi generation we reproached our parents for the cultural and human disaster of World War II. Moreover, as film people, we also had to come to terms with the heritage of the Third Reich. Yet it was Hiroshima that was much fresher in our minds, the kind of progress which contained such catastrophes, the germ of the end of the world. Nevertheless, in spite of all criticism, my generation continued to believe in progress, a fact which thoroughly determined the 1960s. The films produced in these years dealt with the future, with the vision of a society forging ahead thanks to its physical, scientific and philosophical thinking, enabling it to find better solutions for mankind's problems with life.

One keyword which described the idea of progress most clearly to me was speed, the other was communication. These two aspects of the modern age are deeply rooted in film history. Film, which came into being a hundred years ago, is virtually the expression of those two terms. It owes its technical development to the increased speed of mechanical processes. A hundred years ago it was possible for the first time to control acceleration or speed mechanically.

It is general knowledge that the motion picture as seen on screen only exists as such because it became possible to project 24 pictures, one after the other, within one second. This means a machine had to be invented showing a sequence of non-moving pictures so fast that one gets the impression of motion by an optical illusion. Therefore, moments of 'standstill' are joined together to form sequences which we experience as motion. This is an important point often forgotten by filmmakers and viewers alike. Sequential viewing has become second nature in our century. Originally, when there were only live forms of performance as in the theater, the variety or the circus ring, speed was not a matter of interest even when magic tricks were performed. The aesthetics of cinema remain bound to this principle of sequential perception to this day. It is the most important thing for a film to be running. The uninterrupted and irreversible sequence is the basis of cinematic dramatic structure. Everything we plan when making films, all the strategies we think up, are founded on the condition that the film does not tear or break. They are founded on the condition that the machine running in the cinema does not come to a halt. The stopping of the moving sequence would be the end of the cinema.

If we want to tell a story in a film we will soon realise that those stories that are good for the cinema are those that are related to this unrelenting mechanical principle, only then are they 'filmic'. Therefore, the two major topics of the cinema are crime and sex. In crime as well as in sexual passion the inevitable moment arrives when something gets going that can no longer be stopped. These are the passages that grip and enthrall us in cinema stories. Of course there are other topics that depend on the uninterruptable sequence of pictures. I was lucky enough to discover such a topic early on in my career, namely film biography. Stories recounting a life, such as they are told in HEIMAT, bear this mechanical principle of always having to flow on and on.

Consequently, speed is the mother of cinema. It is not by chance that the car was invented at the same time, the aeroplane, the telephone and the radio. Everything that has determined this century of acceleration was invented around the same time, the transitional period between two centuries. Another aspect is that all these inventions were created in order to forge links between human beings. Film was one of the first media of communication. For the first time people were able to take signs of life as information and to separate them physically from human beings, to pass them on separately, independently of place and time. This means that the cinema became a place of secondary experience. By means of motion pictures we have learnt to understand the largeness of the world we have actually been living in. For the first time we bridged the gaps between nations, peoples and cultures in our imagination and it became an everyday experience to see into the hearts of far away and strange people.

Sometimes I wonder how the viewers of the first decades managed to cope with this enormous extension of self-awareness. The relationship between this new experience of omnipotence and the Third Reich should be described one day as a phenomenon of cinema history. Thus appeared for the first time that which we now call the audio-visual age of communication. New media, which we consider to be so momentous and new, actually started with cinema history. We merely experience their continuation. We are presently leaving the mechanical age but nevertheless the aspects of communication and speed remain fundamental. They also apply to data transmission, although there the fight against gravity, which had been so decisive for film history, is no longer important.

In 1961 I shot KOMMUNIKATION. This experimental shot was a by-product of a promotional film for the Deutsche Bundespost (German Postal Service). At that time the Bundespost wanted to show to what extent it had become a child of the technical age and that it no longer wished to conform to the image of the postman going from house to house by bicycle. In the age of electronic news transmission it became obvious that the sector of telecommunications was soon to become the dominating part of this organization, also in economic terms. It was this aspect that my documentary, which has a length of about 45 minutes and is titled POST UND TECHNIK, wanted to emphasize. When I returned from the shoot I had obtained some idea of a world which had been completely alien to me until then. I now had knowledge of the inner world of communications technology. I had taken a second degree, so to speak, whilst making this film. I had to learn to understand communications technology, and did not mind doing it as I increasingly came to understand that my job as a filmmaker was directly related to these questions.

Already at that time there was the technical problem how so many telephone conversations and telex connections could be transmitted by one wire, one channel, so that a worldwide communications network could be set up. There were also attempts of data reduction and multiplex systems distributing pieces of information to wholly different levels, to different frequency ranges or sampling them by means of so-called time-division multiplexers. Technical engineers discovered that during the transmission of telephone conversations there were still capacities for a multitude of information at the same time. This fascinated me because with film we also deal with the fact that 24 pictures per second are projected, but that these seconds in the cinema contain an unbelievable amount of unused time. It is the time between the pictures that I wanted to learn to make use of. A film in a camera is wound on by a gripping device, whereas the projector does a similar thing with the help of the maltese cross mechanism so that for half of the time there is no picture on the screen at all. I started to think about what one could do with this time of dark phases. After all, they fill more than 50 per cent of the cinema evening!

During the following years, at the Hochschule für Gestaltung in Ulm, I carried out many an experiment by trying to project pictures with one projector into the dark phases of another one coupled with it. This experiment resembled those of the 1960s with their belief in progress and their enthusiasm for simultaneous presentations in art. Avant-garde art, which has always considered itself as an expression of time becoming scarcer, has invariably been drawn towards film. For instance, in the 1920s the French director Abel Gance shot his famous NAPOLEON which, already then, had to be shown on three screens simultaneously. Here too, the viewers' time was planned to be used in a multiple way. Film was a time-division multiplex system as I had discovered in the new communications technology. It did not become a central concern for me to make simultaneous films, but coming across communications technology just enabled me to obtain wonderful insights into the ideas of the modern age. It was also important to me that technicians could not think of themselves as crackpots or eccentrics, the way we artists could, that they worked for an all-dominating industry and made big money with their utopian ideas. At last I understood that the world could no longer be seen as a film reel smoothly running through the gate, but that we always have to recognize concurrent contradictory interests and currents. The suitable means of presentation for this insight required a new level of complexity such as already was being investigated in the field of technology. It was this interconnection, this concurrence of movements and events determining reality that I wanted to learn to show.

I find it remarkable that I already came across these questions at the beginning of my film career. I think that the digital technologies and pictures we deal with today are not only the results of new technological means, but that they were already prepared mentally in early film history. It is also interesting that at the beginning of our century artists repeatedly felt a new world was opening up there. Especially avant-garde art deals with the fragmentation of the world. It views the world in the form of small, torn pieces, presented in nets and simultaneous events and confusing forms in which human beings learn anew to orientate themselves.

I worked on KOMMUNIKATION, which only runs for ten minutes, for the entire year of 1961. The editing was enormously difficult because the film contains so many cuts that it often reminds one of the aesthetics of today's video clips. We made innumerable attempts to break out of the then avail-

13) In Edgar Reitz' short KOMMUNIKA-
TION (1961) the new technologies become
a challenge to filmic representation. The
visual techniques deployed are trying to
convey the optimistic perspectives taken
by both the telecommunication industry
and avantgarde artists.

able technical traditions, for instance by filtering out the colours from the pictures. I tried to bring about cuts which were shorter than the single picture and to create overlappings on the human retina which means that pictures were reassembled where they are actually created, on the retina.

KOMMUNIKATION describes an impression of the communications technology of that time. It seems to portray the rather naive beginning of a new technology. However, it also represents an insight into the world that we are actually living in today. We were then in a transitional period shortly after the building of the Berlin Wall. The symbol of the wall appears again and again. At that time, one of the major concerns of communications technology was to overcome the walls, no matter their form or shape. Multiplication is another symbolism in the film. The human sensory organs, eyes, ears and hands multiply.

The manner in which the finished film was received was interesting. Before opening to the public in the cinema the film was presented to the Postmaster General of that time, Stücklen. He jumped up after the projection and announced that the film was not allowed to be shown as long as he was Postmaster General, unaware that he had no control over this. The film seemed uncanny to him. The images that described the future of his technical service were so confusing to him that this untempered remark escaped his lips. KOMMUNIKATION was also new as far as the music was concerned. It is one of the earliest films with added electronic sounds. The music, composed by Anton Riedl, was created acoustically of the same substance the pictures were made of. The basic material is composed of sounds and electronic signals coming from actual news-systems. For instance, I was interested in how it would sound if one heard all telephone conversations simultaneously. In the control centres connections had been made for me with the help of which tens of thousands of telephone conversations could be heard at the same time.

Parts of the material used by Riedl to shape his music was produced in this way. We tried to create a link with the world of communications technology at the acoustic level. When talking of digital media today, of data highway and the consequences of digitization, one has to be aware of the fact that the media are only continuing today what had begun back then. It is also an element of telecommunications that is now entering the aesthetics of pictures. No longer is motion that which is most important but the fact that telemedia understand everything our senses perceive in terms of communications technology and to make its transmission possible – e.g. to invent a global medium of communications technology between people, of which film is only one part. This creates an outlook about which I would like to make a few remarks.

The new keyword is digitization. It is the language of computers that is digital, the possibility to handle all information with the code of the numbers zero and one, or of 'yes' and 'no'. Through these means, everything that can be transmitted between us is dissected into the most primitive forms. This is an immensely complicated procedure and only practical because it is possible to create an incredible speed in the sequence of this most primitive information. Firstly, transmitting a picture in this way is the most lavish method we can imagine because the issue is no longer to understand a picture as a picture but to define innumerable points and to lay down criteria that can be handled with 'yes' or 'no'. On the other hand this form has the advantage that one can intervene in the primitive pictorial basis, the picture elements, and modify it. This means that suddenly every form of forgery has become possible. As soon as pictures, sounds, music or speech have been acquired digitally we have material at hand which makes it possible to access every element from which events can be produced. Our perception of what is real will change fundamentally. Reality and image will have less and less in common. Hardly any image will be able to lay claim to reality. Only the medium itself will still be real.

This acknowledgement of telecommunications as reality has been prepared for over a long time. It has developed, bit by bit, as part of the social perception in this century. The cinema has had a share in this development as well as the telephone, the radio and the television. All media produced by our century have increasingly been taking the place of social reality. We have to assume that in future years everything produced by human culture will be digitized. We have to assume that all music, all construction plans of buildings, all bank accounts, all images, all historical pictures, all films and every kind of painting, will be digitally acquired and that a worldwide network of data banks will develop on the basis of this digital acquisition, establishing a new kind of business. We will be talked into believing that this is a better world, one that puts all data at our disposal. This is the new motto of progress.

Our primary world in which we live physically will increasingly lose importance in our personal biography, as will political decisions which will be made in favour of the data which produced them. The satisfaction will consist in the data that define our existence. The cinema will also have a share in this development. It is highly unlikely that the cinemas of the future will still show 35mm-copies on a projector and that these copies will be carried arduously to the express train or the central store after they have been shown. Expensive film copies are presently at risk because of improper treatment in transport, ageing processes and wear. It is anachronistic that films are only available if the copy has arrived at the station in time. These days are numbered, because it is already possible to digitize cinema films and so transform them to the weightless immaterial state all data have. One day it will be no problem to transmit films to the cinema via data channels and to recall any film at any time. Inevitably, the uninterruptability of the sequence of pictures, of which I said that it was the basis of film aesthetics, will be called into question. This uninterruptability can no longer be the dramatic basis in the digital age since data currents can be interrupted at any time. They do not have any gravity or inertia. Data are so freely available that every event can be linked with the previous event at any moment, the continuous sequence and the chronology of the story will vanish. We can presently only vaguely imagine what, in terms of content, will take its place.

With HEIMAT I made a film which obviously represents an extreme opposite to this technical world of computer aesthetics. The term 'Heimat' (home) itself seems to be the opposite of what has just been hinted at, because it still deals with the fact that each of us experienced a distinctive childhood in a particular place, something which can neither be put into perspective nor be disposed of. My identity was formed in this 'Heimat' and actually most artists often seem to go back to such elementary basic experiences. Artists frequently emphasize that childhood is their only source of inspiration. Up to a certain age we perceive the important contact with the world through children's eyes. Only once can we have this basic experience of having come across things for the first time. The first look through a keyhole into the world, the first love, the first contact with plants and animals, people and things, the first time we eat or drink something particular leaves us with such deep impressions that no other experience of reality can equal it. Each repetition, each later experience confirms this first experience of reality and recalls it.

HEIMAT tries to describe this state which, after all, is also the memory of something forever lost. To this day I know that this is something which cannot be digitized. 'Heimat' is something which primarily determines our relationship to the world. I realise that children growing up today count electronic pictures as well as contacts with telecommunications technology among their very first childhood experiences in the world. In fact it is surprising to see the early age at which children learn to telephone or to deal with television or their game computers that increasingly become a part of children's rooms. Nevertheless, I think that none of these electronic toys is experienced in the same fundamental way as the mother, the house one grows up in, the first friends one makes or the street one goes along, alone for the first time, unaccompanied, from one's parents' house to school. All these experiences do not belong to the world which can be conveyed by means of technology or telecommunication. Yet it seems to be an experience which can be described in the cinema.

This is where the ways of cinema and telecommunications part. It is even said that the cities we live in are progressively losing the character of real places in the direct, personal sense. A virtual space, in which we are slowly but surely starting to live, is replacing it. For all of us, for a long time the telephone has already had the function of replacing reality. If you call your friends, waking them at night, because you are worried about your brother, then you must be aware of the fact that we have been communicating via the telephone for a long time. We do not have the feeling at all that we thereby lose touch with reality. People become closer and reach each other via the telephone with wholly natural conversation. In this respect our lives have been taking place in a virtual space for quite a while and in the course of the following centuries the virtual living space will grow enormously.

I do not intend to speculate about multimedial society, but it seems almost certain that all these new technologies will take place in our homes. The living room, or whatever we consider to be our private place to retire in, will be the place that links us to the world. When I come back from a journey and open my front door I no longer have the feeling of returning to a shelter, a closed room. Previously, we used to look at our mail and open the mail box before we went up the staircase. Now the world is awaiting me at home. First I listen to my telephone answering machine, then I look if a fax has arrived, then I switch on my computer and have a look at my e-mail. Many people switch on their radios or TV-sets straight away so that the world literally streams through their homes. Who knows what will await us when we enter our own four walls in the future.

In this respect the home is no longer merely a place to retire to. Although, it is the place where we no longer participate directly in public life, we are no longer sheltered at home as we used to be. The data lines are holes anyone can slip through, hoping to wangle some money from us when we get home. Incessant commercials await us as soon as we turn on the television-set.

In the future an incredible battle for this participation in the world will break out. On our way home, at the garden fence and on each billboard, we will be urged to switch on our multimedia-sets when coming home: Something is waiting for you there! 'Coming home' will mean booming business for a huge, worldwide industry. The political debate has already moved to television rather than any other reality, and of course our participation in the state and in society will take place in the living room. The living room of the future will be a battlefield. According to Florian Rötzer's *Die Telepolis*, the living room of the future will be called the communications room. Who knows how these rooms of our new homes will be technically equipped? Surely this well-known tv screen will not be the end of it. Very soon it will be possible to have projections as big as a wall at home, too. The relationship between the private and the public sphere will change. Public life will take place at home instead of outside. The classical experience of inside and outside will be reversed. I imagine that this reversal will particularly make young people go out again more often, will make them flee from their flats into the public. If one day there is nothing at home but the multimedial world in the best possible technical quality on all four walls, then going to the cinema will almost be like returning to the womb. Here both topics contrast: The world of communications technology is penetrating into our private sphere and is fragmenting our perception of the world. On the other hand 'Heimat' represents something that we have lost and that we may find again in the cinema, as a substitute for home. It can only be a substitute for home, because we are really in the cinema. Compared with this – according to Ernst Bloch – the real home is a place where nobody has been yet.

Our image of reality is not only determined by the twentieth century, nor was it simply formed by the education we received. It is the product of millions of years of evolution. Our sensory perception is the result of this evolution, a collective experience of the world, which has existed from the earliest times onwards. From the moment primates learnt to speak, surviving also meant learning to distinguish between mediated and true reality. I have every confidence in the fact that each child possesses these powers of distinction acquired during evolution and these are the limits of the digital world. The technological trend offering a substitute for all our sensory perceptions, by means of technical transmission, is called cyberspace. It will surely be possible to offer us a deceptively similar, naturalistic participation in fictitious events. Possibly some day this will no longer mean putting on this terrible gear, such as virtual reality gloves and other bits of medieval armours. Yet, I am sure we will not be able to pass over or forget the steps in evolution. Human existence will always have another, a deep-rooted dimension which is our private perception of reality. To this extent, 'Heimat' is playing an increasingly important role as an alternative concept.

Fin de Siècle of Television

Siegfried Zielinski

I have called my paper '*Fin de siècle* of Television' not simply to provoke, but in order to think constructively about the future of television, bring to mind its present situation and reflect on its place in an audiovisual landscape which is becoming increasingly complex.[1] To do this, allow me to cast my mind back a few years, to the heady hours and days in Berlin and Germany around the ninth and tenth of November 1989. In those momentous weeks, the mass media of the two German states became visible in sharp relief, as probably never before. East German television demonstrated its potential strength for the first time and West German television demonstrated its once again – albeit in a state of rare intensity: the medium was in a permanent state of sensations. It was so much part of the events it purported to be reporting on that for much of the time it appeared to be their chief co-ordinator and orchestrator. At the Brandenburg Gate and other focal points of the rapid East and West German rapprochement, the reality within the medium itself and external reality became as if one and the same.

Television, as programme television, as broadcasting, was alive, or at least one could be forgiven for thinking so, faced with the constantly running film loop of reports on border crossings of all kinds and the permanent partying on the West Berlin streets. But, seen from a media perspective this great moment for broadcasting – even more so for radio than television, actually – was a kind of historic last-ditch stand, the result of the clash of two different social systems, which for a long time appeared to have antagonistic public relations systems. When the collision came about, some of the dynamite originally deposited in broadcasting when it was constituted as a mass medium exploded, but most of it had been getting ever more damp over the last decades to the point of becoming non-combustible. In a recent discussion, the psychoanalyst and Lacan translator Norbert Haas referred to his heightened perception of Berlin as a 'hologram'. Suddenly the quality of the medium was rediscovered and at the same time given the illusion of depth by subjective experience. This came about because the 'hologram' was charged temporarily with real life. 'Berlin – history you can catch hold of', we were told over and over, but also 'just like a film' or 'as if at the movies', which indicates the imaginary quality of perception of the events.

My point of departure is that classical television is historically obsolete. Since the mid-1970s the medium has undergone a tremendous process of

transformation in advanced industrial societies. In the course of this process, traditional television has not disappeared completely, but it is losing
appreciably its once stately significance as the medium of private and famil-
ial audiovisions. Structurally in this sense, it has re-located from the centre
to the periphery. It has become one element, one floor in a highly differentiated and diversified department store where the most varied universes in
sound and images are on offer, competing with and against one another. I
characterize this level with my working concept 'advanced audiovision'.[2]

Since then it has become clear that it did not take much time for this level
of audiovisual communication also to prevail in Eastern Europe. The feroc-
ity with which the shopper-tourists from the East burst into the electrical
goods shops of the West, clearing their shelves of tv sets, video-recorders
and satellite dishes made it easy to predict what a bonanza the fall of the
wall would be for the Direct Broadcasting Television of Rupert Murdoch,
RTL or Bertelsmann, for MTV-Europe and God knows who else, as Polish,
Hungarian and East German housing estates got themselves wired and
hooked up. With an irony that probably escaped the bureaucrats, one of the
very last things the GDR ordered as a sovereign government after the 'turn'
[Wende] was the purchase of 100.000 VCRs from the firm Sanyo. Since the
population of the East had been watching West-television for decades, one
wonders what loyalties they thought they were buying off by buying in
these imports?

The general transformation processes these examples refer to have as
many causes as there are phenomena to illustrate them with. They take
place within a complex mesh of economic, cultural and political relations.
The importance of the audiovisual media has grown so exponentially that it
is clear they will affect the values and norms of both individuals and whole
societies. These media have to literally mediate: between the increasing privatisation as well as the globalisation of our ways of life, between the mobility of our working lives and the rigid regulation of its time structures,
between the highly differentiated life styles of the affluent two-thirds of the
advanced industrial societies and the unrelenting poverty, pauperization
and (self-)exploitation of the rest, many of whom, it seems, would rather go
without shelter than miss out on television.

It is important to bear these backgrounds in mind because our imagin-
ings, ideas and outlines of television's future scenarios are too often influenced only by the foreground. Although what I have to say relates primarily
to our own situation, and concerns some of the technical as well as cultural
aspects of these changes, the underlying socio-economic nexus of globalisation and intensified competition is never far from my thoughts, indeed they
are partially determined by it. With this in mind, I would like to deal with

two aspects in a little more detail, what I call the 'literaturization' of audiovision, and the contradictory forces of 'mobilisation and privatisation'.

The 'Literaturization' of Audiovision

Since the mid-1970s, when Sony with its Beta-sytem and Matsushita with VHS started producing simple, cheaper and efficient recording appliances of audiovisuals for a consumer market that was about to take off, the market for audiovisual products has undergone fundamental restructuring. Until then the choices were between the two film distribution poles of cinema and television. Thereafter, a market with multifarious poles of distribution developed, in which video soon took over the leading position in accumulative power. The connections which interest me the most at the interface between media people and media machines, possess a further decisive quality. In the cinema, the audience bought entrance tickets and thus entered into a kind of rental contract – they merely rented about two hours of film time. Apart from the experience itself and more or less vague memories of it, they possessed nothing of the exhibition process of a film in the cinema. With a television set, they became owners of an appliance for the reproduction of film in a receiver. However, the programmes themselves remained transitory and the owners of the receivers exercised no power over them. It was only with the advent of electromagnetic (and later opto-electronic) storage technology that people came to own, and have at their disposal, film products on a mass scale. Ownership of the reproducing appliance was expanded to include the potential ownership of films as commodities (I include here also television products in the economic sense), long before the arrival of digital video discs.

This opened up entirely new perspectives on how to deal with audiovisions, cultural as well as economic ones. The electromagnetically or – in the case of the video disc – opto-electronically stored film products can be used in a way which had up to then been reserved for literary texts: the possibility to choose the point in time for the act of reception, optional order and speed, possibility of interruption, repetition at will, ability to mark or archive. This is what I mean by 'literaturization' of audiovision. It is not intended to refer to an evaluating classification of the software in the sense of a culturally ambitious canon of literature but to the quality of the process of use. That this concept stands in crass opposition to the prevailing videogrammes and to the prevalent use of VCRs as transit stations for mass produced film commodities, is also an – intended – provocation. It is high time that a start be made on imaginative productions, outside the areas of research, vocational training and further education, which take into account the new use-values of the storage media. In this connection, television as it

14) Using television technology to simulate the theatre experience: an early example of electric cinema.

15) Believe or not, the last days of the GDR were a veritable looking glass war of media attention.

16) Japanese HDTV lounge: In order to enjoy the full delights of HiVision, the subjects are fixed to their seats in front of the 'pictures'.

17) In this Ampex ad, television restages ist claim to be everyone's theater.

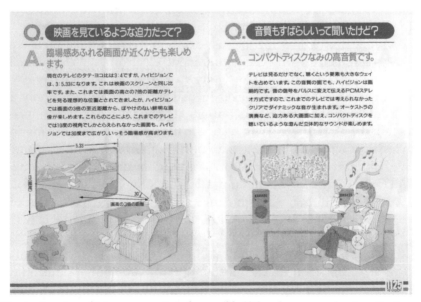

18) The impression of tele-presence is only possible if the viewer remains in a fixed position, as this cartoon illustrates.

exists today in the form of public broadcasting authorities could perform great and innovative tasks. If it fails to do so, this potentially large market will be served in the future by the commercial producers and dealers in storage media.[3]

Mobilisation and Privatisation

These concepts refer and are intended as hommage to Raymond Williams who brings them to bear in one of his last essays, which for me, belongs among his most interesting works.[4] Mobilisation and privatisation, both as 'late modern' concepts of living and forms of cultural organisation, seem to me to be shaping decisively the use of television in the near future and, as vanishing points, now figure intensively and excessively in the projections and planning of the hard and software industries. Mobile telephone, pager, pocket e-mail, portable fax or power book: these are but a small selection of the media appliances available for the manager, politician or scientist who can be reached everywhere and functions communicatively: 'gadgets' for the everyday routine of fast and mobile communication. They are artefacts, signs that have become appliances, of an immense thrust in making technologically-supported communication mobile, but also our way of life. Every air-traveller has noticed the changes in the development of 'Inflight Entertainment' to 'Inflight Infotainment': witness the combination of hyper-fast air travel and individual data as well as audio-equipment, video-screens and telecommunication devices for the jet passenger built into the back of the plane seat in front or the sides of your own seat.

The mobile appliances for the fast-decision-makers have their equivalents in everyday consumer/entertainment electronics: Walkman, Diskman, Watchman, Personal Video, 'Quicks' or 'Tell Me' are the names of the pertinent gadgets which enjoy ever-increasing popularity not only at the relevant international trade fairs but among the younger segments of the population the world over. With regard to film products in a broader sense, which are my own main interest in audio-visions, this means graduation to a state of ubiquity which amounts to a certain placelessness: I no longer go to a film (at the cinema), the moving image no longer comes to me (via television), it goes with me, it accompanies me. This is the realisation of that techno-dream, as for example the author Ernst Krafft outlined it in his small book *Fliegen und Funken* (Flying and Transmitting) as long ago as 1924.

With the appliances and technical systems of mobile audiovisual communication, we have one of the most important vanishing points on which the future supply of 'programmes' will orientate itself. However, there is a further vanishing point, whose relation to the first is both contradictory and complementary/competitive: the intensification and expansion (literally) of illusionism into the private home, in the 'stationary' sphere. I refer to the grand-scale techno-cultural project of HiVision, High Definition Television or Advanced Television or whatever one chooses to call that which is now being discussed and argued over worldwide under the abbreviation HDTV (personally, I prefer the Japanese designation HiVision because these developments are not focused on television, at least not in the sense we now understand this term). I shall not lose words on the conflict between different technologies and standards, which are, as everyone knows, in reality dogfights among the 'global players' for markets!

Beyond the differing concepts being traded worldwide, the parameters of the planned visions may be generalized and condensed to a few definitive and salient points. The issues at stake are:

– A considerable advance in the quality of the horizontal but, above all, in the vertical definition of images, and their essentially fine material structure (also formulated as an immense heightening of 'realism', though it would be more correct to say 'illusionism').[5]

– A change in the relationship of width to height in the direction of cinematographic dimensions, away from the rather square image with a ratio of 4:3 to a broad image with a ratio of 16:9, which would allow Cinemascope film to be reproduced without loss of picture but which also in general, in connection with my first point, substantially raises the impression of 'tele-presence' of that which is being represented. If the viewer sits in the requisite position, the angle of vision approaches that of 'natural', i.e. technologically non-mediated vision. Here it must be stressed that this is only possible if the viewer remains in a fixed position. In order to enjoy the full delights of HiVision, the subjects are fettered to their seats in front of the 'pictures' in the same way that they are in the cinema (or, if you like, as were the prisoners in Plato's famous cave).

– The images are considerably larger than those on traditional television screens, and for the immediate future they will be dependent on projection appliances (such as the video beam), approximating the cinematic apparatus, until the flat screens made of liquid crystals will finally reach the mass market.

In the future there will be radical changes in home interior design, although the 'television room' has already become completely anachronistic in the singles and nuclear family households since the beginning of the 1990s. The space will be a hybrid layout/design, occupied by qualities deriving from the traditional audiovisual media of television and cinema but beyond that with further audiovisions, the contours of which we can at present only just make out – somewhere between the personal computer and the broadcast receiver.

After examining some of the programmes that NHK has been broadcasting since the late 1980s, one can say in general that:

- with the new potential for illusionism, the quasi photographic realism of Hi-Vision, the image makers will be forced to exercise greater care in the composition of scenes and the arrangement of shots. Every detail, including those at the frame's edge, has to be in sharp focus. The attention of the viewer is attracted much more strongly to the whole screen and thus defocussed. In terms of cultural theory this means that the image gains a greater aesthetic (or fetishistic) character as Walter Benjamin understood it, that is, it is charged with *aura*.
- A significantly higher level of quality in the structure of the electronic material makes way for expanded possibilities in the syntax of televisual language: new perspectives are opened up for mixing, for the montage of different materials, but also new working practices, leading to rationalisation in the production process. Extensive experiments in this direction were carried out in the later 1980s in connection with the Canadian series *Chasing Rainbows*. The actors worked almost exclusively in the studio. The historic setting, Montreal in the 1920s, was transposed almost flawlessly onto the studio material with the aid of the Ultramatting process. Prior to the advent of digital effects, it was Zbig Rybczynski who proved to be a master of applying matte work and video matching, as in his celebrated films STEPS (1987) and L'ORCHESTRE (1990).
- The displacement of size dimensions does not only apply to the individual images but is also present within the images: HiVision promotes a tendency towards the long shot, the overview, which is a televisual accentuation of the world of objects. Large and near, the standard distances of traditional television will change, no longer bringing us so many faces (e.g. of politicians), but rather, the perfect surfaces of attractive objects, be they branded goods and consumer products, be they the commodified and thoroughly styled bodies of human beings.
- We will be confronted with a change of rhythm. Where the long shot holds sway, the horizontal panned shot will become superfluous, or at any rate recedes in importance. The individual shot may become calmer and steadier (as in classic cinema) but the hard cinematographic cut will become more important, televisually. Here, important experimental work has also been done, as for example in John Sanborn's and Mary Perilo's CAUSE AND EFFECT (1987/88), produced by Rebo High Definition Studios.

Changes such as these in the microstructure of the individual message will go hand in hand with shifts in the whole range of televisual products. HiVision leads to the setting of new priorities in the genres and programme sections, to the break up and crossing of traditional boundaries. What made this medium great, the ambition to be 'a window on the world', to offer a view on the reality outside of the medium itself, will be pushed back in favour of broad, opulent productions, i.e. in favour of a kind of audiovisual wall paper, a medium for atmosphere, moods and perhaps even for meditation.

Future classifications products will have two poles: on one side the supply of miniaturized mobile communication devices, which will be more utilitarian, i.e. produced at less cost and extravagance, and with fewer superficial aesthetic properties. On the other side will be the special products for the domestic, stationary, highly-developed appliances of entertainment electronics, lavishly produced with high-quality superficial aesthetics. The intersection of both will be the programme genres, which in the future will be even more demand-driven than at present: only those will be supplied that are attractive to audiences in the sense of the highest ratings. As a third factor, there are the 'storage media' (compact disc and CD-ROM), which compete with and complement the appliances mentioned above. The 'content' will come from mobile communication on the one hand (for example, Interactive Programmes) and have special forms of realisation, but they are also the ideal media location for the grand fictions with mass effect (for example, cinema feature films, the taboo subjects of sex and violence) both commercially and with regard to the situation in which use takes place.

All this can be expressed in an analogy from media history: according to this scenario, traditional television would only fulfill the functions in audiovision that radio, with its information and entertainment service, now fulfills in the area of acoustic reproduction. In the case of radio, extravagant musical productions would also gradually shift to hi-fi equipment with its magnetic tape deck, CD and record player.

Kluge's Television[6]

A project which for some years now aims at reacting to the changed structures and classification practices in the audiovisual sector, is DCTP, initiated by the film maker Alexander Kluge. DCTP stands for Development Company for Television Programmes. Over the last 30 years Kluge has played an important role in the German cinema's *politique des auteurs*, he is a jurist and advisor on various committees for the promotion of film, he is constantly looking for new allies in the area of film production and is not afraid of unconventional steps and untrodden paths: all this is in the service of a project whose fundamental principles he formulated with Oskar Negt in the book *Öffentlichkeit und Erfahrung*: 'The problem is that a critique of television cannot be formulated in a literary or published form. Production which is in itself dependent, like television, can only be criticized by a different kind of production. [...] We must let our strength flow into the strength of the opponent.'[7]

DCTP, in which Kluge works in cooperation with several other partners, produces a kind of high quality magazine programme, which is screened on the two most banal commercial channels in West Germany – SAT1 and RTLplus – who in the meantime have achieved high ratings. Kluge made clever use of a loophole in the terms of the broadcasting licenses awarded to these private channels whereby they are obliged to allow third parties access to programming if they wish to occupy terrestrial frequencies. In the Japanese advertising agency DENTSU, Kluge found a partner to finance his televisual experiments. A paradoxical situation: one of the biggest ad agencies in the world makes a type of televisual programme economically possible which must surely have one of the smallest audiences in the world: Kluge's Television. Slotted between the prime time feature film and late night striptease shows or a sex magazine, it really is intimate television, for a club of audiovisual gourmets, with ratings around zero: private television in the real sense, which the large-scale distributor usually ignores, in order to function in a rational economic way.

In *Filmgeschichte(n)*, modelled on Jean Luc Godard's *Histoire(s) du Cinéma*, and in the cultural magazine *Ten to Eleven* (it is no coincidence that the title is reminiscent of Channel 4's/Alan Fountain's *Eleventh Hour*), Kluge and his audience practice televisual seeing and hearing; he introduces people with something to say in intense interviews and develops just by the way – or so it appears – a new dramaturgy of televisual interviewing. By practising the role of an archaeologist in cultural history, he brings to light things that were long lost; he gives his audience access to his amazing private archive of texts and images; he plays with the clip-form as *the* televisual mediation strategy par excellence and combines it with his own passion for opera (he has produced a whole series of opera-clips); finally, he invites other filmmaker colleagues to share the brief broadcasting time – together with SPIEGEL TV just one hour per week – as an expression of solidarity and common purpose.

It is very elitist television – albeit an extreme example, perhaps – which stands for the restructuring process I mentioned at the beginning: televisual luxury goods in the audiovisual department store. Here there is no concern with the integrative or consensual model of traditional television, which in my opinion has in any case become increasingly obsolete. The DCPT cannot and does not want to serve the ominous social average, which only exists, as we know, as an abstract value. DCPT puts televisual time – and thus advertising time – at the disposal of a group of viewers which sees itself as an élite. In this case, the cinéphiles and cinéasts. However, there are, out there, many such groups, constituted differently with certain needs, interests and tastes to be catered for, and with this perspective in mind, the concept of elitist television loses some of its socially disreputable connotations: quality television like Kluge's reflects the simple fact that our societies are increasingly becoming a conglomeration of units of qualified life styles and ways of living, for which an integrative centre has become more and more a chimaera.

Needless to say, television as Kluge makes it could be combined excellently with the hybrid medium HiVision: carefully constructed audio-visions for the intimacy of a post-bourgeois salon. Shortly before his death, the Hungarian video-avantgardist Gabor Body described his preference for this kind of private public space: 'Independence and intimacy: this dualism and its accompanying traits, such as exchanging the grubbiness of movie theatres and the harsh light of installations in galleries for a return to home and hearth, where behind the tv set the house bar and the aspidistra smile at me, while in front of it the comfortable armchair beckons: these make up the glow of this new culture. The programme on the monitor is not the only – though an important – element of being together with friends. It represents a kind of literature that can be read by several people at the same time, though no more than a maximum of seven, otherwise we are back in the theatre or in front of an installation.'[8]

But let us give Kluge the last word: 'The unity of the public and the private would be a powerful form of organisation.'[9]

Theseus and Ariadne: For a Counter-History of the Cinema-Television Relationship?

Vito Zagarrio

Exercises in Historical Fiction

It could have been a different story, as in the best traditions of science fiction or counter-history. Let's try to imagine that ...

The relations between cinema and television developed out of a parallel desire to capture reality. In 1895 the Lumière Brothers staged their famous projection; in 1884 came the first experiments by Nipkow, which were taken up again by Baird and Jenkins in 1923. In 1907 a Russian, Boris Rosing, and an Englishman, Campbell-Swinton, suggested the use of cathode rays; on the other side of the ocean, Edwin S. Porter was making THE GREAT TRAIN ROBBERY. In 1925, while the Soviet filmmaker Sergei Eisenstein was making THE BATTLESHIP POTEMKIN, an American of Russian origin patented the iconoscope. As research advanced both in the field of filmic grammar and in pre-television technical innovation, the great theoretical debate and the resounding technological battle within the two media began. While the sound phase exploded in the film industry, in television a delicate phase of research began: the Very High Frequency band was explored between 1932 and 1940; an increasing number of lines was developed (in 1934, while IT HAPPENED ONE NIGHT was winning an Academy Award, television passed from 240 to 343 lines and to thirty images per second); and a control organism, the National Television System Committee, was established. This is the story as we know it.

But what about the story as it could have been? Here is the twist: Hollywood producers understood the commercial potential of the new medium of television and made an effort to corner its use. The success of the first television shows broadcast in movie theaters laid the bases, as early as the 1930s, for a convergence between the sacred territory of cinema and the new electronic technologies. The first broadcasts were of boxing matches and other sports events, which were brought live to numerous theaters (as the World Cup Soccer Championships would be, forty years later). Gradually, however, attention turned to fiction products to show in several theaters at the same time, and cable television was used to effect simultaneous projections of a given film by a particular major studio in its company-owned theaters — with obvious savings on the printing of copies. Immediately after the Second World War theater television gained a hold, and the majors achieved in the 1940s something that, in another historical dimension, would have been accomplished later, namely, the formation of oligopolies, the integration of movie studios, television networks, oil companies, and news services. In this new industrial stratification, Paramount obtained a 'tied verdict' in the case brought against it by the United States Supreme Court.

And here our historical fiction can ride on the wings of fantasy: Hollywood was no longer 'Panicsville', it no longer viewed the relationship with television in a conflictual manner; television was not a dangerous competitor, it was a fundamental ally. Competition led to an expansion not in width (Cinemascope, Cinerama, 3-D), but in depth, involving techniques (color became a direction of development common to both media) and languages. Common formats were pursued, and above all a great deal of experimentation was carried out on formal terrain — in directing, visual language, and narrative. Television, in its turn, freed from the competition with cinema, no longer directed its efforts exclusively at 'familiarity', at substituting the fireplace, but on the contrary established itself as a moment of aggregation, as a means of stimulus and comparison (for example, through the use of live broadcasts), of integration of different media and languages (theatrical productions, musicals, sports events, talk shows, and live television dramas shown in movie theaters). Thus television became an instrument of interaction between source and audience, rather than a continuous 'flow' calling for a distracted audience and passive consumption. Television series were soon born too, but not in an attempt to pull the studios out of a slump; indeed, serial films made in various formats (film, videotape, or live) created a new cine-television language. Because they were not only destined for the small screen, they did not change filmic grammar for the worse: the aesthetic of the close-up, of which Pierre Sorlin has spoken, did not triumph; and the canned universe of the television set did not win out. High Definition television (HDTV) was experimented with long in advance. It did not become a tool of political battle between the Americans and the Japanese, or between the Japanese and the Europeans, but remained a natural process of technically improving existing standards, making it possible to go to more than a thousand lines. Myriads of multitheaters were created, many with High Definition projectors. Video was one of the many formats in which movies could be made, like Super 8, 16 mm, and 35 mm. Theaters showed avant-garde films and short videos. Cinema did not need Hollywood blockbusters and television did not degenerate into a stupid, hypnotic instrument consisting of quizzes and talk shows. Directors achieved the integration between cinema and television twenty years ahead of time and strange phenomena occurred in culture and politics: in Italy, for example, where there was no movie-theater crisis, the world-famous Italian cinema of the eighties and nineties was born; Mr. Berlusconi, a former singer and department-store owner, went to jail for attempting to establish a privately-owned television network; and all this in a country that had been governed for years by the Left.

The Missing Link

It's just a joke, naturally. An exercise in political fiction in the tradition of novels such as *Contropassato prossimo* by the Italian, Morselli, or of essays like that of Medvedev on Russia (*Was the Soviet Revolution Inevitable?*). But the idea, notwithstanding the extreme conclusions that are part of the game (on the other hand, when a time-traveller changes even an insignificant factor of the past, he ends up changing the whole picture...), is by no means as odd as it might seem. In fact I have taken my cue from an essay by Edward Buscombe: 'Was the Evolution of American Television Toward What It Is Today Truly Unavoidable?'

Although to write history on the basis of 'what-ifs' is obviously difficult and dangerous, to hypothesize a different or alternative development may be of use to the future course of a *possible* history. It is like dealing with the old problem of the extinction of the dinosaurs: what would have happened if that comet (allowing that this was indeed the cause) had not crashed into the earth? The analogy comes to mind, partly because people have been talking since the late 1970s about the 'death' of cinema — a death supposedly caused by television. But while we are speaking of prehistory, let us point our lens a moment at the prehistory of television, and above all at the fundamental period of the television-cinema relationship, the one that has been called 'the missing link' between the two media.

There is a phase of the tormented affair between cinema and television, ranging from the early 1930s to the mid-1950s, in which different 'approaches' to television were tried. There were serious hypotheses of pay television and subscription television, with strong pressures being exerted by groups such as AT&T. The success of these hypotheses would have established a connection between users and the central distribution circuit, very probably by means of the telephone network (it would thus have anticipated the spread of cable by thirty years). But the most fascinating option, as I said in our historical fiction, was theater television, the brilliant intuition of a large-screen television. This, according to authors such as Ed Buscombe and Douglas Gomery, is the true 'missing link' between cinema and television.

Large-screen television technologies began to develop in the early 1930s: RCA, for instance, presented a system with a screen measuring eight by six feet at Proctor's Theater in Schenectady in 1930; after the Second World War, Warner and Fox, two pioneer sound studios, joined RCA to make a modified large-screen system. In Great Britain Baird Television and Scophony successfully experimented with maxiscreens and attempted to enter the American market: they mounted a public demonstration at the 1939 New York World's Fair. These technologies were far from perfect, but they awakened the interest of the companies: Paramount, for instance, in its anxiety to compete with RCA, participated in the foundation of the American branch of Scophony.

At the same time, Paramount tested a system of conversion from video to film (what today is called a 'videograph'). The system (which was called Paramount Intermediate) was an interesting mixture of film and television, a hybrid that somehow recalls the chemical-electronic 'monster' of the steadicam of the 1980s: based on two cathode tubes, it allowed immediate transfer of video imagery to film, which was developed, printed and dried in real time, in order to permit rapid projection.

The system could have been really revolutionary. Many theater circuits were already announcing the construction of small 400-seat cinemas, which would have included television shows in a composite program. As can be seen, the era of the multitheaters of the 1980s and 1990s could have begun decades earlier. In 1947 the Pantages movie theater in Hollywood regularly projected horse races, and Loew-MGM was preparing the installation of television systems in its chains in order to transmit sports events, as were Fox and Warner. But the leading figure of this phase was Paramount, as we have already seen, which even before 1945 had acquired a share of the Du Mont network and possessed several television stations, including KTLA in Los Angeles.

The studio was at the center of the story at this moment: while the spectre of the US Department of Trade vs. Paramount case was in the air (1948), the company publicly demonstrated its system of transfer to film at the Paramount Theater on Broadway. In Chicago, where it owned the important Balaban & Katz theater circuit, Paramount attempted the greatest number of experiments, recruiting well-known artists for shows to broadcast live. The experiments included a spectacular show in June 1949; other public events continued throughout 1950 and part of 1951, the year Balaban & Katz was given up; and in 1952, at the twilight of this experimentation, the equipping of at least seventy-five theaters in thirty-seven American cities for television projections.

Then came the end of theater television, the disappearance of this fascinating 'missing link'. In 1953 the trend that included 3-D and Cinemascope, which stood in opposition to theater television, triumphed. What followed

19) The Italian peplum meets the Hollywood epic, financed with television money: In GOOD MORNING BABYLON *(1986) the Taviani brothers from Italy have recreated the set from D.W. Griffith's* INTOLERANCE *(1916).*

was not a convergence but a wild competition. Fear reigned in Hollywood. 'Panicsville' prevailed, and the cinema-television relation set out down the path of competition and collision that we know so well. Television at this point became a household appliance (a development on which RCA had always placed its bets), the small screen replaced the 'movie-going' of the Depression years, reassuring people with its 'familiarity'. Cinema, by reaction, aimed at very large screens, endeavoring to broaden the gaze and enhance the emotions via three-dimensions, Cinerama, Vistavision, Todd-AO, Technicolor ...

The deadlock began, and the first homicidal and fraticidal metaphors appeared. The Hague conference spoke of 'Cain and Abel'; and an Italian convention bore the title, 'David and Goliath' (where one wondered who was David and who Goliath). But to draw on another Italian myth, why not Romulus and Remus? The two Roman twins, after all, fought precisely over a question of 'invasion of territory'. Romulus (television?) killed Remus (cinema?) after having tasted the milk of the same she-wolf. Who is the she-wolf? The common universe of the new cultural industry, the public of twentieth century media, the *relais* of mass communication and the art of in-

formation. The nightmare of the 'death' of cinema has run through the theoretical debate from the 1960s to the present day. The cinephile myth was
killed by the new electronic cynicism. Cinema is dead, long live cinema!

Let us stick to mythology and look for other metaphorical figures, in order to propose an alternative model of relationship. Instead of the biblical
duo of Cain and Abel (or as John Ellis has proposed, Oedipus and Laios),
why not think of Castor and Pollux, protectors of 'commerce' (are cinema
and television art or commodity?), the Dioscuri of Greek mythology who
were so tied to one another that they lived one day in Hades and one day on
Olympus? Or one might propose Theseus and Ariadne, with their oedipal
and incestuous parental ties. Theseus may be cinema, the new hero who
struggles against the earlier myths. He combats his terrible family — as
Racine, too, narrates — the Pallantide cousins, and then the Centaurs, who
may be the visual arts as they were before technical reproducibility, when
art still had an 'aura'. And who guides him in the labyrinth against the Mi-
notaur, the great mogul of conservation and retrograde culture? Ariadne,
perhaps a metaphor of television, with her magic yet cunning material
thread, her 'cable' in the labyrinth of mass communication. The reader will
object: even the love story between Theseus and Ariadne is brief; Theseus
soon abandons Ariadne on the isle of Naxos and winds up in the not always
tender hands of the gloomy Phaedra. But love stories *are* brief, and the one
between cinema and television, even for a short period of 'falling in love',
could have been overwhelming.

But it was not.

Why? There are various reasons, and it is not our task here to go into an
investigation of the cine-television 'mode of production'. The reader is referred, in this connection, to Douglas Gomery, but also to the other historians of cinema who give less credit to theater television and to the role of
television in general, in the crisis of cinema. According to Robert Sklar, for
instance, the crisis of the movie theaters has been caused not only by the advent of the small screen in homes, but also by the baby boom and, in a
broader sense, by the new way of life that has developed in the post-war period. It is easy to agree.

Whatever the case, the end of the small utopia of theater television can be
traced to economic, social, and institutional factors. Clearly the experiment
did not pay off in the long run; the revenues did not offset the expenses. For
instance, the 1949 World Series, one of the more prominent events transmitted by theater television, was a flop even without counting the large initial
investment it required (the cost of the Paramount system was around
$35,000). The problem should be viewed against the background of the
complex relation between cinema, television, and government that took

shape in this highly delicate phase (see Robert Vianello's essay in this connection).

What concerns us here is to draw some theoretical conclusions from this
fascinating hypothesis of the 'missing link', partly because it brings us back
to the very recent dabate on High Definition as the 'missing link' between
cinema and television in the 1990s. Reading the literature of the 'prehistory'
of television, one finds some extremely modern notes. An article in the *Hollywood Quarterly*, for instance, reports the critics' enthusiasm for 'theater
television' and reveals that plans for 800- and 900-line maxiscreens were already circulating in the early fifties. Well known today is the competition
between the 1175 lines of the Japanese system and the 1250 of the European
(Sony and Panasonic vs. Philips, Bosch, and Thompson). The circulation
strategy of HD imagery also recalls a split that was already present in the
1930s: while Paramount was likely to have been interested in distribution in
movie theaters, RCA aimed at a market for domestic television sets (as it
had done with radio). Something similar can be said of Philips, which has
focused its strategy on the 'convertibility' of existing televisions at the cost
of compromising the quality of the technology, whereas the Japanese have
chosen a higher quality system that requires the replacement of all domestic
sets, or else a different conveyance in movie theaters (small ones like those
that were being planned in the 1940s). The debate that showed signs of developing in the 1930s and 1940s, then, is extremely modern.

But what is most interesting for us is the possible outcome of this debate
on the theoretical ground of cinematic and television language. As Buscombe rightly observes, theater television could have produced a completely different history of television, and hence a different language, a
different grammar, and a different form. There is no way of knowing
whether television would have developed those narrative codes, genres,
and modes of vision that it developed because the 'home box' won, because
the clash (rather than the encounter) between cinema and television gained
the victory. That television turned toward independent fiction shows does
not mean that this is part of an intrinsic condition of the medium. The fact
that American television developed with sponsors and advertising does not
mean there was no alternative (for instance, European-type subscription
fees, especially if they had been developed via cable). Finally, that an indis-
tinct flow of information prevailed, mixing fiction and sports, talk shows
and advertising, does not rule out the possibility that television could have
become an instrument of a different culture, which would have brought, as
Buscombe suggests, a different theory and a different study of the medium.

Television could have become a place of experimentation, invention, and
creation – a medium and an instrument of creative freedom, rather than one

of homologation and constraint in stereotyped grids. One is led to this hypothesis of a counter-history by two subsequent moments of the cinema-television relationship. The first is the 'Golden Age' of American television, in the early 1950s, which witnessed the passage from live television to the invention of videotape; the second is a 'Golden' period of Italian television, in the late 1960s and early 1970s.

The Golden Age

The golden age of American television was another hotbed of technical and linguistic experimentation, a crossroads where history could have taken a different path. To see the composite materials of the 1950s again today reminds one that naïvité was wedded in those years with the seduction of a possible art form. The 'primitive' was joined with creativity, and production and technical difficulties stimulated talent. In the strange mixture of those images, one must view the new level of the clash/encounter between cinema and television. Let us start from an emblematic quotation.

As we have seen in the case of the mythological or biblical couples, scholars have often used mortuary metaphors to describe the cinema-television relationship. In his *Multinazionali e comunicazioni di massa*, Armand Mattelart quotes a curious 'text', a strange episode of the *Superman* comic-book series, which appeared in 1972. In this episode the super-hero has become a poor devil, a paralytic mendicant: his superpowers gone, his hyper-qualities atrophied, at the end of his extra-human wits, Superman is desperate. Kryptonite, naturally, is ostensibly responsible for this collapse of the hero; but the real fault is of advanced human technology, which makes Superman's 'job' superfluous: lasers have replaced X-ray vision, satellites have substituted superspeed, ultrasound has supplanted superhearing, computers have superseded superintelligence. 'The world no longer needs me,' the elderly Superman sorrowfully remarks, concealing himself from the curious and mocking crowds. Mattelart concludes: 'From the ashes of Superman (ashes of the Phoenix) are born the triumphalistic myths of the electronic invasion.'

Mattelart's provocative analogy can very well be applied to cinema: Super-Cinema, that is the great classical Hollywood cinema, has died, slowly exhausted by the universe of television. Like the elderly Nembo Kid, whose powers are no longer useful in a computerized society and who is compelled to beg from passers-by who deride him, the old cinema has retired, in preparation for a sad agony. But Superman dies and is born again (his comic did so, too, recently). So let us remain in the sphere of science fiction (albeit ironic) and return, with a flash-back, to the 1950s.

In an episode of *The Twilight Zone*, the Martians have landed and the police are questioning a peaceful group of passengers whose bus has stopped at a roadside diner. There is one more person in the group than on the passenger list, so one of them could be a Martian. 'Will the Martian please raise his hand?' But the Martian does not make a move. When the police leave, only the bartender and a solitary customer remain. In a *coup de théatre* the customer walks up to the bar and lights a cigarette with a third arm that sprouts from his side. He is the Martian. But then — with a little smile — the bartender takes off his cap and uncovers a third eye in the middle of his forehead— he is from Venus! Who is the real Martian?

Can the Martian and the Venutian be seen perhaps as a metaphor for the competitive relationship between film and television? If we accept the metaphor, the bid-raising (you've got three arms, but I've got three eyes, and so on) could be an ironical representation of a technological deadlock, a conflict that is also a covenant. The Martian-Venutian encounter represents a 'cold war' (like the real one that was being fought in the 1950s) between a 'warm' medium and a 'cool' one, but also a partitioning of the world, a reciprocal glance-casting (with the friendly third eye of the Venutian), an exchange of conventional signs and handshakes (with the Martian third hand).

In the history of the relationship between cinema and television there is in fact a constant, a double thread tying them together, a love-hate bond, the promise of a marriage (unfulfilled) followed by an actual separation, a history of convergences and divergences, of cold war and cold-war thaws. For years a directly proportional relationship between Hollywood's 'crisis' and the ascent of American television was taken for granted. Classic Hollywood was brought to its knees by the famous antitrust decrees (the Paramount case, the end of the integrated production-distribution era) and issued a definitive knock-out by television. A Hollywood in its decline, on 'Sunset Boulevard' – as such it is described by Higgens in *Hollywood at Sunset* and Goodman in *The Decline and Fall of Hollywood* – was the image of the American industry in the 1950s. Decline, fall, and sunset imply a catastrophe (although catastrophes are also positive changes, explosions of preceding logic, disturbances that can lead to new logics and new geometries), a catastrophe behind which television lurked like an incumbent threat, a long shadow.

Television, in contrast, was and is associated with winning, with positive terms, metaphors for life and youth. The golden age (in the mythic sense but also in a more materially tangible, monetary, sense) of television took place in the 1950s and exploded when the golden age of Hollywood (the 1930s and 1940s) had been over for quite a while – as if television had actually sucked the soul, the vital energy of classic cinema. The two golden ages were therefore out of phase, and the development of the two media in America, if they are charted, appear to be in perfect opposition. In 1949, for example, film spectators diminished by 20%, while the diffusion of television increased by 400%: where film went down, television climbed.

But as we have seen in our study of theater television, the struggle was not always a war. It might be considered a game, like the boxing matches transmitted in movie theaters during our prehistory. Perhaps television and film faced off like two boxers who study each other and size each other up before throwing the first punches. But it was a match nonetheless – in the areas of organization (the integration of the major studios with the television networks), of industry (the production of the first television series in the old studios – the foundations for the 'rebirth' of Hollywood one could say lay in its 'death'), of production methods (the emigration of many of the cinema's intellectual work force and craftsmen – especially directors of photography – to television, thanks also to the 'blacklist' and the television apprenticeship of many future Hollywood actors, screenwriters, and directors), and of language (television borrowed techniques, genres, and syntaxes from Hollywood). The double notion of the Hollywood crisis and the Hollywood vs. television conflict must therefore be completely reexamined with new coordinates, tackling the particulars of the two media and their evolution from 1948-1960.

Hollywood film tended in this phase to 'enlarge the visible', to expand laterally, but at the same time it cast itself into a deep hole. Once the mechanisms of assembly line production, the studio system, had been left behind, new expressive trends emerged along with new artists (the Sirks, Rays, Fullers, and Manns). The Hollywood *crisis* was therefore as much a phase of *development*. The glamor of the 1930s had come to an end, but styles, individual poetics, and original reinterpretations of the classic genres (Sirk's melodramas, Anthony Mann's westerns, Fuller's war films) were born, although in a more problematic way. Cinema passed from childhood to maturity, not without traumas, but also with an interesting leap in awareness.

Meanwhile television was experiencing its moment of greatest development, vitality, and energy. Analyzing the golden age of American television, one has the sensation that artists, producers, and sponsors had *carte blanche*, enjoying a unique occasion for research, experimentation, and invention. The television set was not just a limiting container, a claustrophobic mini-universe, as Alfred Hitchcock suggested when presenting the episode, 'Breakdown', in his famous series *Alfred Hitchcock Presents* ('I am always afraid', he said, 'of being a prisoner of this television, and I am especially terrified that you can turn me off'). The television set – and television in general – was also a magic box, an unlimited fantasy space.

The gags of comic Ernie Kovacs, for example, used the television space (including the realm of electronic effects) to reshape a universe of surreal expedients, to remodel the world on its comic strength. In one of his sketches, Kovacs 'designs' reality. He draws a table-lamp and the light goes on; he draws a window and hurries to close it against the wind; he draws an electric plug and socket and the objects in the imaginary house come to life. It is a comic image but also a cosmic one, an image of power – imagination in power.

Free of the conditioning of the ratings system, Kovacs experimented with electronic effects, dissolves, superimpositions, wipes, negative images, sound effects, his voice (once even playing with words and lip movements out of sync), and the camera angles. A revolutionary comic video-poet, he took advantage of all of the techniques of the technology to squeeze out of it an effect that is not fortuitous or commonplace, making television a natural space for invention. Even advertising became, in his hands, a conscious satiric game rather than an encumbrance often comic without meaning to be. The cigars he advertised (there is always a sponsor, even in fantasy) entered the narrative mechanism of the comic discourse, accentuating its surreal aspects.

In the 1950s, in terms of the language, the camera movements, and the grammar of television, auteurs and directors found an enormous potential in their hands. Conditioned in part by live broadcasting, which was characteristic of the years before the widespread use of Ampex, introduced in 1956, screenwriters and directors confronted the space of the television set with new optical effects. They made extensive use of the travelling shot, modifying spatial relationships and 'framing' through a continuity of movement. Unable to use the classic film editing cuts (shot, reverse shot, different distances on the same axis) they invented new techniques, performing television-studio acrobatics to resolve even the most complicated plots.

One of the key moments, one of the switch points to an alternative language track, was live drama. It represents another 'lost opportunity' for the medium, a chapter in the counter-factual history. The live drama had its background in the theater. It required little set decoration, and because of the primitive mode of production, it stimulated fantasy. One of the more brilliant examples of this genre, from the point of view of the use of the television camera, is *Twelve Angry Men* by Franklin Schaffner, where the television camera directly follows the debate of the cloistered jurors, taking the maximum advantage of the dolly, the travelling shot, and the close-up.

In live dramas, the television camera is discreet but present, with bold but seemingly simple movements; it carries the spectator into the midst of a situation, involving him or her in a way more familiar than in cinema. The television apparatus imposes a different way of watching, offering a more reassuring dimension. Thus directors such as Sidney Lumet, John Frankenheimer, Martin Ritt, and Robert Mulligan had a free hand to experiment with a new television language without renouncing the popular narrative discourse, and to engage in formal research. *A Double Life* by Ritt, *Doll Face* by Lumet, and *The Comedian* by Frankenheimer, graft together theatrical and cinematographic forms, manipulating them with the electronic medium.

Exceptional expressive possibilities emerged, even within the logic of serial production (because Lumet, Frankenheimer, et al. produced television shows in an incredible quantity and at an incredible pace). The auteur concept managed to coexist with the needs for producing mass entertainment. The 'free space' was not only formal: subject matter, too, was open. The young lions of television direction could satisfy their fancies without apparent political censorship, inheriting the tradition of social drama that flourished in the Hollywood of the 1930s. In fact, the live drama was almost always a political drama, in which conflicts emerge in the nuclear family, in individual identity, and in the structure of society. There are many examples: *Patterns* by Fielder Cook and *The Last Tycoon* by Frankenheimer, stories of magnates and cynicism that offer a critical view of McCarthyite America; *Requiem for a Heavyweight* (Ralph Nelson), *The Days of Wine and Roses* (Frankenheimer), and *Marty* (Lumet) all focus on private crises provoked by larger conflicts. *Tragedy in a Temporary Town* (Lumet), *A Knife in the Dark* (Frankenheimer), and *A Man is Ten Feet Tall* (Mulligan) are dramas of a more obscure America, that of racism, the working class, prison, and so on. Television in the 1950s was still distant from the means of regimentation and social control that we are used to considering the inevitable norm today. It was potentially revolutionary in its forms and in its messages, and it could have developed in a way very differently from that which led to the stereotypical products, such as *Dallas*, which have triumphantly invaded so many Western markets.

In the power vacuum created by Hollywood's crisis, the New York group of Lumet, Frankenheimer, and Mulligan had a great opportunity to invent a new medium and a new language. Hollywood, however, prevailed in the end. One could say in fact that the poles of the discussion continue to remain — as they have been throughout the history of American film and television — New York on one hand and Hollywood on the other: two coasts, two traditions, two cultures.

New York stood and stands for live television, formal renovation, and an autonomous language as opposed to that of Hollywood. A group of directors (those already cited) and screenwriters (Rod Serling and Reginald Rose, true 'creators' of American television) formed in New York and quickly acquired a vast amount of experimental experience. But they were subsequently forced to emigrate to the West Coast (only Lumet obstinately resisted and stayed in New York), not without feelings of guilt, when the stakes got higher.

Hollywood stood and stands for film, the movies, the stability of film as opposed to the risks and approximations of live television. *I Love Lucy*, the prototype of the modern series, was filmed in Hollywood, paving the way for future generations of 'telefilms', and Hollywood once again came to represent product standardization. Like a vampire, it sucked the energy produced by the golden age of television—screenwriters, directors, actors, cinematographers, borrowing from television new interpretations of classic genres, recycling itself along the lines of the new television model, and ultimately, with the mass production of television series, laying the foundation of its own rebirth. With the new 'blood' of television, the old studios (such as Universal) were reborn.

Whatever else it is, the 'open box' of American television in the 1950s is fascinating, because the products of the golden age constitute a composite material in search of a language and a physiognomy of its own, whose structure is sometimes shocking and indigestable for contemporary spectators. It is a mixture of techniques: programs filmed in 16mm or broadcast live and then filmed in 'Kinescope' (even 'live' broadcasts often used mixed techniques, assigning to film exteriors or certain flashbacks what would have been impossible to do live). It is a collage accentuated by the presence of advertising (live or pre-recorded) that inserts itself directly into the narrative line, such as the refrigerator that suddenly enters and dominates the plot with a movement of the camera, Bogart who sings with self-conscious irony the tune to the Lucky Strike song, or a patriotic ad for Alcoa Aluminum featuring the American Army set in a film about Korea. Its peculiar character derives also from the diverse influences television grafted together: cinema, vaudeville, theater, and especially radio, television's largest cultural inheritance.

It was radio and not film that television replaced, swallowing up the voice, the genres (quiz shows, soap operas, serials), even the role of the mythopoietic object in the midst of the home. The television set was a familiar object, as warm and reassuring as a fireplace, which replaced the discussions and stories that were once heard beside the fire. *Fireside Theater* in fact was the name of a series of live dramas, and the other titles also suggested theater in the living room, a private screening (*Playhouse, Television Theater,* etc.). They were shows — and this is the point — presented by a sponsor who 'offered' his product, plus an entertainment event (*Philco Playhouse, Alcoa Hour, Goodyear Playhouse*) conducted by a guide, a noted personality, a familiar figure.

The host, whose face and voice were reassuring and immediately recognizable, took the viewer by the hand and led him or her through the various situations, as in the famous presentations made by Hitchcock for *Alfred Hitchcock Presents,* by Rod Serling for *The Twilight Zone,* or by Dick Powell and Charles Boyer for *Dick Powell Theater.* Gradually, the host became directly enmeshed in the story that followed, in the narration: Rod Serling appeared on the set where the action in that episode of *The Twilight Zone* took place; Fred Astaire, the host of the *Alcoa Hour,* spoke from the bleachers of a stadium if the film was set in the world of baseball (as was the case with John Ford's *Flashing Spikes*); Desi Arnez, the host of the *Desilu Playhouse,* played comic relief or serious roles with Lucille Ball.

The host received his 'guests' at home, in his theater, to cement the intimate, familiar, living-room rapport established between the viewer and the television set. The host could also be a charismatic figure who guided the viewer through different situations, such as historical events. This was the case of the most famous journalist in America, Walter Cronkite, who took the viewer, seated comfortably in his or her living room, into the midst of a battle or a famous historical event (the death of Socrates, the assassination of Lincoln, the mutiny on the Bounty, the Munich Pact) in *You Are There.* The story was not glamorized in the style of a Hollywood costume film, but was offered simply and directly, as if it were a news report (the historical figures were interviewed by an imaginary crew from CBS). The important thing was *being there.*

You Are There, See It Now, It Could Happen to You, are all titles that directly involve the viewer, who became a voyeur: of historical facts, intricate processes, intimate situations, or great catastrophes. Television invented a kind of voyeurism that was very different from the cinematic one. Film voyeurism is oneiric, due to the dark theater and the luminous screen. Television voyeurism is more economic but more active, less evocative than film but with greater opportunity for participation. Being present, in the front row, at the death of Socrates, is naturally also buying the product advertised. It is a 'domestic voyeurism'.

Clearly, in both cases television could have developed an inner, alternative creativity. Theater television could have avoided the war of small vs. large (domestic reality vs. Cinerama and special effects) and focused its attention on live events, on the reality of non-fiction. But even the domestic

20) In the pioneering days of television, the medium might have taken very different direc-tions from the one it did take, becoming the centre of virtually every family on the globe.

21) Whether at home or in the movie theatre, the family audience is the prize all pro-gramme makers go for. Enjoy your popcorn in the comfort of a theatre, share your pleasure with hundreds of spectators and still enjoy the intimacy of your nearest and dearest: a family at the movies in THE TRAVELS OF MR. LEARY *(1987).*

television box could have focused on its inherent experimental possibilities, emphasizing its specific personality through live fiction, camera movement, one-shot sequences, in short, through the formulation of a more mature film/television language. Paradoxically, television could have been more intellectually minded than 'commercial' cinema. Television *can* be avant-garde, as in Ernie Kovacs' case; it can represent fantasy, freedom, invention, culture, new language, new expression. These considerations call to mind a different period, in a different nation. Let us travel through time, as in science fiction (we started with historical fiction, anyway). Let us pay homage to Italy.

Experimental Television

A decade after the golden age of American television, in Italy there was another gilded period of relations between cinema and television. This phase ranged, more or less, from 1964 to 1975. It was particularly fertile, for many reasons: in Italy television developed differently than in America, more along the lines of the BBC; furthermore, the period was very interesting in general, from the cultural viewpoint, as these were years in which the artistic avant-garde (one example may stand for all: the group of poets of *Gruppo '63*) anticipated the political avant-garde (the 1968 protests and their consequences). RAI, the Italian National Television (there was a government monopoly in the country until 1975) was dominated by the Christian Democratic Party; yet it contained pockets of resistance, spaces of internal contradiction. Among the more profitable contradictions was that of Rossellini, a Roman Catholic who, as a pioneer of the cinema-television relationship in Italy, made movies for television that sometimes brought him into conflict with the 'system' of television politics (this was especially the case with his *Socrates*). Rossellini began with *L'età del ferro* (The Iron Age), a series of documentaries produced for television by Istituto Luce and consisting of five episodes formally directed by his son Renzo, in which subject, script, and supervision were entrusted to Rossellini senior. The experiment revealed the director's didactic intentions, which had be seen earlier in INDIA (1958), a film that rejects traditional style and finish, favoring instead an assembly of various materials (newsreels, archival sequences, film clips, and passages from his own movies, combined in a sort of postmodern self-quotation).

Rossellini used the medium of television to report news, or more precisely, to 'stage' news, to construct a formal and orderly expression of thought on science and history. This marked the beginning of a period of lucid planning and construction for the director, the importance of which would be understood only later, with the making of *La prise du pouvoir par*

Louis XIV (1966) for French television, *Idea di un'isola* (1967) for American television, *La lotta dell'uomo per la sua sopravvivenza* (1967), and the great historical frescoes (usually European coproductions): *Acts of the Apostles* (1968), *Socrates* (1970), *Pascal* (1971), *Agostino d'Ippona* (1972), *L'età di Cosimo* (1973), and *Cartesius* (1974).

Rossellini used the 'cool medium' to tone down the emotions of ideology, filtering them through a more detached, scientific eye. He was not interested in reconstructing the past, so much as in tracing the problems of the present back through history. He evinced an outer formalism, linked to a search for a deeper form. Hence the importance of the cinematographic language that he borrowed to make television, renewing it with respect to its own tradition. One fundamental departure from the grammar of classical cinema was his use of the zoom, an expedient 'forbidden' in traditional cinema, which Rossellini employed both to accelerate his shooting schedule and to give emphasis to his close-ups. The zoom became a tool of poetic expression in Rossellini's hands (as it did for the filmmakers of the *nouvelle vague*, who took a great deal from the Italian director). And it was literally 'in his hands', as Rossellini personally worked a mechanical crank that acted directly on the camera's focal lengths. In this case, too, one had a hybrid instrument, half cinema and half television; a medium typical of television journalism that became an element of the director's style.

Further discussion of Rossellini would take us off our track, which has to do above all with understanding the points of convergence between cinema and television in Italy. In 1964 (the year of Rossellini's turning point), RAI's audience research unit realized that the top ratings were being obtained by two kinds of programmes: the news, and movies broadcast on television. This was a clear indication that viewers demanded a different kind of programme, and it imposed on RAI a new mode of production. Accordingly, the Italian National Television began to use film instead of television cameras, and not just for television news. Politically the phase coincided with the directorship of Ettore Bernabei, a bastion of Christian Democrat power at RAI who, in a famous memorandum of 1969 proposed/imposed the reorganization of the company to meet standards of professionalism and efficiency that had been non-existent previously. A new strategy gained hold that valued information and hence television journalism. The first experiments mixing cinema and television came about in this context, as requisites of competence and talent were set forth that extended to cinema as well as to television, both from the viewpoint of the material support (film) and from that of the organizational model.

The outcomes included investigative television, which was an interesting mixture of the television studio (which hosted a formal debate) and filmed reports, a mixture therefore of electronics and chemistry. Examples include *TV 7*, a famous news program, *Teatro inchiesta* (Investigation Theater), where news reports were fictionalized, and various documentaries that were critical of the Establishment: *Viaggio nel Sud* (Journey Through the South) by Virginio Sabel, *La donna che lavora* (The Working Woman) by Ugo Zatterin, and *La casa in Italia* (Home in Italy) by Liliana Cavani, one of the first female film directors to work with the medium of television.

Then there was actual fiction, which RAI began to produce in various forms. Here, generally speaking, there were four kinds of products: a) regular feature-length movies, which RAI began to produce in the mid-sixties; b) classic serials, which in the late sixties began to be shot on film, as well as with television cameras; c) series and mini-series, which RAI began to create on the American model that we have already seen; and d) *sperimentali televisione*, fiction films of various length that gave many young authors their first exposure.

The 'television experimentals' forged an entire generation of filmmakers who became household names in the 1970s and 1980s. For example, Peter del Monte, the director of the first high-definition feature film (*Giulia e Giulia*, featuring Kathleen Turner and Sting), made his début in this milieu at RAI, with *Le parole a venire*. Likewise Gianni Amelio (internationally known for LADRO DI BAMBINI) made *La città del sole* (1972) and *Bertolucci secondo il cinema* (1974), a spin-off shot on the set of NOVECENTO. Franco Taviani (the third brother of the directors of GOOD MORNING BABILONIA) shot *La sostituzione* (1970). Gianni Amico proved to be one of the more active figures in the field of films produced by television, turning out classic serials (*La quinta stagione*), feature films (*I tropici*), and experimentals (*Il vostro amore è come il mare*). Other authors of television experimentals include Ivo Micheli (*La memoria di Kunz, I corvi*); Mario Brenta (represented at Cannes in 1994 by BARNABO DELLE MONTAGNA), who put his signature to a famous *Vermisat* (1972-74); Luigi Faccini (*Niente meno di più,* 1970); Nino Russo (*Da lontano,* 1971); Manuel De Sica, the musician son of Vittorio (*Intorno,* 1974-75); Tito Schipa Jr., son of the opera singer (the musical *Orfeo 9*); and Ennio Lorenzini (*Cronaca di un gruppo,* 1972). Also of note is Paolo Benvenuti, an interesting author on the Italian horizon, who made *Frammenti di cronaca volgare* (1974), a 'Straubian' film; Jean Marie Straub himself, who made *Mosé e Aronne* (1975) for the experimentals; the 'revolutionary' Glauber Rocha, who created *Cancer* (1972); Liliana Cavani, already well known at the time, who made *L'ospite* (1971); and Marco Ferreri, who shot the documentary *Perché pagare per essere felici?* (1974). All of these are 'difficult' films, forming a cultivated and politically engaged island of production (the experimentals were run by a leftist Catholic, Italo Moscati), which formed just when grand cinema was snubbing television. A few years later, cinema would have been lost without television....

History's judgment of the experimentals varies. Some speak of them as an experience that was relatively important notwithstanding the fact that it was 'quantitatively limited'; others view the experimentals as an unrepeatable moment in the cinema-television relationship. Here, too, we may find ourselves confronted with a 'missing link', limited to Italian and European history, perhaps, but no less meaningful for that reason. In this case it is television that renounced its mythical identity and, taking the initiative, drew near to cinema, a cinema of fiction, free from patterns and conditioning factors linked to the market. For example, it was not necessary to make a one-and-a-half-hour feature film for movie-theaters; brief films, shorts, mixes of documentary and traditional film, etc., could be made, thanks to the vehicle of television.

But other fields are also worthy of note. Concerning films as such, we can mention FRANCESCO D'ASSISI by Liliana Cavani (who later did a remake with Mickey Rourke); LA STRATEGIA DEL RAGNO by Bernardo Bertolucci and SAN MICHELE AVEVA UN GALLO by Paolo and Vittorio Taviani, two classic films that dealt with the history of the left, within a politically conservative Christian Democratic television; LA CIRCOSTANZA and I RECUPERANTI by the Roman Catholic Ermanno Olmi, another pioneer, like Rossellini, of cine-television relations; IL DIARIO DI UNA SCHIZOFRENICA by Nelo Risi, a poet and director, brother of the better-known Dino, master of the classic Italian comedy.

From this initial productive passion began the trend that led in the late 1970s to films like those which triumphed at Cannes in 1977 and 1978. These films – PADRE PADRONE by the Taviani brothers and L'ALBERO DEGLI ZOC-COLI (The Tree of Wooden Clogs) by Olmi – historically legitimized the cinema produced by Italian television. After this time cinema was heavily conditioned by television sales, which became a decisive factor of production; RAI and Berlusconi's Fininvest became the duopoly of cine-television strategies.

But what happend in the meantime? RAI's monopoly came to an end in 1975: a judgment by the Constitutional Court declared it illegal, paving the way for a proliferation of private television stations unregulated by laws. These television stations, with their indiscriminate circulation of films, on the one hand provoked the collapse of the consumption of movies in theaters, and on the other emphasized the magnitude of the demand for fiction. Hence the appropriation of cinema by Italian television that took place after 1975. But this is another story – one that culminates in Berlusconi's conquest of political power.

Another consequence was the reorganization of RAI mentioned previously, which brought the Italian National Television to new standards of professionalism and efficiency and placed an unprecedented premium on television journalism, even where this meant fomenting a counter-culture within the ranks of the system itself. An example is Cavani's *Galileo*, which caused her more than a few problems with the executives at RAI. Where series are concerned, the question is also one of definition. By 'series' I mean productions like *Perry Mason* or *Dynasty*, that is, film products of roughly an hour which feature the same characters in different stories (as in *Perry Mason*) or in situations that evolve from one episode to the next (as in *Dynasty*). In Italy one of the forerunners of this genre was a series starring and directed by Ugo Tognazzi, parodistically entitled FBI (which stands for Frank Bortolozzi Investigatore). But in Italy the series is also a container of film products having different situations and characters grouped around a common theme: for example, *All'ultimo minuto, Storie italiane, Oggi in Italia, Una porta sul buio* (the latter written by Dario Argento), in addition to the famous *Racconti del maresciallo*, based on stories by Mario Soldati.

With regard to 'classic serials' on film, it must be said that the moment at which RAI chose cinema over video is particularly important. Classic serials had used cinema for certain sequences, above all those shot in exteriors, for some time previously; but only after the mid-1960s did the interest arise to make classic serials in episodes entirely shot on film (with a ten-year delay compared to American television). The most striking product, in this sense, were adventure stories, exemplified by Franco Rossi's *Odissea*, for which RAI turned to an expert of the movie industry, Dino De Laurentiis. The first classic serial made with film was *Mastro Don Gesualdo* by Vaccari, based on a story by Giovanni Verga. Other titles include *La baronessa di Carini, Eneide, Mosé, Gesù di Nazareth, Coralba, Il diario di un maestro*. But most of all I like to recall a serial based on an Italian classic, *I promessi sposi* (The Betrothed) by Manzoni, which was made electronically in 1967 and remade on film in 1989 (after numerous take-offs, such as that of Mario Camerini and the 'Italian comedy' version of Monicelli, *Renzo e Luciana*, featured as an episode of BOCCACCIO '70). 'The Betrothed', of course, brings me to the metaphor with which I can conclude these notes on the 'missing links', lost opportunities, golden or gilded ages between cinema and television: a would-be 'marriage' in which Renzo may be seen as cinema and Lucia as television, or vice-versa. Whichever way round, the fact remains that there is someone, an evil Don Rodrigo, who does not want them to marry. But they remain 'betrothed' nonetheless, and who knows if there is not a good Fra' Cristoforo out there who will perform the miracle. Who knows: as with Manzoni and as in Hollywood, there may well be a happy ending.

Scanning The Horizon: A Film is a Film is a Film

Conrad Schoeffter

Though our title is 'Cain and Abel', I shall resist the temptation to get bibli-cal. It would get far too messy, given how much incest there is between the two brothers.

Imagine that you are watching television, and a tennis game is taking place, say at Madison Square Garden or Wimbledon. Why do we watch this sort of thing? And why do we not watch, say, a man climbing a mountain? Why do they not stage mountain climbing at Madison Square Garden? Well, the mountain is always just that: a mountain. When you climb a mountain, you are up against a static conflict. The tennis game presents a situation of dynamic conflict. Not man against rock, but man against man. Unlike the rock, the man (or woman) fights back: actively, with a deliberate strategy. He keeps you on your toes at all times. You never know what the opponent will do next.

Remember the film CLIFFHANGER? What is interesting about it is that we do not watch Sylvester Stallone climb a mountain. To get away from the static conflict – the mountain – they invented a second set of climbers. Those were bad guys with guns. The two sets of climbers pursued mutually exclu-sive goals, like the two players in the tennis game. This way, the conflict be-came dynamic: What is each side going to do next?

Without making too much of this, one could almost argue that a game of tennis is a better movie than CLIFFHANGER. In tennis, both sides seem wor-thy. Both sides are engaged in a righteous struggle to reach an honorable goal. In action movies, only the hero tends to be good while his opponents are rotten to the core. Let us consider a fictionalized version of a tennis game, for instance, from a film called THE GREAT SANTINI. There they are playing basketball actually, but the principle is the same.

The tennis game was a live event. Not so this basketball game. THE GREAT SANTINI represents an artificial reality where we have everything under control. The events unfold just the way we want them to. Being in control al-lows us to introduce elements that make THE GREAT SANTINI even more en-grossing than live tennis. For instance, in our television broadcast of the tennis match, the players are usually almost indistinguishable, they even dress alike. The usual broadcast does not give us a real feel for the two women. We notice their concentration, but do we get a feel for their emo-tion? Deep down, is the one who is winning close to tears, the one who loses actually happy? Why are they out there on the court at all? We have no idea what motivates them – in their lives, or on this particular day. The tennis game is about tennis and nothing more: who will win? That's all there is to it. THE GREAT SANTINI, on the other hand, was not about basketball. The game was merely a device, used to express something else. This something else is called subtext. Though we see father and son play basketball, we get a sense that there is more at stake than the number of hoops. The scene is about ageing: The colonel is being retired and he cannot handle it. Now he lets it out on his son. 'Good writing lies below the surface,' as William Goldman puts it. In good writing, people act in oblique ways; they will lie – even to themselves – rather than admit the truth. Facing up to reality is often painful. Think about it. It requires self-recognition and a certain amount of greatness. Both are difficult to rise to.

That is what films are all about: the painful path to greatness. Filmic characters have weaknesses, emotional hang-ups from their past. Their past haunts them in the present. At the beginning of your film, your protagonist will not realize what is keeping him from fulfilling his true potential. In fact, he will not even know his potential. He will have a wrong perception of himself. His past has left a mark that impairs his judgment in the present. In CLIFFHANGER, Sylvester Stallone is haunted by feelings of guilt from an accident that happened years ago. In THE FIRM, Tom Cruise grew up poor. As a consequence, he came to believe that money brings happiness. This leads him astray. The senior partners in THE FIRM literally have a few skeletons in their closet. All films have a back story. The back story is everything that happened before your film begins. A film starts at the point of crisis where the past comes to a head, where the volcano erupts.

A tennis game is really only the climax of a film, with the beginning and middle parts missing. Think of a karate movie: The beginning will set up the opponent and the hero's desire to win. The middle part will be about training for the final confrontation, about rising to one's true potential. Structurally speaking, the tennis game is incomplete. That's why the sports people like to bring you interviews before the game. The ones after the game are *post mortems*, but the ones before affect your enjoyment of the game: they convey a sense of the individual behind the action. During Olympics broadcasts, you'll see a mini-documentary about the Ukranian long distance runner at home, meet his fiancée and his mother and hear him talk about his desire to win in honor of his deceased father: his motivation. This conveys a sense of the stakes. It makes us root for him, take sides, like in a movie. For each player, they will also give you the odds for not winning. They will insert the doubt because doubt creates suspense. You will hear about knee injuries, the strength of opponents and streaks of bad luck. Aah, 'bad luck' –

it's static from an undigested past. You won't know the trauma though, the inner hang-up that kept the sports figure from winning. Not even the sports figure may know. It would take a movie for him/her to find out and rise above it!

In simple action films, you will find not one but two confrontations with the opponent. The first one is near the beginning and will be won by the opponent. The other one comes at the end. In between, the hero's trainer – writers call him the intermediary – has taught him his kicks and a little Eastern philosophy along the way. In the end, when the hero finally beats the crap out of his foe, we cheer along: the hero has grown. The way he has grown, of course, is that he has overcome his character flaws and hang-ups from the past. He has a new perception of self that allows him to tap his full potential.

Just to be clear on this: the intermediary – the karate trainer – is not the same as a sidekick. The intermediary is someone close to the hero who recognizes the hero's flaws and traumas and helps him to overcome them. The STAR WARS trilogy used mentor figures to this effect ('Trust the force, Luke!'). Oftentimes, the intermediary is the hero's love interest. Every film has an intermediary: he/she is a dramatic necessity. A sidekick, on the other hand, is merely a convenience. Consider that film deals in external symbols. Unless the hero has someone to talk to, it is often difficult to convey what he is thinking. The convenience of having someone to talk to is called propinquity. Sidekicks are used for propinquity not just in film, but on television as well. Sitcoms use them all the time. They need them because the sitcom format is all talk; very little is conveyed visually. Where you have to talk all the time, you need someone to talk to: to feed you the straight lines and react to your punch lines. That is another use of the sidekick. You can let him react off of the hero, thereby giving the viewer a cue as to how he is supposed to react. Many talk shows use sidekicks, too. Johnny Carson had Ed McMahon. David Letterman and Jay Leno use their respective band leaders.

On a structural level, a sidekick can provide a parallel story. Let me explain this. Drama, as we all know, is a choice between two courses of action. You are at a crossroads, and you could go either way. If your movie is well written, both choices will look equally tempting and rational (or equally unattractive). That is why CLIFFHANGER was not a very sophisticated film (albeit an effective one). There were no real crossroads, no real choice, no doubt that the bad guys were evil and had to be destroyed. The only temptation came from the money, but no immediate need for money had been established on Stallone's part. Now in THE GREAT SANTINI, the boy's opponent is his father. Here, the choice is no longer so easy. Nor in POINT BREAK, where the criminal you are after is your friend. Those are tough choices…

22) IMAX 3D: 'The cinema auditorium of the future will be a modified flight simulator...'.

23) *Conrad Schoeffter demonstrating the roller-coaster principle in the chase scene with the mining trolley from Steven Spielberg's* INDIANA JONES AND THE TEMPLE OF DOOM *(1984).*

which is where it gets interesting. When your hero reaches a crossroads and you give him/her a sidekick, you can let the sidekick take the alternate course of action. Your hero chooses one path of action, his sidekick the other: their ways part. As the film progresses, the sidekick's fate serves to illustrate what would have happened had the hero not made the choice he did. Compare and contrast, like in a school paper, or in documentary films.

What all this amounts to is the notion of a deliberate narrative structure. Structure is something very firm. Tennis games have a firm structure. There are 'sets' and 'games' and what-have-yous, and it is all regulated and monitored by an umpire up on a high chair. Think of structure as grammar. You can make yourself understood without it, but to reach a level of poetry you need to observe certain rules. Filmic structure starts on the scene level. Every scene is a variation of the same sequence: bridging-in, rising conflict, reversal, climax and bridging-out. Many sequences in feature films make sense in themselves, they function as a miniature version of the film as a whole. Bridging-in is the equivalent of a beginning, rising conflict equals the middle part and the reversal is a plot point that propels your story into its climax. The bridging-out part is your ending. The key element in all this is the reversal. The one thing you do not want is for your scenes to develop in the direction they were set up to go. Your film would become predictable and boring. What you want to do is to lead me in a certain direction, and then let something unexpected, though not implausible, happen; something that forces your hero to reasses what he is doing, to readjust his strategy for reaching the goal. The basketball game in THE GREAT SANTINI starts out as just another friendly game. But then, it turns ugly and ends in tears. Reversals are the most repetitive and predictable device in films. You'll find at least one reversal in every scene. Yet they are the very thing that keeps your film from becoming predictable. Reversals guarantee change. You need change because a static process is not interesting to watch. We are back to why the mountain is not a compelling opponent. 'Even' in a documentary, you need reversals. Capturing the moment of change is probably the biggest challenge a documentary filmmaker faces.

Whether it is a documentary or a work of fiction, be it for television or the cinema, you have to structure your film into scenes and your scenes into a plot. A plot is a structured story: story plus structure equals plot. At the core is always the story. Structure is your strategy for telling that story in the most compelling manner possible. There is more than one way to give structure to your story. You will probably work with three acts if you are doing a feature film, with two if it is a half hour television sitcom. A 52 minute television movie will be structured into four acts, a daytime soap opera into seven. But the basic pattern is always the same, and it is rooted in the scene. Currently, what is popular among writers are narrative structures derived from mythological plot patterns. They focus on character growth, on an overreaching arc rather than so many segments or acts. Typically, they reach from a hero's need and desire to obtain a particular goal to his/her self revelation and personal growth. This may be Hollywood movie talk, but its application is universal. The larger the audience you are trying to reach, the more judiciously you will work with structure.

For example, what could be further removed from a feature film than the nightly NBC television news? Let us assume, they were reporting on the (annual) brush fires in Malibu. Now remember, this is just your average news report, slapped together quickly under tremendous deadline pressure. Nevertheless, here is how it was done. The segment opened with some spectacular footage of flames shooting sky high. Quite aside from providing shock value, this established an immediate need: an emergency situation. It also led to a strong desire: to do something about it. Next, they introduced the protagonist: the fire fighter. They had him explain the opposition, what his team was up against, namely winds, sparks, dry shrubbery and shingled roofs; and his plan: how he was going to battle the blaze. Then we got to see what was at stake. You saw charred homes and interviews with their weeping owners. This was contrasted with homes that were still intact but whose survival was in question.

Another point: if you feel sorry for the weeping home-owners, it was because they were in what is called 'undeserved jeopardy'. Undeserved jeopardy is also important in feature films, for instance, in THE GREAT SANTINI: no son deserves to be treated this way by his father. After all, it is not the kid's fault that dad is over the hill. Or take HOME ALONE. The parents go on vacation and poor Kevin gets left behind accidentally. You can find an element of undeserved jeopardy in most successful films. A case of injustice makes us take sides and root for the hero.

The issue is this: You have to tell a story, and you have to structure this story. 'Even' the documentary filmmaker is always looking for good stories to tell. That is why he will not make a film about the social security system. A system is a topic, not a story. Nor are the dykes a story. You have to find a story and structure within your topic. Most often, this means personalizing the topic. Not the social security system, but the old lady who depends on it and the young man who defrauds it. Not the dykes, but the man who risks his life to keep them from breaking during a storm. As a filmmaker you will be looking for people with goals and the willpower to pursue them, so that your film contains conflict and change. It's just like in fiction. It is all the same. A film is a film is a film.

There is one important difference, though. In documentaries, what you are showing is perceived as more or less real. Consequently, the minute you personalize your topic, your documentary tends to become somewhat voyeuristic. The documentary filmmaker is always working for television, and television has learned to thrive on voyeurism. We look at the little box as if through a peephole. The polite way of putting it would be to say, on television we want to invite our neighbors into our living room. The fact is, we like to pry on them in theirs. That is one reason why the majority of American television movies are fact based. Usually, they are straight from the headlines: Lorena Bobbit who cut off her husband's penis. The Menendez brothers who knocked off their showbiz parents for their inheritance. Maybe the ultimate exercise in voyeurism is *Court TV*. The thrill of watching the obese mother of a serial killer break into tears as she begs to be strapped into the electric chair in her little boy's stead!

What also works well on television are the melodrama and high romanticism of those thick yet lightweight bestsellers that become mini-series. They may not be voyeuristic, but they appeal to women. Much of television programming is targeted at a largely female viewership. At home, it is Mom who has the last word on what to watch. Television values women highly also because they tend to stick with a show, whereas men tend to zap wildly from channel to channel. In the cinema, on the other hand, it is hard to be successful with stories centered on women. It is the male who suggests what film to go see on a date. Hence, theatrical films are directed by and large at a male audience.

These are important considerations. What is the appeal of your story? Is it better suited for the cinema, or for television? The answer will determine how you will approach it, from cost to cast to script. If it is television, then what is the time slot? For example, if you are writing a series to be broadcast in early fringe (what the Germans call 'Vorabendprogramm'), you will want to write it in little vignettes, with only a slow, almost lethargic progression of the overall storyline. You will be writing for people who come home from work and tune in halfway through; and who do not concentrate on it because they are setting the table and preparing dinner.

It used to be that theatrical films were targeted almost exclusively at a young audience. The assumption was that young people want to get out of the house while older people tend to stay home and watch the tube. But the universe evolves. Today you can actually make money with films like THE REMAINS OF THE DAY and SCHINDLER'S LIST -not just CLIFFHANGER, THE FUGITIVE and BATMAN FOREVER. A limited number of films with an older, more sophisticated appeal stand a chance again, not in the least because that segment of the business has been taken over by the majors and is being backed by their marketing muscle. The television universe has evolved, too, even though young people still tend to go out and older people stay home. But older people do not spend money as freely as the younger ones do. The more that television is being advertiser driven, the more it will target young people.

Either way, your work must be entertaining, even where your television station's charter may be cultural and educational. Pay heed to the principles of drama. You need a good story and a tight structure, otherwise you cannot sustain viewer interest over the running time of your show. You have to make it a little movie, no matter what it is that you are making. Making it a little movie is not always easy. Take talk shows. They are like a stand-up routine by the host. We tune in to watch David Letterman, not the chainsaw juggler and the bestselling author who are tonight's guests. Structurally speaking, the problem with talk shows is that they are a rambling sequence of gags and anecdotes. They have nowhere to go. Unlike a movie, they do not escalate ('the plot thickens'). That is why the format has evolved into *Donahue, Oprah, Morton Downey, Frank Meisner*. The talk show becomes a tennis game between opposing viewpoints. You let it escalate by provoking the other side. The key is conflict, like in a movie; or, because it's television, voyeurism. Some of these shows are becoming freak shows: married transvestites whose children are also married transvestites. But in the end, you are still tuning in to the host.

We are conditioned to perceive even the evening news that way. In a multi-channel environment, we watch Peter Jennings or Diane Sawyer, not simply the news. The news themselves are generic; the better show is with the more likeable anchorperson. Or with the more likeable politician. That is a kind of information voters did not have access to, before the advent of television. But now they do, and it is here to stay. President Kennedy, as we know, was the first to use television as a political tool. His charisma and the show at Camelot overshadowed what he did, namely, very little about the Berlin wall; letting budget deficits spin out of control; getting the United States into Vietnam. Look at how television reporting influences US foreign policy. Somalia is a textbook example of humanitarian concerns raised by television imagery taking precedence over the national interest. We no longer fight enemies. We fight the wrong that we get fed in television images. The decision where to intervene is made for us – by television.

Part of television's influence stems from a tacit pact with its audience. It is a pact that is very different from the conventions of cinema. Cinema is fiction. The film school I attended carries a sign over its door: 'Reality ends here'. Television, on the other hand, is reality based, not just where news and documentaries are concerned. As I mentioned, most television movies are rooted in fact. Talk shows are perceived as real. In game shows, real people truly win or lose. By extension, we take a lot of things we see on television at face value. It used to be, 'if it's in print, it must be true'. Nowadays, 'if it's on television, it must be true'. In fact, sometimes it is not true *until* it is on television. Think about it. It is frightening.

The power of television is enhanced by the perception of television as a friend. For as long as the tube is on, you are not alone. The characters on the screen are there with you – not in a movie theatre that you go to and leave when it's over, but in your own home. They become a part of your life. After a successful mini-series, the actor who plays the villain can bet on getting harrassed in public. That is not going to happen to the actor who played a villain in a feature film. After watching *Beavis and Butthead*, a kid set his parents' house on fire; his little sister perished in the blaze. Beavis and Butthead are not even portrayed by live actors – they're animated cartoon characters.

Though the overall influence of television on people is open to debate, incidents like this one have led to a backlash, particularly where portrayals of violence are concerned. Remember the news reports about the two little boys in Liverpool who abducted a toddler? They dragged him across town and killed him. Their crime had nothing to do with television. The trial is over, the boys are locked up. But now suddenly, someone discovered that their father had rented a violent video some weeks before. No one ever said that the boys had seen this video. In fact, it has been proven that they did not. But it has led to calls for a parliamentary inquiry into violence on television and its effect on children.

But let me give you another example, not from television, but from the cinema, Steven Spielberg's INDIANA JONES AND THE TEMPLE OF DOOM. You may recall the scene of the chase in the abandoned mine, and the line of dialogue that runs: 'Whatever you do, don't take the tunnel to your right.' Only one of the characters gets this information, which means that you and I know more than most of the people up on the screen. It is a technique called superior position. The hero thinks he is acting smart but we know he is taking a wrong turn. But the way it is filmed, the placing of the camera, the sparks on the tracks as the mine trolley careens along and then goes over the edge – what a difference, compared to television! We are right there. We do not 'look at' this. We experience it! INDIANA JONES AND THE TEMPLE OF DOOM is designed as an experience – for all of us. This, too, is characteristic of cinema: it is a collective experience.

It is a visual experience. If you merely listened to the soundtrack, you would not get the story. This is no talk radio, like television. The content of a television movie you can get with your eyes closed. Television is an oral medium, to the point where people get uncomfortable when their little box does not talk to them. Even in an expensive American mini-series, much of the action is related rather than shown. It is like on stage, where the messenger comes running, shouting 'we have won the battle', but we never see the battle. A theatrical feature film better *be* the battle. If you expect me to spend ten dollars, plus the cost of a babysitter on your film, you have to deliver: stars, production values, grand spectacle. A feature film has to be an event.

Indeed, the scene from INDIANA JONES I referred to is the opposite of a peep show. It is not all close-ups and medium shots. The camera even incorporates the very room we sit in. If you are an aspiring photographer, you learn to visualize the finished print, not just observe the live action in front of the camera and press the button. In television, it is the same: you have to abstract from what is 'out there' and learn to see what is 'in the shot'. In cinema, you add a second step. You extrapolate beyond the edge of the frame into the room in which the film will be shown. That is why a Spielberg designs so many interesting camera angles. They are designed to pull you into the action.

Once you have me by the collar, if you can then take me to the limit, all the better. Not just visual, but visceral. Scare me a little. In real life, you would not have wanted to be on that ride through the mineshaft. Nor on the tram that took you around JURASSIC PARK. But then, 'it's only a movie'. It may take a little daring to keep your eyes open, but at the bottom of your heart you know it is safe. We have checked reality at the door. That is what makes it fun, as opposed to a nightmare, which is another point of the scene from INDIANA JONES: cinema is violent. Or at least, in cinema the violence is shown; it is right up there on the screen. On television, the violence is implied. They tell you rather than show you. Or they lead up to it, and then you get a reaction shot or they cut away. Remember the two kids in Liverpool, the ones who abducted and killed a toddler? The television coverage showed you next to nothing: a stretch of railroad tracks and a few seconds of grainy, nondescript footage from a shopping mall surveillance camera. None of it would have got you to first base in a horror movie. But this was not a horror movie. It was television – we 'knew' it was real. Combined with some grizzly voice-over, the mere suggestion of mayhem was more gruesome than any horror movie. At the cinema, all we ever get is make-up and special effects and some clever editing. It is all pretend, and I know it. That is a problem. In the cinema, you have to make me forget that it is fake. The key to successful cinema is the suspension of disbelief. Cinema is a flight of fancy. It makes us believe in the impossible. And it takes us places: to the land of Oz, or to the planet Tattooine. Television stays home, right here in our back yard. Cinema takes us on a ride... through JURASSIC PARK, or a rollercoaster ride in INDIANA JONES AND THE TEMPLE OF DOOM.

The literal interpretation of cinema as a rollercoaster ride is brought to the fore whenever a new technology comes along. A new technology comes along whenever television becomes too big. There was a rollercoaster ride in THIS IS CINERAMA. One of the first films in Sensurround was called ROLLERCOASTER. One of the first IMAX films featured rollercoaster and similar rides. Indeed, the cinema of the future will be a simulated rollercoaster ride. Go see *Star Tours* at Disneyland. That is the prototype. The cinema auditorium of the future will be a modified flight simulator. You will literally fasten your seatbelt for the ultimate flight of fancy. That is why you're seeing alliances forming between the motion picture and aircraft industries.

At home, too, there will be changes. The motion picture industry is aligning itself with the telephone companies. Why the phone companies? Because they know how to throw switches, how to make a connection between two or more points. This makes cable systems interactive. There has been much talk about the fact that the digitized transmission of signals will allow systems to carry 500 channels or more. It is probably wrong to think that there are truly 500 new programs on the horizon. What you are likely to get is one movie on 8 channels, starting at 10 minute intervals; a dozen or so shopping channels including an interactive version of the Sears catalogue;

and a channel where you can call up the rental movies you used to get at your local video store.

However, to the phone companies, the entertainment business is only a small piece of the pie. What they are really interested in is the upgrading of, and new uses for, the telephone business. Every time you use your fax, cellular phone, beeper or modem, you will spend a nickel. That is where the big money is. Be aware, too, that the entertainment revolution on the home front is not about new programming but the repackaging of existing libraries. Nevertheless, the mere idea of it has led to a production boom, at least temporarily. Once the first excitement cools off, the boom is likely to subside. By the way, though we're talking cable, the boom is not in television. It is in theatrical feature films. A feature gets promoted by its theatrical distributor and reviewed in the press. To the cable industry, that is the value of your film: the hoopla that surrounds it. They could not care less about your *chef d'oeuvre* as such. What they buy is the audience awareness of it. After all, it is this awareness that will make you tune in.

Likewise, and maybe surprisingly, the cinema can sometimes exploit the audience awareness of television shows. I say 'surprisingly', because why should you pay good money to see something that comes free into your home once a week or even daily? Yet there are several successful STAR TREK movies, two ADDAMS FAMILY films, THE BEVERLY HILLBILLIES, THE FLINTSTONES, THE BRADY BUNCH MOVIE. Oh yes, and MTV has formed a theatrical wing – the lure of those 500 channels! – and they are bringing us BEAVIS AND BUTTHEAD, the feature film.

Who needs 500 channels, anyway? You cannot possibly watch them all. Just look at the three networks (ABC, CBS, NBC) plus Fox. They are all that is really called for in that particular segment of the market. Their audience certainly is not growing. But still, both Warner Bros. and Paramount are launching new networks. Who knows whether both will survive. People will watch if the newcomers create a better program. But can you create a better program? There is only so much talent that combines both craft and creativity. The supply is limited and spread thin already. Commercialization has added quantity, not quality.

So you need gimmicks – like *Court TV* – and specialization – like MTV and *The Weather Channel*, or *The Bible Channel*. Which leads me back to 'Cain and Abel'. Who is Cain to Abel: bro' or foe? I'd go with bro'. Film is their family name. They feed off the same dramatic principles and the same narrative strategies. Yet each has established his own identity. If you made a list of their characteristics, what you would end up with would look like a high-school sampler of opposites:

Television	Cinema
Daily habit	Event
Low budget	High production values
Local	Escape
Fact based	Fictional
Dialogue-oriented	Visual
Viewed	Experienced
Modular	Dramatic arc

There may be additional criteria, not to mention exceptions, but the polarity is apparent. It is the result of competition, the way you are likely to find it between ambitious brothers. Each forces the other to excel and to find his niche. In our case, television is the driving force. Television made the cinema what it is today. The ride, the immersive experience, the special effects and digital sound systems are there because television has not got them. A cynic might say it is more like an arms race: Every move on one side forces a countermove on the other. Cinema throws around high budgets and hardware like a waning superpower hoping to preserve a modicum of dignity and market share. But the situation of network television is remarkably similar. That is because a third sibling is growing up fast and putting television under pressure. Let us be politically correct and say she is a sister: video rentals, videogames and computer time (internet). It is one big soap opera, lurid and incestuous. Everybody is at each others' throats, yet everybody is also in bed with everybody else. Just look at the amount of co-production, cross-promotion, cross-ownership and other corporate entanglements. In light of this, do you really want to stick with the family analogy? It would take us right back to where we did not want to start this off: into the realm of the morally objectionable. Maybe it is best for me to get out before the censors step in.

Television and the Close-up: Interference or Correspondence?

Pierre Sorlin

One of the biggest problems a filmmaker faces is the choice of his framing: how shall I frame this character or this object? There are eight different listings for the concept of framing, but I think we need only look at three of these: the long shot, the medium shot and the close-up. The former two are generally considered 'more natural'. The long shot, as we see it on the silver screen, reminds us of the landscape seen from a hill or a church tower. Although we must always remember that the image is not exactly the same, for there is a significant difference between our peripheral vision and the cinema's wide-screen or panoramic vision. Nevertheless, we can compare the long shot to something that can be seen from a distance. The medium shot is what we perceive in our daily lives, that seen from the height of a man or a woman.

The close-up, however, is very different. We do not normally see things in close-up in our daily lives. It can happen that something is being looked at, using a magnifying glass, although normally, this is fairly rare. Therefore, it comes as no surprise that cinema has always been very reluctant to adopt the close-up, and however strange it may sound, close-ups are still rarely used in films. Some years ago I made a shot-by-shot analysis of D.W. Griffith's BIRTH OF A NATION. I counted 1600 shots of which only 26 were close-ups, less than one out of sixty. There are few close-ups in this film, but because they are extremely important, the impression is created that there are many. I confess that I completed the boring task of counting shots in other films. Briefly checking Hitchcock and John Ford films revealed that the proportion is more or less the same. Basically, film avoids close-ups unless it is used for a precise reason, such as the shot of a gun that will shortly be used to kill someone.

Why is cinema so reluctant to use a trick which is after all very simple? The close-up is both intrusive and unpleasant. It is a way for a filmmaker to enter into the film, to try to catch the viewers attention and then direct that attention. Hitchcock, a master in the use of close-ups, produced PSYCHO which provides a good illustration for my argument. The film tells the story of a woman, Marion Crane, who has stolen $ 40.000. Early on, in the third sequence, we see her getting dressed, facing a closet, and while she is dressing the camera pans and shows us in close-up an envelop that contains the money. Whilst showing us this detail is very important, it also suggests that the money is going to be the theme of the following drama, which is not the case. Hitchcock uses the close-up as a tool of manipulation, and therefore he never, or rarely, uses the technique subsequently. Such an effect can only be achieved once, but not ten times during the same film.

Furthermore, the close-up is very unpleasant, as it portrays things we normally rather not see that big. Imagine an insect on the silver screen, it is a monster, a different animal, not the one we are used to seeing in our kitchen or our garden. The close-up of a face is repulsive and, to certain extent, absurd. The skin seems to be made of big craters edged by huge fleshy ears, and thus presenting a fairly disgusting image. Therefore, close-ups are used only for a precise reason, one that mostly tortures the spectators. Remember one of the most famous examples of the close-up: Dreyer's JOAN OF ARC. The judges' torture of Joan is obvious, not because she has her legs broken, but because we see her face in close-up, the different expressions fleeting across her face expose to us her horrendous, evil judges. It is her torture, but also that of the spectator. The use of the close-up by Eisenstein in BATTLESHIP POTEMKIN is restricted to scenes of mourning, with the exception of the meat shot at the beginning of the film. When the leader is killed, the different faces of his comrades file by, one after the other. Here it is not obscene, but sad and it is used precisely to make us feel this way.

Filmmakers who are not as willing to impress us as Dreyer or Eisenstein mainly try to neutralise the close-up. Take the example of BIRTH OF A NATION. The few close-ups are used very carefully, just before the death of the young sister, Flora. She is walking in the woods and we see the black who does not kill her, but causes her to commit suicide. At that precise moment we are shown the close-up of a squirrel, creating a moment of emotion. It is a form of suspense. At the same time, of course, the squirrel also symbolises the youth and innocence of the girl. But mostly, a close-up is neutralised by the shot-reverse shot pattern, which inserts it into a kind of dialogue, so that it is no longer the picture of an isolated face, but merely a picture which is used to accompany dialogue.

My argument is that television has introduced a tremendous change in our conception, both of film and of the human body, by increasingly using close-ups. Close-up is not the only specific feature of television, on the contrary, there are many other features which are typical of television. However, the close-up is one that is frequently and very cleverly used on television, whilst more and more filmmakers are influenced by the televisual facial.

Why is it that close-ups are so common on television? A few specific explanations spring to mind. The first of these is technical. The television set is often called the small screen. Conrad Schoeffter's example of a tennis match illustrates the point perfectly. I was struck by the fact that, although it is a contest which pitches two different people against each other, the producer is compelled every now and again to show us the faces of the two players. Were it not for the periodical introduction of close-ups, we would not be able to tell them apart. We cannot recognise someone on the small screen unless we are given a very close view of them. An interesting question would be what is going to happen now that we have the television wide-screen? Of course, I cannot answer this question as it is impossible to say what is going to happen within the next ten years. There will be so many changes that it would be absolutely meaningless to attempt to answer, and even if big television screens entered the living room, the functions of television will remain more or less the same. Television is a domestic appliance. People come in, switch on their television and then go somewhere else. Television creates a permanent presence in the home.

It is for this reason that it is important to have a good soundtrack with music and voice. Voice is closely linked with the most common use of television and, consequently, speech is an important element of television programmes. There is another reason. When radio was introduced in the 1920s, radio networks were run by people who thought they were on a mission; they had to communicate something that would improve the cultural standards of the population. This element has disappeared. People working for television networks have no mission at all, except that of making money. Therefore, there is no obligation to develop cultural or informative programmes, while television has become accessible to an ever larger group of people. Increasingly, people from the audience or in the street are invited to talk on screen, which means that the 'talking head' is becoming the typical image on our televisions. Visually criticised for being boring and off-putting, there are also a few possible uses of the 'talking head' which can be really interesting.

Take for example the well-known British sitcom *Eastenders* (BBC, Great Britain), which is broadcast every week, and consists almost entirely of close-ups. There are a few establishing shots which are used to introduce the actors, but most of the time we watch people talk. At first it resembles what can normally be seen in films. But a close look reveals an establishing shot, followed by a few close-ups of people, taken at random, often of someone who is not even talking. It ends with the same shot that was shown in the beginning: this would not be done in a film. A film tries to insert characters into a context through the use of different methods. First, by trying to create some sort of surroundings, for example by showing something of the room. More importantly, a film achieves this by layering the image, putting two or three people in front of each other, for we often observe an action from the point of view of one of the characters. This changes every time there is a reverse shot, but mostly we remain with one of the characters. There is a direction in the way people look at each other, and this establishes the lines of force on the screen. In the case of the sitcom, the three people on screen are taken in a row, although they are meant to be talking about a deal. It would make more sense if they were seated around a table. This is typical of the way people are now filmed. Instead of trying to create a link between the different characters, the camera merely jumps from one to the other. In this manner the relationship between what is said and what is seen loses importance, we merely have a face on a screen.

This may appear to be very critical, but it is merely a way of demonstrating the difference between filming close-ups on television and doing the same in the cinema. However, it does not mean that television is limited to speech when showing the shot of a face: emotion is an important element in television close-ups.

A more crucial point is that television is becoming more and more international, the same programmes can be seen all over the world. Take, for example *Cronaca* (Retequattro, Italy 10 Jan 1991): it is a European programme (but the same could no doubt be found on United States television) about an interview with a woman whose daughter has been killed by an unknown person and the murderer was never arrested. Conrad Schoeffter has said: 'on television we don't see, we hear.' This is the perfect example: it would be difficult and indecent to try and reconstruct the death of the girl. Therefore, we do not find out how she was killed, nor what happened. Everything is concentrated upon the encounter between the interviewer and the mother. The programme only lasts about 12 minutes. One soon realises that the poor woman has nothing to tell, that she does not want to tell anything, she only wants to mourn and we are faced with that mourning. Is this voyeurism? I am reluctant to use the word for two reasons. Firstly, in psychoanalysis, voyeurism has a precise meaning, which is taking pleasure, usually sexual, from the use of vision. Somehow I do not think this could apply to the present case. However, the woman did agree to be filmed, she could have stopped it at any point, and even after, she could have forbidden to have it broadcast. So there is an agreement, an unspoken agreement, between those on screen and those watching it. Formally, what is important, are the different looks which are directed at this woman. The division of this person, the fact that we see here her hand, her neck, her face, some bits of her surroundings, photographs mostly. Her home, her body are divided into small bits and all this reconstructs the feeling of someone who has experienced extreme loss.

24) *The mise-en-abyme of the close-up: Wim Wenders playing off the different image media in* NOTEBOOK OF CLOTHES AND CITIES, *as film, video, television and photography combine to the create the media image of our everyday lives.*

25) *With television having invaded the home, the private and domestic has become public: telephone sex while feeding the baby in Robert Altman's* SHORT CUTS *(1993). We have come a long way since Louis Lumière's* REPAS DE BÉBÉ *(1895).*

More directors are becoming interested in the purely visual aspect of a close-up made in this way. I could have cited many other examples. Think for instance of Stanley Kubrick, who went from BARRY LYNDON, which is made up mostly of long shots, to FULL METAL JACKET, which, with the exception of the attack at Da Nang, is made almost exclusively with close-ups of soldiers and officers. Someone newer to the industry is the Spaniard Pedro Almodóvar who consciously uses the television method in his films. In TACONES LEJANOS the actress Victoria Abril mostly appears as a face in front of the camera; the character in itself has little to tell.

The story line is about a complicated murder inquiry and in the end we can guess as to the identity of the murderer, but we are never sure, since much is left to our interpretation. Here, what counts is not what is said, but the way it is said. The face of Victoria Abril is very important. Shown without a background, we can see her teeth, her nose and there is a sharpness, a voluntary sharpness of the filming, to make us look only at who she is whilst she is acting and trying to be emotional. There is of course a big difference between the television programme just mentioned and this film. In the television programme the woman cannot act, she has to be herself, she cannot be more than herself. For this reason, it takes a long time before she finally accepts to cry and the camera can catch the tears, whereas an actress is able to be emotional on cue. However, in both instances the method of trying to introduce us to the study of her face is the same. To a certain extent, this means that television is obliged to find faces. There is a permanent interplay on television between reporters, who try to make people talk, and people who accept and do not accept to talk. We could say, up to a point, television has to hunt down faces. An example of this strange form of hunting, in which the hunted may accept or refuse to become the prey is *Zur Person: Günther Gaus im Gespräch* (ZDF, Germany, 1963-1966).

In this example it is interesting that colours and architecture are used to frame the character. Of course, this was not done on purpose, but out of probably half an hour of interview material, it is not by chance that the producer chose this segment and that it was edited in this way. It was chosen because it shows how a face can be inserted into a frame, that of the place where the boy lives, and that the colours are those basic colours of his surroundings.

Almodóvar uses the same tactics in his film, whereby a small part of the same face can be seen, showing various colours, and giving an almost kitsch effect. This is the case in the scene where the judge tries to hunt down Victoria Abril after she has been released from jail. The visit in itself is pointless, the magistrate has no right to question her again and he has nothing to expect from a new meeting. From a purely narrative point of view the scene was not necessary, although it retains interest because it is a way of having the two face-to-face. The magistrate forces Victoria Abril to sit down in a strange armchair, strange in colour and shape whilst forcing her to talk. There is a similarity between the interview techniques used to make other people talk, and the way this magistrate tries to make Abril talk.

At its root, TACONES LEJANOS is a televisual film, purposely made in this manner, about a woman who is a presenter on a television channel. Television plays an important role in the plot, for it is on television that she first confesses to having killed her husband, and the film is filled with extracts of television shows. Abril's mother, a famous actress, is to be interviewed for television. In exactly the same way a television programme would, the film shows the arrival of a big star in Madrid with someone waiting for her at the airport. As she arrives, for example, there is a brief evocation of the past, moments of her life portrayed as if taken from a television archive. Imagine she was being followed by a cameraman or a reporter, he would more or less have filmed her in the same way. She is then taken to her hotel and we follow her in the car. This sequence inside the car is broken up by a few shots of the street, just the sort of shots we would see in a television programme, shots that do not say anything and only aim to show us the city, meaningless shots of cars in the street. Just like the shots that have been put in to cut the dialogue that was too long. And while she is in the car, we see the star on one side, but cut by the frame. On the other side is the daughter, also cut by the frame. It evokes the interviewer and the interviewee all over again. Furthermore, there is no attempt to harmonise the image, and the centre of the screen is distressingly empty, there is nothing but the two half faces on both sides of the screen. Throughout the film, there is intentional and clever use of televisual tricks to create an atmosphere 'with a difference'.

Cinema is motion, there would be no cinema without motion. Whilst film is a way of creating motion, at the same time this motion is channelled in order to make it appear harmonious and well organized. These two aspects cannot be separated, there would be no film without motion, and there would be no 'correct' film if motion were to be recorded at random. So, there are two possible other ways that have always been avoided by cinema when filming people. One is an excess of motions, too much movement, stemming from a refusal to channel motion: this is what is more and more the case on television. Music videos, for instance, extensively use motion which does not count, or at least does not seem to be motivated.

The second way of using motion is in filming people, human beings, where motion is connected to emotion. Emotion, what does that mean? It means that we are out of motion. Emotion is to a large extent stillness, we are stricken by fear, hope, by different possible feelings and we no longer move. It is only our face and some parts of our body which express, what is extremely intense, but what is at the same time internal. Emotion, after all, could be the main topic, the central topic of film. And it is what directors like Almodóvar are trying to use. He is not alone, I could give you a list of other filmmakers that work in the same way. But it is not a question of giving an extensive list of names. It is a question of trying to understand what is happening. I think that what is happening is another way of looking at human bodies, of analyzing and understanding. You could say, after all, Cain killed his brother, and he reduced him to pieces. The body in pieces, maybe that is where we are.

But I think I would rather use another biblical example. It is the example of Jacob. Jacob was not the eldest son, but at a given time he got the inheritance. That does not mean he killed his eldest brother. He took what he had to take and went away. Do you not think that this is what is happening between cinema and television? Television is just taking its share, obliging the cinema to give it its blessings.

Cinema and Television: Laios and Oedipus

John Ellis

The title of 'Cain and Abel' implies an enmity between cinema and television, an enmity so strong that it offers no hope of reconciliation. The purpose of this paper is to argue against this grain, to look at the complexities of the relationship. So, against the grain, I propose a counter-myth to guide our thoughts. This is not a Hebraic, Biblical myth of origin, but a Greek myth of family life, latterly appropriated by psychoanalysis: the myth of Oedipus, the son, and Laios, the father.

Now in this myth, as in the myth of Cain and Abel, one party kills the other. I am assuming for the purposes of our discussion that this convenient narrative closure does not operate. Cain, the cinema does not kill Abel, television (or vice-versa); neither does Oedipus, the son (television) kill Laios, the father (cinema). The myth becomes even more interesting as a result. All that we know of Laios and Oedipus is their relationship. Laios is so deeply suspicious of his offspring that he casts him off into the wilderness. Oedipus is so blithely unaware of his parentage that he can attack his father and marry his mother. Yet, behind all this, they are bound together nevertheless. It is a relationship of mutual dependence. Their place in our imagination, and the imagination of centuries past, is the result of their being contained together in one powerful myth. You cannot have one without the other. And so it is with cinema and television in the second half of this century. They need each other. They advertise each other. They depend upon each other.

Television needs cinema's glamour. It needs cinema's superior production values. It needs cinema's adventurous approach to narrative and characterisation. It needs cinema's culture. Cinema needs television's audience. It needs to sell itself through television. Individual films use television to recruit their audience through advertising, and through the growing number of programmes about cinema, some of which I have spent the last few years producing. And cinema needs television's money: crucially in Europe and the rest of the world, and even in the USA to some degree. Cinema and television, therefore, are bound in a relationship of mutual dependence: each needs, in particular ways, the other's money, and the other's cultural position. That is the first aspect of this relationship.

The second aspect grows out of this. Laios had been warned how his son would turn out. Laios was suspicious of Oedipus. Laios himself knew all about usurpation. The classical version of the myth has it that Laios carried off the son of Pelops whilst teaching him to drive a chariot. Like father, like son. Television may have supplanted cinema; but cinema had already supplanted a whole range of popular media: music hall, vaudeville, shadow theatre, fairground entertainments.

Oedipus, if we believe Freud, or perhaps just the evidence of our own behaviour, was intensely rivalrous with his father. The mutual dependency between cinema and television is not that of an ecological system; it is that of thieves or usurpers. Cinema and television are desperately jealous of each other, they want what they perceive the other as having, and they are prepared to steal it. Television takes cinema films and shows them as its own creations. Think of television slots like *Film on Four* and of Channel 4's great boasts about its role as a creator of films. Think of Canal+... without whom, it appears, scarcely any films would be made in France. Cinema, for its part, takes television's money; but, with a certain amount of face-saving pride, it uses television's money to make things that it knows television will be unable to show. For evidence, look no further than the achievements of Peter Greenaway and his Dutch producers in taking television's money to fill the screen with naked bodies, arcane conundrums and scenes of surpassing cruelty. So this is the second aspect of the relationship: both sides, both Oedipus and Laios, are out to grab whatever they can from the other. And both know it.

But Oedipus did supplant Laios in the affections of Jocasta. Oedipus became king of Thebes. He married Jocasta, Laios's wife, his mother. For our purposes of course, Jocasta represents the popular audience. We know little of her apart from some aspects of her taste, just as we know little about the popular audience.

Now it is undoubtedly true that Oedipus/television usurped the place of Laios/cinema in the affections of the popular audience. And what a difficult ruler this Oedipus has turned out to be. He subjects the audience to a non-stop barrage of things that he hopes might appeal to them. Desperately insecure, television has to ceaselessly re-calculate public taste, to push neurotically at the boundaries of what is acceptable, and edge away from anything that might be genuinely disturbing. So insecurity is one of the characteristics of television's relationship with the popular audience.

Another aspect is the way that television is using up the patrimony of cinema. Television spends recklessly all those wonderful films that cinema kept stored away in its treasury. But it seems that Laios/cinema did not die at the crossroads after all. He faked his own disappearance. Freed of the responsibilities of power, freed of the need to care for the masses, cinema went off to enjoy itself at last – until the money ran out. There are moments,

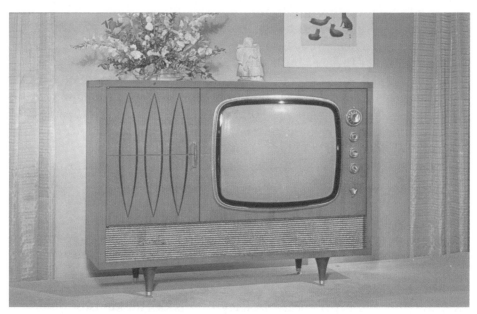

26) The single, imposing television-set as the media-altar at the centre of home and hearth: a phenomenon of the 1950s that seems to belong to a different century.

27) The cinema as the place of lost innocence, the recovery of childhood and the memory of companionship: a nostalgic look at a lost world of bliss, community and contemplation from CINEMA PARADISO *(1988).*

too, when Laios returns to haunt Oedipus in his dreams. Taking on the guise of Steven Spielberg, Laios reasserts his old power over the audience. All that Oedipus can do is watch with awe, to babble away about the artistry of the master. If it works of course, because sometimes these dreams do not have the desired effect, especially when they concern Peter Pan and his problems as a grown-up lawyer. But when Laios cares to make an awesome demonstration of power, to undertake an occasional re-seduction of Jocasta, it serves only to make Oedipus's regime more hysterical.

Oedipus then tries to reassert control by imitating the outward appearances of Laios. He dresses in his father's clothes. Television tries to make movies, or lavishes so much attention and care on its tv-dramas that they take on the appearance of movies. But this is a doomed enterprise. For the game has changed. Laios only returns occasionally to taunt Oedipus. His real pleasures lie elsewhere. Cinema continues to have the potential to be more adventurous than television. Its audiences select themselves. The ever more sophisticated marketing allows audiences to know the kind of thing they are about to experience, and television issues all kinds of hints and warnings to help the process along. Quite simply, cinema can risk what television dare not, be it Hannibal Lector of SILENCE OF THE LAMBS, HARD TARGET or STRICTLY BALLROOM.

This is partly a matter of theme, subject matter, modalities of human experience. But it is also tied into a simple fact of marketing: each film has to emphasise its difference from all others, even while it boasts its similarities to others. Every film is a new product, and one of its attributes has to be novelty. However, television regards novelty as a necessary evil. The institutions of television do not like the risks involved. Their business is that of amplification and repetition. Novelty is a strategy of last resort, to be attempted when all else fails. Such are the responsibilities of power, the price of winning the affections of the mass public. So the third aspect of this Oedipal scenario is the relationships that each have to the affections of the mass audience.

But taking also involves giving. Cinema has received a good degree of restitution over the years from television. I would suggest, straying for a moment from the strict comparison with the Oedipus myth (you may well have had enough of it anyway), that there are two areas where cinema has received from television.

First, television has produced a greater sophistication in the audience, greater than cinema on its own could ever have achieved. The general level of audiovisual literacy in Western culture is much higher than it was even twenty years ago. Ordinary people know how images are created; they have some idea of how images are selected, and how they can (in the common view) distort things. They are well used to sophisticated media 'in-jokes'. They can deal with elliptical narratives, ambiguous characters, leaps and discontinuities that would have puzzled the cinema audience of years ago. And it is cinema that profits from this audiovisual literacy, whenever its executives allow it to.

One key aspect of this has been the way that television acts as a vast, chaotic archive of cinema. It sometimes seems as though afternoon and late night television had been scheduled by some deranged ghost of Henri Langlois. Every movie whose negative Hollywood had contrived to keep, plus every scrap of entertainment from the domestic film industry of whatever country it might be: they all get their brief moment of reflected electronic glory on the television screen sooner or later. So, at last, films can find a truly cinematically literate audience: thanks to television.

I expect that, late at night, Oedipus would reminisce about the father he never knew, telling his retainers embroidered versions of his exploits, some full of exaggeration, others making surprising connections, unexpected juxtapositions. This is the effect of the jumbled history of cinema that daily graces our television screens. And now, since we find ourselves back with these mythical characters again, let us explore another angle. Who are these people? What does the myth tell us about their characters, or rather, what can we read from the myth about their characters, as is the way in our televisual/cinematic culture, since myths are not known for psychological depth and complexity. Laios was forward and decisive. His was a regime that began with a revolutionary break. It had to establish new rules. Cinema emerged with a programme, a way of doing things. This model of narration which developed in Hollywood produced in its moment of birth a less coherent (but perhaps even more interesting) opposition to itself. These predominantly European forms gave more value to performance and acting, and carried a central concern with artifice, that undertow of self-awareness that seems to elude the American culture as a whole. Where Europe could never produce as blatant an Oedipal fantasy as BACK TO THE FUTURE, America could never produce as devastating a critique of the very activity of cinema as PEEPING TOM.

I say this simply so that I am not accused of championing the critical orthodoxies of Bordwell, Thompson and the 'Wisconsin School'. It is also to characterise in a few words the regime of narrativity of cinema, because television does not have the same economy of narration at all, unless it is television that is making itself according to the model of cinema (and even then there are differences). Television narration learned more from Joseph von Sternberg than it did from Howard Hawks or John Ford. Television narration has a certain fetishism about it: it is condemned to repeat rather

than to move forward; to go over the same ground; to return to the scene of
the crime; to keep before our gaze the same insoluble problems; to refuse to
let us off the hook.

Television invented the situation comedy, a form impossible for cinema
to contemplate. Each week: the same situation, a return practically to zero.
And for aficionados of the form, Channel 4 has occasionally produced the
ultimate situation comedy, *Nightingales*: three security guards stuck in a
surrealistic limbo. Week after week in a world that literally has no outside
and no meaning.

So these are the two stars of our tale: Laios the decisive; Oedipus the obsessive repeater. What of the other characters? First, there is the Sphinx.
When Laios disappeared, this character terrorised the citizens of Thebes until Oedipus came along and guessed the answer to its riddle. When you
study the story, you very soon realise that the Sphinx's riddle is a pretty te-
dious one: 'what walks on four legs, two legs and three legs?'. We could all
do better than that, but it was probably the way he told it. For the Sphinx
represents the spirit of variety, of the stand-up comedian, the music-hall artist, the popular entertainer of the live stage, exactly the people whom cinema found it most difficult to integrate into its performances, yet whose
natural home, the variety theatre, cinema relegated to a secondary role in
popular entertainment. No wonder that with Laios suddenly gone, the old
spectre of the stand-up comedian came back to haunt the population of
Thebes with his terrible gags.

Oedipus comes along, slays the Sphinx, and offers much better material.
Game shows with fifty gag writers. The Sphinx could never match that.
Stand-up comics doing a different routine every Saturday rather than every
five years. No wonder the Sphinx disappeared. As for Jocasta, I said that we
know very little about her. But this is not strictly true. We are all haunted by
a question about Jocasta, one that only she could answer. Did she recognise
Oedipus as her son? Or, if she did recognise him, did she confuse the characteristics that she recognised in him with those of her husband? If Jocasta can
represent the popular audience, then we have to ask how far the experience
of television and the experience of cinema are interchangeable. How far
does television satisfy the need for cinema; how far does cinema satisfy the
need for television; and how far are they, in fact, separate needs?

Perhaps this is where the analogy will collapse. Those of us who analyze
films know that the figure of the woman is usually the most problematic
point, the point at which definitions blur or are recast. So it is with our Jocasta. We know that she rejected Oedipus as soon as she knew that he was
her son, and had done away with her husband. At this point, too, Oedipus
goes away and blinds himself, which at least proves that the regime of sight

plays some kind of role in this whole scenario. Yet had Jocasta not been made aware of Oedipus' identity, then the situation could have continued indefinitely. For I believe that cinema and television offer different modalities of entertainment to the popular audience. If anything, their differences are becoming more marked.

I think we all have a relatively good idea of what cinema can offer, but how do we characterise television? Our critical languages force us to conceive television in the terms that are appropriate for cinema. Television inevitably comes off worse from such an encounter. It appears to be an inferior version of cinema: the son of cinema. But what if we can see that the son has his own separate identity, a radically different identity? Television is part of everyday life. Its rhythms are those of everyday life. In this, it is radically different from cinema, whose performances are special events. Television is permanently available to us, constantly with us. It is familiar and domestic. Its aesthetic is a new one, and we do not have the critical language to encompass it. Our culture is used to finding aesthetic value in discrete and separate items: in texts, in objects, in events. Cinema films can, with only a little difficulty, be fitted into this aesthetic.

But there is nothing of this in television. Its aesthetic is the aesthetic of ordinary, mundane human existence, rather than of special moments, of epiphanies, of a separated realm of the senses. It is a nonsense to talk of television programmes as if they were films: the very texts themselves resist this, because they are held in a network of explicit repetitions and variations. They have a different relationship with their audience: one of casual encounter, of habit, of the infinite postponement of narrative closure. And, above all, they have a different relationship to time. Cinema has a magical ability to expand and contract time at will. We pay no attention to the casual elisions that an editor will make: the famous example is the act of opening a door and stepping through it. And we are aware of the opposite possibility only to the extent that we enjoy it: that cinema can expand time through the multiplication of points of view, of different set-ups. And we all know of the impossible chronology of THE BIG SLEEP, to which can be added many other examples.

But for television, time does not expand and contract in this spectacular way. Television time is the time of the metronome, ticking away prosaically and regularly. Television exists in the same time continuum as its audience: its time is co-present with that of the audience.

Television belongs to the present, to the immediate; cinema belongs to the historic, to the photographic. This allows television a different relationship to the audience. It shares the audience's everyday realities; it comments upon them, accompanies people about their daily business. It is frequently mundane, but more often inspired, able to reach out to make the ordinary into something to be reflected upon. Television has made intimacy into an art-form. This is the basis of its aesthetic: it is at once private and public, ever-present in our domestic space without ever being completely a part of that space.

The idea of space takes us further in defining what I am trying to get at. A cinema is a special space, one to which we are permitted a limited access. It is not *our* space, it is a controlled public space which we enter according to set rules – the payment of money, arrival at an appointed hour – and agree to behave according to still further established rules. These rules certainly vary according to the particular culture in which the screening is taking place, but in Europe our established convention is that we sit, we do not talk, and we attend to the spectacle. We submit – and, having submitted, we can enter into a different modality of existence, into a realm of fantasy. This process is essentially a *sacred* one. It is not in itself religious, but it is close to the activity of a religion. Collective submission to rules and rituals allows the individual a degree of epiphany. No wonder that, in this special space, cinema can walk on the wild side.

Television, on the other hand, occupies a different space entirely, one that has no sacred dimension to speak of. We have television of right in our society. It is a social necessity in the same way that indoor plumbing is a social necessity. It defines the basic level of culture in modern Western Europe. Those few households (under 2% in Britain) that have no television are radically cutting themselves off from the normal social intercourse of society. They find current events difficult to follow, newspaper reports full of lacunae, because television has such a basic and central role in the way that our society talks to itself.

Television is a right and occupies the same domestic space as we do. In Britain, the attempt to set up collective television viewing clubs has always been seen as a kind of perversion, an inversion of established values like that of Luis Bunuel's LE CHARME DISCRET DE LA BOURGEOISIE in which eating is a shameful, private activity and shitting a normal public one. However, in the Netherlands it seems that viewing clubs have been successful, for *Inspector Morse* and other such television shows that are not available through broadcast channels. This argues an awareness of what is happening on British television that is quite formidable; but it is also interesting that *Inspector Morse* falls exactly into the category of television attempting to be cinema, in production values, in duration, and most certainly in pacing.

It is generally true, though, that we have no ritual around television. The viewing of films on video at home can incite us to emulate cinema (low lighting, food, a sense of event, a special start time), but television does not attract such rituals any more. There is no sacredness, and so the release into phantasy is correspondingly low. Television accompanies you through life, it does not take you to another dimension. It is secular rather than sacred. Its activity is not that of enabling a little epiphany to be experienced by the viewer. Its actuality is different, but equally important. Television is concerned with *working out*, in the specific sense of repeating and working over, gradually giving more and more form to an experience, to a fear, to a puzzle, to a problem, until it becomes acceptable: understood in part, rejected in part, repressed in part, misperceived in part, but acknowledged in whole. Pierre Sorlin's important perception of the unstructured movement of much television (compensated by the enormous use of close-up) applies especially to those parts of television which are most close to the initial experience that television is just beginning to work upon. This is the area of news, of talk shows, of studio-based 'personal problem' television, and then of soaps with their perpetual present. Later comes analytic television: highly edited documentaries, formalised drama, films for television. These provide more structure to the initial incoherence. Through television, then, the tensions of the outside world can become domesticated. As I have indicated, this is not an easy process, and is subject to multiple repressions and distortions upon the way. For this reason, it is in no simple sense social integration according to any grand design of social repression. The results are too unpredictable for that. But it does explain to a significant degree why forms that used to be marginal in cinema – news, documentary and social realist drama – take up a large amount of space on television, and can, in certain cultures at least, command very large audiences.

Television's programming strengths lie in this fundamental characteristic. It is able to do best what cinema does least well: it can satirise, it can report. Television can take the continuous present, the present in which we perceive ourselves as existing, and give it back to us in a formalised set of routines of meaning. This is where television and cinema are most different.

I believe that we find this difficult to perceive. We are misled aesthetically by the history of the relationship between the two media; the development of cinema before television; and the fact that cinema's material can easily be shown on television. Had television been invented first, we would not have had this debate, though I believe that the public exhibition of complex fictions on large screens to paying audiences would still have developed. I believe that cinema and television have very different aesthetic experiences to offer, and very different ways of translating our perceptions of reality into audiovisual creations. But, like Tiresias, I do not expect anyone to believe me.

This essay is dedicated to the memory of Esmond Ellis (1925-1994)

Cinema and Television: From Eden to the Land of Nod?

Michael Eaton

The following is no more than a set of personal reflections on the process of working as a dramatist for film and television in a time of international co-production and the 'film for television'. You may treat it with the customary disdain reserved for someone who, in my industry, is axiomatically referred to as 'just the writer'.

And Abel was a keeper of sheep but Cain was a tiller of the ground.
Like many another witty aphorism emanating from the same source (Jean Luc Godard): *Cinema and Video – Cain and Abel* seems superficially pertinent. But is it really? The phrase suggests that video has come along and slain cinema, David has toppled Goliath. My thoughts will focus not so much on the successive technologies of film and video, but rather on the increasing mutual interdependence of the institutions of cinema and television.

True enough, the story in the fourth chapter of Genesis does seem to speak of a struggle between representatives of two communities, two ecologies: the agriculturalist and the herdsman, but these are co-existent life styles. Cain is the oldest brother and the one who survives – this is not a dynastic or generational struggle. This is not an Oedipal story of succession, of supplanting.

Neither does it seem, as some historians of the detective story have maintained, to be the world's first murder mystery – if it is, then Yahweh is a rather uninvolving sleuth as he knows all the answers already. This is a story not of selfish, jealous, murderous revenge, but of a ritual sacrifice and ritual expulsion. Therefore, maybe it is not so *im*pertinent to our business after all.

And in the process of time it came to pass that Cain brought of the fruit of the ground an offering unto the Lord...
Certainly since I have been working as a screenwriter from the middle 1980s, most British films have been at least in part financed by television. We could go further and argue that most British films have never (at home, at any rate) been shown in cinemas. I for one would be committing professional hari-kiri if I were to regard television and cinema (if not video and

film) as rival ecologies engaged in a murderous struggle of succession. We all of us eat from the same trough.

But it wasn't always so. A few personally refracted considerations about the historic role of the script in both film and television drama are perhaps in order. For instance, I get the distinct impression that the script was a relative latecomer to the movies. The earliest scripts were little more than sets of shot lists and plans and inventories of what was required in terms of settings, properties and personnel to achieve them. Metaphorically, little has changed: at base the document we call a 'script' is a blueprint for a budget. The format of the international language of the screenplay is not something that is ever read by our audience. Rather, it serves as an architectural blueprint by which our fellow professionals can understand what contribution they need to make for the realisation of the piece. And the first thing that is done with it is that somebody goes through it and starts to put pound note signs next to everything you've written. The script does not exist primarily to be read (at least that's what it often feels like) but operates as a palimpsest onto which other workers write in their specific technical languages. This is something that novelists and, to a lesser extent, playwrights coming into the world of the screenplay often find creatively limiting if not demeaning. Personally it's something I take a certain pride in. If nothing else, my words form the basis of other people's employment.

And Abel, he also brought of the firstlings of his flock and the fat thereof. The script in television drama has a rather different pedigree, emanating from the early days of live television with its three video cameras in a studio-bound setting, perhaps with a few minutes of film which would usually have consisted of exteriors already shot (with a cine-camera) and inserted where appropriate. Any experimental use of film in the early days of television was more likely to be found in documentary rather than drama. In this sense, television drama was essentially from its origin a hybrid form. It borrowed its dramatic construction entirely from the theatre but its syntax was that of classical continuity editing in terms of camera angles, movements and cutting, more because of lighting conditions than any limitations of technology.

But in its early days the new medium also drew on some of the studio techniques of radio drama. All of the classic genres of television drama: the situation comedy; the long-running serial drama; the adaptation of classic novels and the one-off original, commissioned drama developed out of radio. Although, it could, of course, be argued that the scope of radio drama then was wider than what was possible on TV. Certainly, from a budgetary standpoint it is no heavier on resources to produce a space opera or a period

28) Going out to stay home, or dressing up for television: in the 1960s the television set was promoted as a focal point for social gatherings in the home, an idea that must seem touchingly naive to the generation of the couch-potatoes with their tv-dinners.

drama on radio than it is a contemporary naturalistic play – two halves of a coconut are even cheaper than a car horn.

It is frequently argued that one of the foremost distinguishing features of the role of drama within the institutions of television, during its subsequent evolution, has been a prioritised investment in the *series*, which has a certain continuity occupying a particular weekly or daily time-slot, which makes use of familiar faces and characters and which can build and maintain a following over a period of time. In Britain, the season for a series' run has characteristically been no more than six episodes, usually the work (in the first season at least) of one writer, whereas in the USA these seasons may be at least 26 weeks, and so are naturally the product of team work often with the series editor being the person who originally developed the franchise for the series. The whole point about the series format is that it can be reproduced indefinitely. The Starship Enterprise's five-year misssion subtly encodes a truth of US televison ecology: at the end of five years the first series becomes available for profitable syndication whilst the current series is still playing the networks.

On a formal level, therefore, the drama of the series has characteristically involved a sort of inside/outside structure with narrative elements entering the familiar world only to be expelled by the end of the episode, leaving the basic set-up untouched. Clearly, this indicates that the major investment of the long-running TV series is in the characters rather than the narratives, although both of these aspects have a tendency to become all too familiar as the run progresses.

But if we take a historical perspective it becomes obvious that the series is in no way a uniquely televisual form. Even if today's cinema no longer invests in long-running series detectives like *The Saint, The Falcon, Sherlock Holmes*, or comedians like The Three Stooges and The Young Rascals, which were staple bottom-of-the-bill fare in the 1930s, nevertheless we only have to look at the proliferation in our cinematic lifetime of the sequel to realise that it is not just the television institution which banks on the familiar. To some extent the very notions of genre and star are bound up with that play of repetition and difference so characteristic of the television series.

Also, like cinema, television from its inception always produced one-off, stand alone dramas, even if these sheltered under a series umbrella, as in the USA with *Colgate Theatre* and *Dick Powell Presents*, or in Britain with *Armchair Theatre, Play for Today*. This was the place in the schedules where television's debt to the theatre was perhaps most apparent and it was the spot where the work of the writer was, in that Edenic time that I was never fortunate enough to live through, paramount. And it is from this privileged locus that the television film, (a contradiction in terms?) certainly in the UK, developed.

A final category in the typology of TV drama might also be mentioned: the *serial*, which was also a cinematic staple in the pre-television era. The serial is a kind of hybrid of a hybrid. Bounded in form with a definite Aristotelian beginning, middle and end, it plays over a number of episodes so still capturing a particular time-slot: a kind of stretched out one-off. It is hardly coincidental that so many of these (significantly labelled 'mini-series' in some territories) are adaptations of novels, since it was the novel and the feuilleton that pioneered this form in the 19th century. Interestingly enough, the BBC has a Head of Series *and* Serials whilst a different person commissions one-offs, a fact which might well be indicative of some sort of institutional categorisation.

Gradually, from the 1970s onwards (another Eden I missed out on, when the ITV companies had, as Lord Thompson famously put it, 'a licence to print money', due to their advertising monopoly) all three of these categories of television drama increasingly left the studio, were increasingly shot entirely on film, increasingly approached cinematic budgetary levels and increasingly adopted the language of film, not only in the technological sophistication of lighting and editing codes at that time unavailable on video technology, but also in the dramatic structure itself. Scenes became much shorter, action sequences became more elaborate, settings became more naturalistic, less 'theatrical'. It was coming to look as if Cain and Abel were always both tillers of sheep and keepers of the soil.

Am I my Brother's Keeper?

When in the early 1980s (a golden age in which, finally, I have been able to share) Channel 4 started commissioning, there was a final recognition that a broadcaster could produce drama for both theatrical release in the cinemas and subsequent television screening. But, of course, there was the inherent risk that this product would become neither fish nor fowl, neither Cain nor Abel, a criticism so often levelled at British cinema.

Nevertheless, it became possible for writers in Britain to write low-budget film scripts without going near the film industry at all – the university-educated, BBC-apprenticed writer never had to deal with the blazered spivs of Wardour Street – not for a while, at any rate. Here, the mataphor apparently holds: cinema was populated by fly-by-night no-mads, all too willing to flaunt their out-group status mark, whilst television types settled down on the farm. Secure in their growth of a variety of sta-ples, they could hazard the occasional luxury. But then, who was Cain and who was Abel?

A trivial, but telling anecdote, indicates that a savage survival from the early years of television drama is still current in an age of the television film, an age when the one-off strands are no longer packaged as *The Wednesday Play* or *Play For Tody* but *Screen One* and *Screen Two*. When a script of mine, written and submitted in the screenplay format familiar to filmmakers all over the world, goes into production at the BBC it is retyped into an antedi-luvian script format which was developed exclusively for the three-camera studio shoot. A script of 100 pages mutates into an unwieldy document of about 250 (all those poor trees). When working on a co-production with the US company HBO, the American continuity person did not know how to read it, did not know how to do her work upon it. Old habits die hard.

And the Lord said unto Cain: Why art thou wroth? and why is thy countenance crestfallen?

Just as cinema had to learn how to talk, television drama had to learn how to be visual. It could be argued that in learning how to talk, cinema, at least ini-tially, became less international, and in learning to be more visual television became more international. To get a television drama, in the age of inde-pendent production, off the ground has become no different from getting a movie into production. Money has to be raised from a variety of sources, often internationally, with all the concomitant exigencies of production and differing demands from the co-producers that this involves. Neither Cain nor Abel but Cable.

I hear more venerable writers than myself constantly bewailing the fact that young writers today do not get a chance to fail, do not get the opportunity to see their work go out on 'the box' season after season. Was it inevitable that, in coping with the different demands of two institutions with very different histories and needs, films would become more like television and – this is the more important point – television would become more like film? In a global marketplace which promises mutual benefits for both television and cinema, has a certain type of television drama – more topical, more provisional, more experimental, more political – been branded with the mark of Cain and exiled to the east of Eden?

This parasitic hybridisation is even experienced at the level of viewing. Today's cinema audiences have grown increasingly to resemble the television viewers, munching on junk food as they give a running commentary on the action on the screen. If they were to instal powersockets in cinemas they would probably get up periodically and make the tea. Neither Cain nor Abel but Babel.

In Britain today, films would not be made were it not for the investiment of television. Television would not have been so consistently good were it not for the aspiration to be more like film. But maybe the time has come that we should take another look at the historical roots of cinema and television drama in terms of what separates them formally rather than in what unites them. Maybe it is time that films should be more like films and television more like television. If this involves ritual sacrifice and expulsion, then both brothers will have to bear the mark.

And Cain went out from the presence of the Lord and dwelt in the land of Nod.

It was Jonathan Swift who first used 'the Land of Nod' as a synonym for sleep – a state more usually associated with watching television than going to the cinema. A more recent Biblical translation speaks of Nod as meaning a wind-blown place. It is my fear that the type of television drama that I have been privileged enough to work on will become increasingly hard to finance as audiences fragment, national networks become less significant and even more broadcasters will be needed to put together a financial package for expensive filmed drama. The cultural significance of television drama will be a thing of the past. In that case, where is East of Eden? I'll see you in a wind-blown, desert place in a state of catatonia.

Fantasy Island: Dream Logic as Production Logic

Thomas Elsaesser

Play it again, ...

As we know, serialization in literature and visual narrative dates back already several centuries. In the series, a particular economic and technological organization of production finds its most direct rhetorical embodiment. When Dickens wrote instalments of *Oliver Twist* against the fortnightly deadline, he was writing against his publisher's need to keep his printing presses rotating, and the news-vendor expecting to feed his family. In the cinema and television, the serial form was meant to tie an audience to a star, or to make viewers come back for the 'Further Adventures of Dolly'. On television, it is to educate an audience into being 'loyal' to a show. From a formal point of view, on the other hand, we tend to think that serialization, as practised in soap operas, the classic serial or in cult programmes like *Twilight Zone* or *The X-Files* is merely a version and variant of classical (Hollywood) narrative, with an extra element of indeterminacy and openness written into its 'closure', much as, for instance, Tsvetan Todorov had defined the literary genre of the fantastic.

What interests me here is to see how the double logic of narrative form and economic organization articulate themselves into the 'compromise formation' which is the television serial, suspended not so much between 'classical' closure and the (avant-garde, serial) 'open' work, or the great philosophical figure of repetition and difference, but between certain economic constraints inherent in the fact that television and cinema sustain each other by a curious kind of symbiosis, in which the production process can take on a textual form. It is this symbiosis, it seems to me, that is responsible for a phenomenon which critics have, perhaps too quickly, characterized as 'post-modern', namely that television, in many of its genres, but especially in the series, 'addresses' its spectator as at once a knowing, a believing and a disbelieving subject. At the same time, in the cinema, a similar trend appears to manifest itself, not only with the STAR WARS cycle, or the INDIANA JONES films, but in the phenomenon observable for some time, namely that more and more feature films are given an 'open' ending, presumably in order to have the option of a sequel. Yet is this the case and does the same logic obtain? Why are there also open-ended films, with no sequel in sight, such as DRESSED TO KILL (Brian de Palma), BLADE RUNNER

(Ridley Scott), SILENCE OF THE LAMBS (Jonathan Demme), CONTACT (Robert Zemeckis)? An exploration and a case study, with no evident end in sight...

Serialization as a War-Zone

From a historical perspective, several factors support the assumption that the television series has structural features whose rationales reach beyond the generic in film and television. The economic determinants, from sponsors and advertisers, to fans and loyal viewers as targeted consumers of tabloid news and gossip sheets are invariably built into the formulas that make a given show a 'success'.

From this it also follows that the pressures behind making series 'popular' reflect the changing fortunes of a given institution, be it publishing or television: one might even argue that, beyond being a staple of the mass-media, it is also particularly responsive to crisis, that it is a sensitive barometer of the rapport between an institution and its clients, between a medium and its consumers. If we cast our minds back to the emergence of the serialized novel during the 1840s and 1850s in England and France (Dickens, Eugène Sue) its first great successes came at a time which saw a tremendous increase in the power of the newspaper press over book-publishing. The serialized novel was part of a struggle of control, in which writers and authors came under pressure from the printers and distributors, those who owned the raw materials, the sites of production, and those who controlled the markets. Instead of authors or publishers creating a product and seeking a market for it, the relation was the other way round – newspapers had created the space, and they needed attractive product to fill it. The serial novel thus marks one of the key points in the history of commodity production in the sphere of intellectual labour, with authors merely filling a given form or space.

The case of Dickens is exceptional, because thanks to his popularity as a speaker and orator, he was able to wrest a certain amount of autonomy from the machinery that held him in thrall. Dickens turned the process to his advantage, by imposing his own fame directly on the market as a brand-name, but someone like George Gissing is an instructive example of this rather radical displacement of authorship and control which entered fiction writing in the age of the serialized or instalment novel. The whole ideology of the serialized novel, and its mechanisms of suspense, its particular construction of enigmas, bifurcating narratives, depends very evidently on the technology of cheap printing and rapid circulation, in other words, on new forms of distribution and sales outlets – for how else sustain suspense if it cannot be at once satisfied and re-awakened within days or, at most, a week or two?

In the cinema, this technological and economic structure of rapid circulation was of course in place prior to the existence of feature-length, internally coherent narratives. The serial represents, between 1916 and 1921/2, an attempt to generate longer narratives out of the one- and two-reeler format, to which the audience had become accustomed. It was an elegant solution to the problem of how to make best possible use of the economic power inherent in the rapid turnover of films supplied to cinema chains. But whereas in Europe – one thinks of Feuillade in France, or the Joe May and Fritz Lang serials in Germany – the serial had an important history by itself, in Hollywood, Griffith's BIRTH OF A NATION both solved the narrative problems of which the serial had been a symptom, and transcended it, by finding the (formal) means and (epic) subject for generating a longer narrative as well as creating the kind of total experience of duration which had been the serial's attraction.

For it is evident that, besides the technical reasons, the serial had an institutional function: to bind the spectator to a particular mode of entertainment, to make going to the cinema a habit, creating a compulsion to repeat, and thus uphold a power of attraction not by the cinema's novelty value (around 1904 the cinema experienced its first major crisis, when people ceased to be astonished by the performance of the cinematograph as a technical wonder), but by a more psychological fixation. And the kind of paralleling of plot, the cross-cutting and alternation which Griffith developed, for instance in INTOLERANCE, are also the structural elements of the serial, worked into an overall, overarching narrative, where the principle of division and separation, of fragmentation and flow was taken into a mode that could sustain the rhythm of enigma and resolution, bifurcation and hesitation across a unified narrative space.

A similar case for the relation between a crisis in the institution cinema and the re-emergence of the serial could be made for the late 1940s and 1950s, when, in the face of the emergence of television, the cinema undertook to compete with its rival either by outdoing it in size, colour, production values and spectacular effects (such as 3D), or by offering products that seemed comparable. Television, whose mode of reception is the conjugation of discontinuity known as 'segmented flow', found in the serial both a model that reproduced in miniature, as it were, its own organizational time structure, and (as with the newspapers in the mid-nineteenth century, under the pressure of establishing a new medium as the dominant and paradigmatic one) evolved the continuous discontinuity of the serial as its form of binding an audience to its own institution. The function that advertising and sponsorship had in the imposition of the serial is in this respect quite crucial and well-documented.

So far, I have merely wanted to outline a proposition which considers the serial linked to an institutional and technological crisis situation of the cinema and of television, where it appears as key phenomenon of balance and compromise, negotiating between an economic regime and a regime of pleasure. This crisis-compromise theory of the serial with regard to the cinema could be demonstrated with some felicity in the case of the German cinema in the 1960s, at a time when the collapse of the commercial film industry was particularly acute. What could be observed was that a particular kind of film – mainly soft-core pornographic films and adolescent comedies – were produced in series, some of which were simply numbered consecutively, like the SCHULMÄDCHENREPORTS, while others were known generically by their literary source: as an Edgar Wallace film, or a Karl May film. Here in its most denuded and brutal form, an economic necessity (to produce cheaply and quickly) gave rise to the series, as a way of wooing back a fickle public, but with a commodity that was almost as cheap to produce as television, since actors, props, sets and plots could be recycled. The commercial cinema in its moment of agony fought back, with the weapons of televisual form, but with a content – sex and violence – that television at that time hardly dared to touch: trying to have it both ways, it lost all when the new technology of the video-tape and the VCR entered upon the scene.

Thus, my 'media war zone' theory of the series needs to be modified if it is to account for its resurgence into prime time television in the 1970s and 1980s. Analyzing the narrative strategies in evidence in long-running classic series, such as *Coronation Street* on British television, or observing the multi- and cross-cultural audience appeal of, say, *Dallas* and *Dynasty*, critics tended to pay less attention to the underying globalization of the media, of which the *Dallas* success story was a startling harbinger. A struggle there was, but it was not in the first instance between cinema and television; the more momentous shift was taking place between two kinds of television, say, between the BBC (or CBS) and CNN (or MTV), creating a new constellation, within which serialization had to be reinterpreted.

Repetition and Multiple Choice
Crucial to the long-running series in the 1970s, I would argue, was a distinct non-congruence between the boundaries of the textual unit – the individual episodes or the time slot into which they are programmed – and its boundaries as a unit of discourse – the 'world' that the series created, spilling over into magazine articles, soap characters as 'media personalities', the comings and goings of actors. Anticipating the demand for interactive storytelling which we now associate with the digital media of the 1990s, serialization already constitutes a significant textual form in which similar changes in nar-

29) *Fantasy Island and the revenge of nature on culture: King Kong climbing to the Radio Tower. The airplanes may have defeated him in 1933, but he will be back...*

30) *.. digitally remastered as a tornado, gripping not Fay Wray, but stray cows and heavy-duty utility vehicles that cross his path: the spectacle of wronged nature in* TWISTER *(1995).*

rative logic manifest themselves as we find in multiple choice, open-ended, or so-called 'interactive' narratives. Serialization rests, I would argue, as much on multiplication as it does on repetition, in the sense that repetition is the result less of mass production and formulaic combinations of elements, and more of the media-specific form that multiple choice and divisibility take in the age of miniaturization. The linearity of serial-time is, as it were, merely the foreshortening effect of a multi-dimensional strategy of partici-pation and dissipation. What one witnesses is the convergence of the pro-cesses of splitting, cutting, separating and dividing not only in the work of art as we know it from avant-garde practices such as surrealism and dada, but the industrial application of such aesthetic principles in the productive sector and the economic sphere.

That this signifies more than an extension of the division of labour and of rationalization to texts and narratives is indicated by the fact that the series appears in this context as an instance of embedding, of mise-en-abyme, whereby the progress of the episodes is guaranteed not by an internal logic, but by reproducing the (economic and technological) conditions of its exis-tence, but also the menu of options it offers to the viewer.

I would like to illustrate this by an example from American television, a series called *Fantasy Island*, very familiar to viewers in the US in the 1970s and – together with its companion piece *Love Boat* – still broadcast occasion-ally as re-runs of TV Gold or similar cable television-fare. Usually airing in the early evening, it is a hybrid between series and serial, because the format hovers between open-ended episodes, where characters undergo a change of state – and thus open to current events, audience feedback – and the self-contained adventures of the serial. One's view of this depends on whether one is a 'minimalist' viewer, attending to the slightest detail and nuance in the behaviour of the regular cast, or whether one is more interested in the adventures of the newcomers each week.

The basic formula is that a castaway or visitor comes to a mysterious but familiar island, inhabited by a dandyesque figure – half Dracula, half Pros-pero – in a white tuxedo, surrounded by servants and a chorus of very lightly clad young ladies. The visitor or visitors – usually television person-alities well known to the average viewer from other network shows, get in-volved in what turns out to be their favourite fantasy, which suddenly becomes real. As often as not, this may also be something of a nightmare from which the visitor has a narrow escape. The ambience of the show is one of broad comedy, the happenings are beyond all credibility, the events seem incoherent to the outsider, the jokes often feeble, the allusions embarrassing or in bad taste. But the very format of the show is one of embedded narrative and self-referentiality, since each episode enacts its own premises. *Fantasy*

Island was a long-living show, without apparently being all that popular. I have never met anyone who actually admitted to having watched the programme regularly, but I know a number of teenagers who adore the re-runs, finding them both camp and scary. Its familiarity to most Americans had probably something to do with its time slot – either just before or after the main evening news – so that the fact that viewers were watching it while impatiently waiting for something else (those were the days before the 'freedom' of the remote control began to terrify programme makers) or that they had just watched something engrossing seemed built into the show. There is thus a certain displacement – of attention, of interest – almost endemic to the very viewing space of *Fantasy Island*, which is perhaps one of the reasons it began to interest me. As a foreigner and an outsider to American television mores at the time, the rationale of *Fantasy Island* was virtually impossible to construct. It had none of the compulsive speed and suspense of police-series like *Streets of San Francisco*, or later *Hill Street Blues*. The love interest was perfunctory, and it was not, properly speaking, a soap opera either; the grandee host, played by Ricardo Montalban gave the programme almost the allure of a talk-show, although a talk-show that, instead of interviewing its guests, made them the object of practical jokes, chance encounters and random adventures.

What, even in the context of American network television, made *Fantasy Island* an oddity was that it situated itself at the very limit of narrative. It seemed almost totally under the regime of repetition, with the episodes building up neither character nor suspense, but following merely the logic of contingency and accident. With the one difference, namely that the incidents and adventures had a curious recognition effect, as if one was being told scenes from half-remembered films. Both the word 'fantasy' and 'island' seem important indications of the hidden fascination of the show and its inconsequentiality, for while the contents of the fantasy were immediately recognizable as the stock inventory of American popular entertainment from music hall and vaudeville to B-pictures and television entertainment, the logic of the series seemed as incoherent as that of dreams, and indeed, for the casual viewer like myself, the episodes were about as interesting as one's own dreams are to one's friends: told to others, they lose all mystery or urgency. Nothing seemed more natural than the idea to treat the peculiar non-logic of *Fantasy Island*, the isolation and discontinuity, the essentially displaced position of its viewing schedule and time-slot, as that of a dream – and to pose myself the question of who, in this case, could be the dreamer. It is the old problem of bringing to cinema, television or popular culture notions derived from psychoanalysis: where to place the desiring 'subject' of the text, once there is no author (and once one abandons the idea of a coherent, single source of intentionality) and once the mass media are not seen as the collective unconscious at work. If *Fantasy Island* lacked in some important respects the 'secondary elaboration' that characterizes classical narrative and its symbolic codes, what then were the discursive or psychic energies animating a piece of light entertainment that had no pretensions to being anything other than part of television's internal cohesiveness of flow and alternation, repetition and deferral? In other words, what does the mere existence of such a programme tell us about the 'political unconscious' or hidden agendas of television, as a social space and institution? Especially, if we assume that television's primary function is to manage for us our ideas of time, of experience, of pleasure and event?

A Studio Tour

Almost exactly a year after I chanced to see two or three episodes of *Fantasy Island*, I was invited to one of the Hollywood studio tours, not the famously popular Universal tour; instead, it was the more select tour of the Burbank Studios, covering the area once occupied by Warner Brothers, and now in the possession of a joint holding company which rents the space and the facilities to the two major shareholders, Columbia Pictures and Warner Brothers, who use it almost exclusively for television production and advertising commercials. After visiting the sound stages, the recording facilities and prop departments, we were taken to the set – yes, you guessed it – of *Fantasy Island*, where an episode was just being filmed.

Ricardo Montalban, more familiar to me as the Indian chief from countless 1950s Westerns, is sipping some hot liquid, limping to his folding chair wearing an anorak and a scarf. Next to me, a Mexican dwarf in white tails is making annotations to his copy of the script. The set is hushed. Montalban, taking off his anorak and scarf reveals a teeshirt with a gleaming white stiff collar and bow-tie. An assistant helps him into an equally white dinner jacket: he now looks the part of the dignified dandy keeping up civilization amidst the jungle wilderness. The Mexican dwarf is stood on a soap box so they can both be in frame together. Montalban acknowledges us, the gawping visitors, with a benevolent wave. He and the dwarf rehearse three lines of dialogue each, in a scene that lasts maybe seventy-five seconds. The first full take is also the final take, and the crew is getting ready for the next scene. All in all, our presence lasted about three minutes. Not many film or television programmes can be more efficient and economical in their shooting ratio, more businesslike and sober, more time, labour and cost-conscious than those three minutes of *Fantasy Island* which netted some two minutes of air-time.

In this minute's worth of dialogue, I began to grasp not only the episode which was being filmed, but the concept behind *Fantasy Island*. Repeated explanations by Montalban to the Mexican dwarf that end with the question 'do you understand?' seem addressed to the casual television viewer or eavesdropper like myself, and when Montalban says 'if not, then *Fantasy Island* as we know it would disappear' it begins to dawn on me: while Montalban self-referentially repeats the rules of Fantasy Island (the place) to the newly arrived guest (or newly tuned-in viewers), I suddenly understand the rules of Fantasy Island (the show). The guest-celebrity is allowed to live any fantasy whatsoever – so long as it coincides with a 'property' the studio owns, that is to say, so long as it can be 'made real' with the various pre-painted sets, props and costumes that the studio has on the lot. Hence the efficiency, the smooth moves from scene to scene. *Fantasy Island* is, I realize, the mise-en-abyme of our own studio-tour (and vice-versa), using property, personnel and time when such an expensively maintained, well-organized production site with costly overheads would otherwise stand idle. *Fantasy Island* is fitted into the gaps of other programmes' production schedule. Like some undemanding organism, the show lives in the crevices of more glamorous, more prestigious series, such as *Dukes of Hazzard* or *The Thorn Birds*, also shot at Burbank, also visited by us.

Nestling thus inside the organizational structures and economic priorities of a production-line studio-system, *Fantasy Island* is marked by these structures with a clearer imprint and less complex ideological baggage than its bigger brothers and sisters. But it is remarkable that the quasi-fortuitous encounter and coincidence of television celebrity's booking schedule with the Burbank Studio's own booking schedule of its sites and props should give rise to a programme called *Fantasy Island* when the fantasy is the result of extremely shrewd cost-calculation, and the island is merely the name for dead or empty time in the studio's facilities, and on the network's programming schedule: an island indeed, and an accountant's fantasy.

Television abhors a vacuum even more than nature. This perhaps explains why as a medium it is so successful in naturalizing its own rationale of total rationalization and integration. *Fantasy Island* in one sense is nothing other than the recycling of commodities no longer in demand, or if you like, the alternation, the matching up and oscillation of two kinds of property: that of the celebrity, and that of the decor which the studio happens to have on hand. It is this oscillation that gives it the semblance of life. The narrative is generated out of a fantasy which is only the façade, fronted by a celebrity who endorses this façade as if he was endorsing with his appearance and name a branded product in an advertising commercial, and thereby labelling as 'personal fantasy' what is in fact a piece of corporate real estate. The principle is of course that of every talk show and its roster of guests: promoting their book, plugging their film, or being famous for being famous.

In this respect, *Fantasy Island* appears naively anachronistic: the 'pitch' is still packaged into an elaborate charade, a 'fantasy', even if this fantasy is nothing other than the coincidence of two apparently totally disconnected or even antagonistic realms, which once brought together, startlingly but also subliminally make apparent their secret connection and unity: it is the dream-logic of a surrealists collage, which also, as we know, often results from the clash of mass-produced or industrial objects, taken out of context, stripped of their primary utilitarian function. The unity lies between the economic and the fantastic but precisely not in the sense that one is necessarily the condition of the other (with the economic demands of Burbank determining the order of representation on *Fantasy Island*, ie some sort of base-superstructure machinery). Instead, they are as it were, the recto and verso of each other, each being the unconscious discourse of the other. If in some sense the capitalist logic of recycling real-estate is repressed, displaced, off-frame, it returns in the product as a fantasy, and thus subject to a different economy as well – psychic, libidinal, oedipal. I am almost tempted to make a bold analogy: what Marcel Duchamp's Armory Show 'Urinal' was to the cultural symbolic of the art world, *Fantasy Island* was to the accumulated capital of Warner Brothers movie classics – except that *Fantasy Island* did not have its Duchamp to enact the definitive displacement.

Television Time as Materialized Fantasy Space
Never before has the necessity for property to circulate in order to realize surplus value struck me as quite so closely related to the production of fantasy and pleasure, possibly because the property here circulating has such a complex reality-status. This reality-status one is tempted to call the aggregate or transitional states of the commodity form, most abstract where concrete as in televised spectacle, most concrete when theorized, as in terms like repetition and serialization.

The apparent paradox is that in classical capitalist economics, profit realizes itself as a movement through space and time, whereas on television, time and space are actually created by the medium itself. Repetition, dead time and past time are replacing the resistance that 'real' space and time offer and oppose to the circulation of commodities, a resistance which (as labour) generates what capitalism turns into surplus value. *Fantasy Island* is such a clear index of this shift, because it reproduces the new category of television time and space as exotic fantasy, located in no time and no space other than that of the show and spectacle, the world of cinema and television itself. For this effect it is of course essential that the fantasies which the visitors are granted are echoes from old movies – for some of which no doubt the studio not only has the right props but the rights, too. Visitors' fantasies include bootlegging and beating prohibition in 1920s Chicago, tap-dancing with Ruby Keeler, going on south sea island voyages with swashbuckling pirates or playing Robin Hood in Sherwood Forest.

The concepts of 'fantasy' and 'island' are thus also symptomatic in another respect. In both cases, something is submerged, the connections with everyday reality and the mainland of economic practice. They are the repressed that returns in the show, and an imaginary space constructs itself out of the logic of a symbolic, from which it is forever separated. In this case, at any rate, the concept of the serial, of repetition inscribes itself in a compulsion – proper to the dream or the neurotic symptom – to repeat a traumatic situation: hence the logic of the visitors having nightmares as well as wish-fulfilling fantasies. Yet, in the practice of the programme 'visiting' the various sets, *Fantasy Island* also traces a veritable cycle on a quite different topography, namely that of the Burbank Studio and its separate buildings and stages.

If *Fantasy Island* may be an extreme case of the direct rapport between an economic order of recycling and a narrative order of repetition, this formula for bonding is nevertheless open to further elaboration, as seems evident by what I hinted at about the logic of the talk-show and its guests. Because it does not altogether dispense with narrative, *Fantasy Island* closely intertwines the economic and the narrative without there being a causal link, as, say, in product placement in a *James Bond* film; rather, they are figurations or 'allegories' of each other. Both are subject to a kind of arbitrary, contiguous, fortuitous matching, so that one begins to suspect that the relation between serialization on the textual level and the arbitrariness of exchange at the economic level might in fact be what binds television as an institution to the spectators' imaginary, and thus constitutes what ultimately creates the viewers' 'loyalty' to the show, and thereby makes the analogy with a commercial trade mark more than a metaphor.

A brand name is the successful welding together of a company, a logo, a line of product, and an image – preferably with each element having as little to do with the others as possible. It is the job of advertising to generate the heat that makes the welding stick. In *Fantasy Island* we can observe this process in *status nascendi*, in a more primitive form perhaps, but also in an area other than soft drinks, cars or denims. Since television is not a market in the traditional sense, regulated by supply and demand, it is 'time' – significantly called 'air-time' – that has to be filled, sold and traded, and the arbitrariness of what fills it is checked by a factitious but rigid system of constraints, which is on the one side circumscribed by the 'vertical' time

slots of a given channel, and on the other by the horizontal axis of inter-
network rivalry, competing for ratings. We tend to think that the purpose of
a commercial television programme is to put across the sponsor's message
to the largest possible number of viewers: 'television does not deliver programmes to audiences, but audiences to advertisers', as the famous phrase
has it. But one could argue that the system functions even if the 'support' for
this message is no longer materially present, if the product is named neither
on the show nor in the breaks, for in television it is 'air' and 'time' itself that
have become the concrete support for the construction of an imaginary, a
fantasy island. Any television programme is itself in fact the 'message' of
another structure, in our example, an economic one of real estate and cinematic properties, sustained by and sustaining a textual one of narrative and
repetition.

What we see in *Fantasy Island*, then, is the 'branding' of film culture and
movie history itself, across the material intermediary which is the studio lot.
What appears arbitrary and fortuitous from the perspective of television as
a textual entity has its logic in the copyrighted 'film property' – itself a word
rich in material and immaterial resonances. Cinema and television have, as
we know, a history closely associated with the acquisition of real-estate, investment in technology but also investment in stories, characters, images,
concepts, formulas. The props and sets stored at Burbank (up to the 1970s at
least), which Warner Brothers and Columbia were recycling in cheap television shows like *Fantasy Island*, owe their value, their real-estate status, to fictions, to cinematic fantasies and narratives, built and acquired as they once
were in order to serve as material supports for filmed images and filmed
views. Hence, the economics that realize themselves in the film and television industries are themselves dependent on a visual imaginary: that of our
cinematic, narratological and iconographic patrimony. The aggregate states
of the commodities put in circulation are thus material and immaterial in
turn. But with digital techniques becoming more sophisticated, those lots at
Burbank and elsewhere are no longer in demand, they need no longer be
stored, kept and maintained at great cost, and therefore need not pay their
way with televisual or actual studio tours. The days when the material
could not exist without the immaterial, and vice versa, seem to be numbered.

The Disney Principle
Self-referentiality, repetition, revamping of genres, reiteration of formulas
is thus the endless chain of stand-ins whose mechanisms of transmutation
are simple enough but also subtle enough to give the impression of an almost necessary, natural cycle. Serialization in the electronic media is like

water: it rains from the sky, seeps through the ground, feeds rivers that flow into the sea where the sun heats up the surface which evaporates to form clouds that again come down as rain. History, and especially movie history, has become this 'natural history' of television, where it evaporates and co-agulates, as repetition, montage: a permanent mill of metaphors, the stand-ups authenticating the stand-ins.

The series as an organizing principle in the cinema has also seen a con-temporary revival: the STAR WARS saga began it, but other notable examples are BACK TO THE FUTURE, the TERMINATOR films, the two ESCAPE FROM... films, and the ALIENS cycle, at the last count on its fourth instalment. The temptation is great to construct for it a similar dream logic of recycling eco-nomically obsolete property values, this time with cinema feeding off tele-vision's past, its sci-fi matinees, 'Alfred Hitchcock Presents', and late night Twilight-zones. Here the dream logic would have a generational base: the return not only of the childhood of television, but of the television of child-hood as the new all-family movie entertainment. In this respect, the Disney principle looks set to be the global master plan: each generation of Ameri-cans since the 1930s has in effect not only grown up with Disney cartoons, but has had its first and formative encounter with the cinema thanks to one of the company's key films, from FANTASIA to SNOW WHITE, from BAMBI to CINDERELLA, from THE JUNGLE BOOK to THE LION KING, from ALADDIN to THE HUNCHBACK OF NOTRE DAME. And since the late 1960s, the rest of the world has not been far behind.

While in the classic studio-system, film production was organized around the exigencies of the exhibition sector, filling release dates of cinema chains with product, not altogether unlike television filling its time slots with programmes, the modern Hollywood production machine is quite dif-ferently organized. One can argue that the serial principle we have been dis-cussing has shifted sideways, away from production, to become the dominant distribution and retail model of cinema. Unlike the television se-ries, where the 'arbitrary' relation between one signifier and another signi-fier is held together by the rigid vertical integration of the programming schedule, the field that constitutes itself around a mega-film-production is held together by an altogether different totality, of which television as an in-stitution is of course an integral part. In the film-cycle, it is not the flow-pattern of the television channel, but the ever-more synchronized and yet necessarily distinct and separate media channels or media technologies that generate repetition and serialization.

The concentration of capital and resources has first of all meant that fewer films attract a larger share of the overall investment, leading to the dozen or so blockbusters a year, which now are the work-horses of the industry (with the price tag and temper of a full-blooded race horse), pulling along the whole wagon train. At the other end, initiating a film, putting together a concept, developing a project and getting it financed is now a much more dispersed and decentralized process, in which individuals (the deal makers of the talent agencies, for instance, or director-producers like Steven Spielberg and stars like Bruce Willis have a greater say than in the days of the studio-bosses and their executives, the producers).

At one end then, the personal, authorial input seems to have made a come-back; at the other end, this creativity is designing a juggernaut. Each major film is today both the reason and the pretext, both the cause and the effect of an operation that on the production side is tantamount to founding a company and building a factory for a single film, and on the distribution side, the occasion for what can only be compared with a military campaign, involving tactical thinking on a global scale. The marketing strategies, the publicity machinery, the release dates, the interviews on television, the special features in the press, the franchising of the main characters' clothes and accessories amount to a war, with each blockbuster both rehearsing and enacting the battle for world conquest, by the most diverse and sophisticated, but above all, also *material* means imaginable. On the face of it, this diminishes the attractiveness of the series. The battles are really separate wars, the citadel which is the global audience has to be stormed each time, and the deals have to be put together all over again. In the old studio system, the economies of scale with the series were more evident: with studio-facilities in place, one could work more economically with the same parts and set-pieces. But the modern, deal-driven picture making is more like the Japanese 'just-in-time' production model, especially since more and more specialized labour and time goes into so-called post-production, given the input of special effects, digital technologies of sound and image. At the other end, the centri-fugal tendencies predominate: in the marketing campaigns, for instance, which target not only the film itself and its outlets, but the whole field of consumer culture and the entertainment landscape. A film, an object we usually consider to be a self-sufficient work, possessing a narrative with its own mode of closure, is being crafted rather more like a land-mine: to scatter on impact across as wide a topographical and semantic field as possible. Whereas a humble television series like *Fantasy Island* functioned more like dada-tv, with seemingly incompatible fragments of reality condensing themselves in the regular half-hour time slot of a television channel, the blockbuster breaks up the film text into as many part-objects as possible, which then cascade through the whole entertainment and information space, bouncing off the multi-faceted surfaces of the social mirrors that englobe us users of the audio-visual media.

Not many films are distributed today without a sound-track available as a CD or an audio-tape, and a book version is usually sold as a paperback. A maze of spin-offs and subsidiary rights precedes the sales to cable and the video-market, or the path to the games arcade. It emphasizes the degree to which the uniqueness of the individual film vanishes before the diversity of the forms and media of consumption through which it circulates, in order to attract further investment and further profit, but also generate further emotional investment and pleasure. It suggests that the blockbuster is no more (but also no less) than the lubricant that keeps the sub-systems, such as publishing, tourism, advertising, toy-manufacture and fashion design, smoothly working amongst each other and attached to the global systems. The specialized skills and technologies that have to come together to make this interdependence function present themselves to the object of all these efforts, the mass consumer, as a total and totalizing synthesis. For the commodity 'film' scintillates and glows so powerfully today, not least because it allows for roles other than spectatorship: becoming participant in the verbal, acoustic and visual environments represented by the hardware and software that echo, repeat, and retransmit the film experience. In the process, the old division of markets and consumer groups has given way to a division in the social spaces of consumption, where one type of recreation reiterates others, making even a simple narrative become complex, rich in information because of the several separate systems of sensory experience that give it 'body'.

The Return of the Digit
The condition of popularity for a feature film in the mass market seems to be that it must be divisible not so much into consecutive episodes, but in its internal, constituent parts. Time has become space, repetition is either serialization or 'semiotization'. The open endings or ambiguous narratives of contemporary Hollywood films – with or without sequels – with which I started act like palindromes: you can 'read' them backwards, which is to say, you can see them again and again and again. In which case, the two modes of the 'stand-alone' of the classical and the 'serial' would, after all, be aspects of the same kind of logic. Whereas in classical aesthetics 'the work' has its own internal coherence and self-sufficiency, regardless of whether we consider it tied to an author or not, the series has not so much multiple authors, but rather more significantly, it derives its own coherence, the motor and motive force from the many acts of authorship it can entice its audiences to enter into. The work is thus not an end in itself, but rather the transitional form, the temporary state whereby a whole series of socio-economic processes and textual practices are put in motion. This intermedi-

ary, fluid form – fluid in relation to the many different values (economic, demographic, gendered, subjective, semiotic) which are invested in it – means that the work finds its ultimate destiny not in the act of being viewed, but in its function as 'transitional object' (in Melanie Klein's sense), which includes the echoes, after-images and after-effects created both in the subject (the temporal trace of memory, fantasy investment, projection and identification) and in the social sphere (the spatial presence of objects such as badges, toys, posters, tee-shirts, tea-mugs, calendars).

Our traditional discourses compel us to condemn these phenomena as evidence of crass commercialism, as lack of originality, as the disappearance of the author. Interestingly enough, this is exactly what George Lucas, the creator of the STAR WARS trilogy did: he disappeared as a film-author, as director. He could have retired on the several billion dollars it earned him. But since when do artists retire – or for that matter, billionaires? Instead, he founded Industrial Light & Magic, which has been the state-of-the-art in the field of cinematic digital effects for the last fifteen years. Lucas is busy re-inventing the cinema, or so his many admirers say. He himself is more modest, arguing that digitization is just a tool. And yet, in 1997 alone, Lucas made a cool $400 millions re-issuing the first part of his STAR WARS with added digital effects, some of them done, it is said, on an Apple Powerbook. Repetition and serialization have taken on a new meaning, as the immaterial of film-fantasy is not de-materialized as in *Fantasy Island*, or re-materialized as in the toy-shops, but de-immaterialized in the form of digitization: the 'Return of the Jedi' as Digit. I think we may once more be entering a new war-zone among the media, but is it the Empire of the digital, or of the cinema that 'strikes back'?

'I See, if I Believe it' – Documentary and the Digital

Kay Hoffmann

Pictures have always been deceiving. The idea that film and television show what is real – that they deliver an appropriate copy of the world has been proven to be wrong and discredited long ago. The more surprising, therefore, was the journalistic irritation in Germany when the television author Michael Born was convicted of faking over 20 documentaries for various television channels in 1996. He merely followed the hard rules of the media market in coming up with more sensational and spectacular films by staging them himself. There was the German Ku Klux Klan with homemade white robes, the cat-snatcher or the wonder drug from a frog. At his trial Michael Born said: 'We are on our way from infotainment to infofiction and the kick has to be produced, because television is no good at providing information.'[1]

However, the Michael Born incident did not lead to a discussion about our relationship to images we can no longer trust, but only to the call to order for journalists'professional ethics and a call for stronger internal controls in the nations' television newsrooms. There had already been similar reactions in Japan, in 1992, to the faked television documentary *NHK Special – Mustan: The Forbidden Kingdom Deep in the Himalayas*.[2] After all, Born was still a forger from the analogue age. He produced his stories with paid extras in front of the camera. In future this extra expense will hardly be necessary: One dip into the digital archives will suffice to build all the images one wants. Reason enough to think about the changes digitization brings to the documentary format.

Digitization creates a bridge between the photographic and electronic world. Up to now digital tools have mainly been used for commercials and in special effect scenes of big motion picture productions. But during the last few years, a revolution has been going on in postproduction which will have an enormous impact on our relation with the moving pictures. As it is believed too difficult, time-consuming and, of course, expensive to change such a large amount of pictures, many viewers believe what they see on film or television and take it to be real. This is especially true of documentaries and news, where the notion that a technically recorded image shows reality in an objective way is still deeply ingrained in most viewers. After all, the

technical possibilities of 'faking' images convincingly are of a relatively recent date.

Conversely, it is barely a hundred years ago that mankind first had the illusion that a moving image could be an accurate record of the real world.
Up to the early nineteenth century most people only knew paintings or
drawings, which, however life-like, were always perceived as subjective. In
the 1830s followed photography, about which people learned, after a few
decades, how easy it was to fake individual pictures and how willing some
were to abuse photographs for political ends.[3] With the digital revolution,
another qualitative change is said to have occurred. As William Mitchell
puts it: 'Although a digital image may look just like a photograph when it is
published in a newspaper, it actually differs as profoundly from a traditional photograph as does a photograph from a painting. The difference is
grounded in fundamental physical characteristics that have logical and cultural consequences.'[4]

But even the idea that a moving image is very hard to manipulate has
never been very credible. As is well known, a documentary always follows
a specific artistic concept and its production, if not scripted, has nonetheless
to be strictly organized. In addition, the most important decisions for the
structure and dramatization of a film are made during the final cut when the
images that will eventually be shown are selected. Consequently, no objective pictures of reality are possible: selecting views means subjective views.
Most directors of documentaries are quite aware of this and therefore visualize these strategies, making the production process itself enter into their
work. Yet, as Marshall McLuhan has said: 'It is no longer "I will believe it, if
I see it" but "I see, if I believe it"'. This implies a complex reversal of our relationship with the image. It would seem that the whole idea of 'visible evidence' – the very foundation of a documentary filmmaker's work – has to
be questioned.

Digital effects are still very expensive. In commercials or breathtaking
special effect-sequences the viewers get used to all the possibilities of digital
compositing, morphing and electronically multiplying extras or props. Sitting at a computerized editing-suite, one can find a totally new aesthetic for
images. But not only an aesthetics: one can 'rewrite' history. In Wolfgang
Petersen's IN THE LINE OF FIRE (USA, 1989), a young Clint Eastwood is
shown standing beside John F. Kennedy. This was done by taking a sequence from DIRTY HARRY, the famous Don Siegel/Clint Eastwood film
made in 1971, and then isolating Eastwood electronically. To fit him into the
Kennedy 1960s, Eastwood was given the first 'digital haircut' of film history, as producer Jeff Apple always liked to remark.[5] Young Eastwood was
then matched with archive-material of President Kennedy. In other scenes

actual footage of the presidential rallies of George Bush and Bill Clinton from 1992 were manipulated and integrated to segue into the story of the movie. This method was chosen because it would have been difficult to set up, if a film crew had actually shot on location, not least because Eastwood would have attracted more public attention than either of the candidates. In a sequence of the President arriving with Air Force One the body of George Bush was used, with only his head replaced by that of the actor who plays the President in the film. Other computer-generated images, which the viewer could not recognize as artificially produced were also included. For instance, thanks to the computer, a few hundred extras became a crowd of several thousands, standing and waiting alongside the street, applauding the President on his rally through town.

Again, the technique itself is not that new. For some decades now, it has been possible to achieve similiar effects with analogue pictures. The best-known example is probably Woody Allen's ZELIG (1983), where the eponymous hero, played by Allen, is shown meeting prominent people in different situations and at different times throughout the twentieth century, usually by posing with them in newspaper photographs. However, in 1983 this was very time-consuming work, because on the optical bench one never has real-time control as one does today. If one analyzes ZELIG carefully, one can see how ingeniously the technicians manipulated the photographs and how cleverly the editors did their work, in order to create the impression of this living chameleon. The film also works because strategies borrowed from the documentary form were used, such as using as eye-witnesses such well-known personalities as Saul Bellow and Susan Sontag ('He was the phenomenon of the Twenties').

In FORREST GUMP (1995) by Robert Zemeckis, the manipulation of historical news footage was even more elaborate. One will recall that the central character, a Vietnam hero played by Tom Hanks, meets different American Presidents, gives them a handshake and even talks to them. Our concepts of a discrete chronological time and a unique historical space are undermined. The computer literally puts the words of the script in the Presidents' mouths. As we get used to such techniques, the stakes are getting lower. Every day brings surprising new effects in television commercials, which present the state-of-the-art of digital technologies right within our living rooms. It is as if the whole history of visualization is being reinvented, with commercials often showing off a very broad palette of different techniques. Besides dazzling the viewer with colour, there has also been a renaissance of black-and-white images, to attract the viewers' attention, simulating a photographic past when a historic setting is suggested, as in advertisements for Levi's Jeans, or Jim Beam Whiskey. In future, the digital manipulation of images will become a day-to-day affair and in a few years everybody will be able to change images with his own personal computer and so redefine the past. One benefit might be that not many people will be left who place their (at any rate misplaced) trust in the evidentiary truth of the moving image.

Documentary filmmakers have to think hard about the consequences that this entails for their work. One possible answer is to obtain credibility and reliability, not from the images themselves, but from the information about who made the film, and how it was produced. This process has to be shown in the films themselves, so that not only the 'perfect' results are shown, but the making of the film itself becomes a topic. As Brian Winston has pointed out: 'Grounding the documentary idea in reception rather than in representation is exactly the way to preserve its validity. It allows for the audience to make the truth claim for the documentary rather than the documentary implicitly making the claim for itself.'[6]

I am firmly convinced that this new concept will liberate the documentary. At the Documentary Film Centre in Stuttgart we organized a conference on this precise topic in 1996.[7] Among the films shown, there were a number of examples of how film directors have been using the new technologies, while also launching their ideas for a new aesthetics of the documentary form. Leo Lorez from Hamburg showed a series of films, made in 1990/91 – he called them cultural videograms – which are about the Russian constructivists of the 1920s, such as El Lissitzky, Konstantin Melnikov and Alexander Rodchenko. The topic lent itself especially well for new possibilities of visualization. For example, he built a model, based on the architectal drafts of El Lissitzky for a new type of house, then made paintings of the building and integrated a computer simulation into footage of today's Moscow in a very stimulating and thought-provoking way.

The visualization of objects that do not 'really' exist is a very powerful tool, especially if it helps to tell a story or support a strong argument. Nevertheless, the question did arise whether the use of these possibilities is acceptable for documentaries. How far can and should a film maker go? Should these tools be banned in a particular genre? Can such a demand be a realistic option? Who will or should 'police' the digital world? In my opinion, the example of EL LISSITZKY shows clearly that these tools can be very helpful and can give the documentary a new openness not just aesthetically, but for new content and argument.

Joachim Faulstich is another director who has specialized in docufictions on political, scientific and ecological topics. In 1994 he made the science fiction film CRASH 2030. In the year 2030 the environment is so heavily damaged that a public prosecutor of the European Community is asked to investigate the causes of the ecological disaster, and what could have been

31/32) In CRASH 2030 *(1994) by Joachim Faulstich an impending environmental catastrophe is illustrated by digitally manipulating photographic images from the present, using simple paintbox software. The goal was to inform and activate the viewers by simulating the future 'realistically', which is to say, providing a perspective the viewer can identify with.*

done to prevent the catastrophe in the 1980s and 1990s. CRASH 2030 is a sub-jective comment on our times, and uses an interesting mixture of different materials. It incorporates quotations from news bulletins and television-features, classical documentary footage and graphics, while the sequences with the prosecutor are staged, as are the eyewitness reports. For the viewer a differentiation between the sources is no longer possible. However, it is clear that, given the underlying scenario, the images are subject to a strong argumentative structure provided by the director. Some images, especially the so called 'reconstructions' are made with a simple paintbox-system. What is most interesting is how Faulstich uses the new digital possibilities to develop a forceful commentary on ecological politics. Insofar as it started fruitful discussions on the topics it raised, the film can be considered as very successful.

The Swiss film BABYLON 2 could also be called extremely subjective. Made by an Iraqi-born film maker, Samir, who has lived in Switzerland since the age of six, the film concerns the second generation of immigrants and their situation today. Samir uses different materials such as documen-tary images shot by himself, old news footage, private amateur movies and videos, fictional scenes, photographs, graphics and even written text and words. The editing was done on an Avid compositor, and Samir blended the material in an interesting and original way, also creating a very sophisti-cated and complicated soundtrack for the film. Given that there is usually more than one image simultaneously on the screen, the linearity of tradi-tional film is overthrown. Such a layered structure is extremely suitable for this particular topic, as the young people featured in the film are, of course, also divided and have multiple presences: negotiating their identity be-tween their new home, Switzerland, and the country their parents origi-nally came from. Yet despite these potentially intrusive technologies, Samir made a very personal film and opened a new horizon with his concept. As a critic wrote: 'The result is a documentary which is literally the most multi-facetted film of its kind to have come out of Switzerland. Above all, how-ever, BABYLON 2 is a montage which is not content simply to compile otherwise pre-existing material, but seeks to draw the varied spectrum of material into an interplay of confrontational relationships. This confirms Samir's belief that as individuals, not only the immigrants in the mass resi-dential areas of the Swiss suburbs, but all of us, are damned to remain help-lessly isolated.'[8]

Such new aesthetics and editing effects were, of course, also possible with traditional tools, but complicated, more expensive and giving the film-maker often only poor control over the results.

33/34) *New imaging tools can result in a fascinating new aesthetic, as shown in* BABY-LON 2 *(1993), a film by the Swiss-Iraqui director Samir, who puts together a literally 'multi-layered' portrait of linguistic and geographical exile.*

BABYLON 2, by utilizing the full range of effects now available manages to overcome the old educational concept of the documentary, opening it up to a more subjective way of handling even political topics. These films are refreshing, not least because in the 1970s and 1980s there were so many politically engaged documentary films whose strongly didactic, educating intent ended up alienating the viewer. In this respect, the political 1970s were not a good decade for documentaries: previously, there had been more interesting examples of ironic and subjective films, such as those coming out of the documentary department of the Süddeutscher Rundfunk, known as the so-called 'Stuttgarter Schule'. There, already in the mid-1950s, a group of young filmmakers, strongly influenced by the German news magazine *Der Spiegel*, were searching for ways of renewing the television documentary. The targets, against which they tried out their ideas, were the time-honoured 'Kulturfilm' (natural history film) and the 'Wochenschau' (newsreel film), genres that had been abused for political propaganda in the Third Reich. After an initial period of trial and error, Heinz Huber, Dieter Ertel and his colleagues found a new form, featured mostly in the series *Zeichen der Zeit* (Sign of the Times), broadcast between 1957 and 1972, at a rate of several films per year.[9] They tried to present current aspects of German society, commenting often ironically and with a sense of humour in the editing, which is rare, if not unknown today. In the 1960s the group was strongly influenced by the American Direct Cinema, which is one more reason why these traditions should not be altogether forgotten and why the films deserve to be rediscovered.

In conclusion, it is worth repeating that our trust in the moving image as an index of truth is of fairly recent standing, and has always required a healthy dose of scepticism and critical intelligence. With digitization we may have to adjust to a new magnitude of constructedness of the image, when it comes to how 'reality' is presented to us in film and television, but the principle and the problem are as old as the cinema itself. This applies to documentaries and news footage, just as much as to fiction films or television broadcasting, where the same critical stance is needed that we have already developed towards photography and printed information. This may be one reason why, since the 1970s, film and television are no longer as hostile to each other: they probably know perfectly well, that, in the face of our sharpened awareness of what they are up to, they need – and need to support – each other.

Theatrical and Television Documentary: The Sound of One Hand Clapping

Brian Winston

The dominant British (or, better, Anglo-American) documentary tradition is one of social realist work dedicated to public education and information – a tradition I shall refer to, in shorthand, as Griersonian. In considering it, not much understanding can be gained from examining the difference between cinema works and television works since the tradition has, for the reasons John Ellis has suggested, at best only a *pre*-history in the cinema.[1] The documentary has developed in Britain, in essence, as a television form so that the idea that film and television documentary are locked together in some Cain-and-Abel conflict makes little sense in the British context. It is more like one hand clapping.

John Grierson defined the documentary as 'the creative treatment of actuality', but of these three terms 'actuality' came to dominate.[2] Beyond art, which is what creativity implies; beyond drama, which is what treatment means; the documentary is also evidentiary, scientific. The term 'documentary' depends on the presence of 'actuality' in this definition. 'Document', to quote the Oxford English Dictionary, is 'something written, inscribed etc. *which furnishes evidence or information*'. It is crucial because Grierson also allowed 'creativity' and 'treatment', both of which work against any truth claim. Only 'actuality' sustains the non-fiction status of the documentary.

The 'etc.' in the Dictionary embraces photography. The concept of the photograph as document, despite the contemporary positioning of photography as an art, arises from the camera's basic status as a scientific instrument capable of producing evidence. There are two main reasons for this. First, there is the long history of pictorial representation as a mode of scientific evidence, a history which conditions, in part, the research agenda that produces the modern camera; and second, there is the tendency of modern science to produce data via instruments of inscription whose operations are analogous to the camera. The camera, in effect, joined 'the thermometer, barometer, hygrometer'[3], and the telescope and microscope in 1839 as nothing so much as the latest of scientific instruments. The photographic document offers *prima facie* evidence of the real.

Not only that, but the data produced by these instruments of inscription led the way in creating an 'avalanche of printed numbers'[4], of statistics, at first scientific and then, by analogy, social. The new concept of '*l'homme moyen'*, which was the most potent creation of this avalanche, legitimated new forms of social investigation, such as those of the English journalist Henry Mayhew into the conditions of the London proletariat in 1849/50. His methods involved calling mass meetings of workers to determine pay levels and terms of trade. Even the 'first person' biographical portraits of individuals for which he is best remembered were written up from formulaic interviews. As Robert Colls and Philip Dodd have pointed out, there is a strong line of continuity from Mayhew to Grierson via such pictorial works as Sims' 'How the Poor Live' (1887) or Reynold's 'A Poor Man's House' (1907): 'The titles and subjects [...] might be those of documentary film...'[5] The crucial point for the Griersonian documentary is that the statistical frame which originally legitimated such work came to be implied, because, in general, the numbers, as it were, could now be taken as read. Grierson endowed the documentary with, exactly, Mayhew-style social significance, thus bringing the form within this statistical realm.

Griersonian actuality becomes an evocation of evidence and evidence eventually takes the Anglo-American documentary tradition, via the law, to journalism. The law is the source of a critical documentary technique – the interview. The filmed interview is descended from the British legal reforms of the early nineteenth century which introduced the modern evidential procedure of the court-room cross examination. Almost as soon as this was in place, it was borrowed for journalism and, as we have seen with Mayhew, for social science. It was then borrowed again for radio and the cinema. It can be said that the camera produces a record, legitimated as such by general reference to the legalistic model, of the events filmed – even down to legal-style interrogatories, interviews. The legal tradition casts the documentarist as witness to the original scene (and, even more overtly, the interviewee as witness to data unfilmed or unfilmable).

I am arguing that all this is implied by Grierson's use of the term 'actuality'. These scientific, legalistic and journalistic implications operated as a constraint on the development of the British documentary. They meant, in effect, that a documentary of spectacle could not be pursued. Nor could the tradition easily embrace the poetic or impressionistic documentary, the personal or politically engaged documentary or a documentary which mixed these forms. But Grierson had positioned himself where he had no alternative. He had sought governmental and corporate sponsorship and that money was tainted in exactly the sense that it closed off these other possibilities. It also somewhat limited journalistic possibilities insofar as engaged or investigative modes were not possible. What these paymasters demanded were films of social integration; that is films which looked and felt journalistic in that they apparently dealt with some of the major issues of the day in a supposedly unglamorous way but were, despite this, essentially supportive of the existing order – films, as Grierson termed them, of 'public education'.

However, what neither Grierson nor his sponsors got with this agenda was an audience. There is no question that in the silent period the possibility of a commercially viable documentary cinema of spectacle was very real. NANOOK OF THE NORTH (Robert Flaherty, 1922), BERLIN: SYMPHONIE EINER GROSSSTADT (Walter Ruttmann, 1927), MOANA (Robert Flaherty, 1926) all confirm this; but the sound cinema was unable to exploit this promise, especially where the Griersonian aesthetic with its public education mission took hold.

The great repressed issue in the study of the Griersonian cinema is that hardly anybody ever saw the films. Although Grierson claimed his intention was 'cumulatively to command the minds of a generation', by 1933, faced with real public hostility to the films, he began to talk of alternative distribution systems.[6] The products of the documentary film movement had failed to make a mark in the commercial cinemas. In fact only DRIFTERS, the film he himself directed at the outset of the project in 1929, made back its costs. The evidence is that the public did not wish to be hectored about how the great and the good were actively improving their quality of life when, in the midst of the Great Depression, they knew very well this was more or less a lie.[7]

Nor did the alternative 16mm distribution Grierson proposed in the face of this disaster achieve much of an audience either. The 'Documentary Film Movement's' films were gathered into libraries and distribution was established; but Grierson's initial claim for a non-theatrical audience of four million a year appears to be wildly overstated, perhaps by as much as a factor of ten.[8] The point is that, even at four million, this audience was minuscule when compared with the numbers buying tickets for the cinema. By the most optimistic estimates, non-theatrical exhibition in the UK delivered one-fiftieth of the cinema audience. The actual figure, certainly before the war, was likely to have been closer to one five-hundredth.

It is in this sense that the cinema history of the Griersonian film might be considered a pre-history of the British documentary. It is the coming of television that liberates whatever public education and real journalistic potential the Griersonian documentary had, creating a sustaining audience.

In the early 1930s, as Grierson was creating the GPO film unit, the BBC had established a radio 'Talks Department' which took as its subjects much the same material as he did – HOUSING PROBLEMS (Elton/Anstey, 1935) and the like – but dealt with them in a much more engaged way.[9] Indeed, so outspoken was this output that a species of 'purge' took place in 1935 with pro-gramme makers being dispersed to the regions.

As the European crisis grew ever more grave in the second half of the 1930s, the most striking thing about the work of 'Talks and Features' in Lon-don was an *absence*: the lack of any programmes dealing with major political issues of the time.[10]

In other words, the BBC eventually achieved exactly the same result as Grierson's sponsors had managed from the beginning. By 1937, when major Griersonian documentaries on malnutrition and self-help for the unem-ployed were released, the President of the British Board of Film Censors could boast: 'We may take pride that there is not a single film showing in London today which deals with any of the burning questions of the day.'[11] The journalistic sting had been drawn in both media.

The BBC's concept of public service broadcasting was as integrative as were Grierson's ideas about public education. The radical Talks Depart-ment was an aberration which flourished for a moment in the early confu-sion as to what a radio network might be. After 1935 the two rhetorics, public service and public education, meshed seamlessly and continued to do so with the establishment of television after the war. Despite some small hiccups, such as the Griersonian Paul Rotha's unhappy stint as head of BBC Documentary Department between 1953 and 1955[12], the British documen-tary tradition was transferred to the small screen in the 1950s, most ably by Denis Mitchell.

On the other hand, the memory of audience antipathy to Grierson's pub-lic education documentaries constituted something of a hindrance. Twenty years on, in the early 1950s, the spectre of such audience neglect was still apparently haunting the Documentary Department, counter-balancing the appeal of the Griersonian Documentary Movement's impeccable public service credentials. The answer to this problem turned out to be an empha-sis on the journalistic.

Special Inquiry which ran from 1952 to 1957 was the department's first major series, disliked by Rotha because of its mixture of studio and film in-serts. Norman Swallow, its executive producer, was influenced by *Picture Post*, the British version of *Life* Magazine which had, during and after the war, achieved a very high reputation for journalistic integrity and by *See It Now*, the CBS news-documentary series widely credited with, among other things, contributing to the downfall of McCarthyism. It is significant that, of the Griersonian output, Swallow recalls only HOUSING PROBLEMS as an in-fluence.[13] This film was, arguably, the least 'aesthetic', most journalistic of the pre-war GPO documentaries. Via such series, the journalistic promise of

35) *Traditional concepts of documentary veracity have always been highly ideological, since shooting and editing a film is a matter of choice and selection, even of trial-and-error, as this improvisation on an assembly-line shows.*

36) *Video-artists have often had an ambiguous relationship to television, both to the medium and to the institution. But Ant-TV's spectacular protest statement from 1972 has itself become an icon of the television age.*

Grierson's 'actuality' was finally released as the only way to combat the essential unpopularity of the old public education remit.

This ploy was to a large extent successful. Although the documentary strand in the output was not among the most popular television offerings, it nevertheless worked well enough with audiences, and certainly in public service public relations terms, to justify a steady place in the schedules. Over the past four decades, the BBC has regularly reported remarkably consistent percentages of programming described as 'documentary', something in the order of 20 – 25 per cent of its total television output.[14] This steady stream has conditioned what British viewers have come to expect a full-service television channel to offer, whether it be publicly or commercially funded. The commercial terrestrial channels' schedules therefore also feature high percentages of documentary (by world standards).[15] Channel 4 devoted 22 per cent of its time to such programming.[16] Even the mainstream commercial channel (ITV) has consistently reserved around ten per cent of its output for documentaries across these decades, in contrast to other commercial channels, especially outside the anglophone world, which have virtually no sustained documentary production strand.

It was, however, not until the 1980s that documentaries finally began to figure among the highest rated television shows in the UK. The precursors of this were to be found in the occasional 1970s documentary series, normally devoted to fairly dramatic subjects such as the Hong Kong police, which achieved ratings comparable to middle-ranked entertainment shows. Roger Graef's 1982 *Police* marked the culmination of that process by being the first such series to break through into the top ten prime-time list. However, we must not get carried away. For all that millions of British homes might watch, documentaries are still by and large less popular than most other programming. Any documentary audience above five million was, and remains, exceptional. The point is that television audiences of this magnitude, bought by stressing the documentary's journalistic (if not its sensationalist) aspects, have secured for the Griersonian tradition a place on television never achieved in the cinema, although at some cost.

The line between the documentary and the journalistic – which in this mode is termed 'current affairs' in British television parlance – has all but disappeared. The hand-held camera and portable tape recorder – the very equipment used for the dominant documentary style of Direct Cinema (or for 'Vérité, that peculiar television mixture of Direct Cinema and older techniques) – were developed initially for the news.[17] Careers which were once spent on one or other side of this divide (that is, in either the Documentary or the Current Affairs Departments of the BBC and the other television organisations) now hop between the two. The result, though, is unequal. It is the one-way importation of news/current affairs values, techniques, styles and ambitions into the documentary output which is significant, not the reverse. As a result documentary's capacity for engagement, for satire, for poetry, for personal expression, have all been attenuated.

This has not gone unnoticed. At the 1996 Sheffield Documentary Festival Dick Fontaine, head of the Documentary Department at the National Film and Television School of Great Britain proposed the revival of the big-screen British documentary. A small group including producers Sandy Leiberson and Roger James as well as the distributor Jane Balfour emerged to mount a bid for production funds from the National Lottery specifically for non-fiction theatrical projects. Although unsuccessful in the first round of commercial franchise awards, the group hopes that it will acquire some £2 million to fund a programme of production starting in 1998.

For Fontaine, who has spent a large part of his career in America, there are clear distinctions between the theatrical and the television documentary: 'In the theatres you watch a documentary as a community. It is extremely different from watching television in your house. I got that from observing people for years in New York.'[18]

The Americans, like the British, have a tradition of 1930s state-funded public-education documentary production, which also transferred to television after the war. However, in contrast to Britain, a television audience never really developed despite the *succès d'estime* of series like *See It Now* and *CBS Reports*. Even more than in the UK, the US networks ran documentaries as a sort of 'cultural loss leader'[19], a kind of long-term network public relations exercise. Documentaries were being marginalised even before 1984 when the Reaganite Federal Communications Commission removed the guidelines which had encouraged the public service element (including documentaries) in the schedule. The prestigious network documentary departments have all been disbanded while the new dedicated documentary cable channels, which some suggest have replaced them, have, like all cable channels, very small audiences. The Discovery Channel, for example, has a cumulative rating of around one million (of some 96 million) television homes.[20]

Perhaps in consequence of this failure (at least in part), the small specialised cinema audience, which has influenced Fontaine's thinking, emerged. Funded by the arts and humanities councils as well private foundations, an intermittent stream of feature length documentaries began to emerge almost in synch with the decline of television network output. Such work has become an established element in art house cinema circuit programming, sometimes with not inconsiderable commercial success. HOOP DREAMS (1994), for example, took $5 million at the American box-office. Even more rarely, the most notable example being Michael Moore's ROGER AND ME (1989) which was distributed by Warner's, a documentary feature will even make it on to the screens in the local mall. Fontaine believes that this could happen in Britain, if the production pump could be primed with public funding: 'I have a vision of a non-fiction film having at least as much appeal as a Mike Leigh film – that is, serious, but popular appeal.'

Such films might differ from television documentaries in a number of ways. 'It is primarily a question of scale and ambition', Fontaine argues. 'Some television developments have been positive, like Direct Cinema which did hold attention of audience but now television has turned that into nothing but a constantly gratuitously moving camera. The problem is that the documentary form can't sustain its value if it is dependent on television. Intrinsically the small screen has no scale and little ambition. It is diminished. Television is aware of this so we have to point people at every nuance. Narrative commentary is there to shock you into paying attention.'

In Fontaine's view a move to revive the theatrical documentary in Britain would not necessarily require the recovery of the more poetic strand in the Griersonian *oeuvre*, much less the importation of alien forms such as the sort of personal documentary associated with Chris Marker – although he points out that the BFI and the National Lottery funded GALLIVANT, an extremely personal full-length theatrical documentary. Instead, it is more likely that the journalistic would be recaptured for the big screen. Even the dominant Direct Cinema mode might be transferred and thereby given a new lease of life: 'Direct cinema on the big screen is a as powerful as it ever was but it is not on the small screen. Audiences' jaws fall open with big screen documentaries like HOOP DREAMS. We are in awe of the big screen. The whole thing is about creating an awesome experience.'

'It is no accident that 100 critics in the States wanted HOOP DREAMS to be nominated for an Academy Award as the best picture, because it was the best piece of narrative that year. Contrast the simple-mindedness of characters in mainstream fiction with the people in HOOP DREAMS or 32 FILMS ABOUT GLEN GOULD. It is not a question of aesthetics.'

Nor is it, within the British context, primarily a question of politics. Although under considerable pressure, the journalistic element in British television documentary work long ago recuperated some measure of the engagement found in the earliest radio tradition and has managed to maintain that, regularly if intermittently producing controversial programming. But, according to Fontaine, this very success has had a negative impact which the big screen could correct: 'The way in which television diminishes and removes from sight the large issues by overkill could be arrested by serious narrative investigative films which would make people think about political issues.'

If Fontaine is right about all this, then even a revival of the theatrical documentary in Britain would not result in a significant confrontation with the television output. More would still be shared than would divide. It would still be rather more one-hand-clapping than Cain-and-Abel.

On the Big Screen every Doctor gets a Starring Role

Joyce Roodnat

When a film critic wants to show that he or she found a documentary on television particularly pleasing they write that it was 'good enough to show in the cinema'. Sometimes the praise is even higher, with such comments as 'very beautiful' or 'brilliantly gripping and so wonderfully filmed'. And then comes the 'pity...': 'pity that this film was only shown on television'. If I were a filmmaker I'd burst out laughing at all this praise. You make a beautiful film, you get a good press, and all you read is that your film was thrown away. Disposed of. A lily on the dung heap that is television. Pearls before swine – the TV viewers, that is. Because in Filmland documentaries only count if they are shown in the cinema.

In going to the cinema to see a documentary you are signing a sort of unspoken agreement, one which promises that in buying a ticket you shall be transported into the world of the film you are about to see. The filmmaker, in turn, does his or her best to deliver the goods. If all goes according to plan, the spectators will be reduced to tears, or left screaming and shrieking, either grief-stricken or joyous, at the filmmaker's behest. They might even manage to distance themselves from everything and everyone, and withdraw into the abstract beauty that the filmmaker offers them. Whether the audience's reaction to a film is one of anger or utter delirium is beside the point. As long as 'reality', as the spectator experiences it, is blocked out in favour of the reality of the film. That is what the spectator came for, after all. If the filmmaker fails in this respect, then his film did not work. The documentary filmmaker is after something completely different, however many times his film may be screened in the cinema. The documentary filmmaker does not want to block out the spectator's reality in favour of his dreamed reality. What he is showing *is* reality.

If you watch his film from the comfort of your cinema seat you'll very likely be swept away in the same way as you are when you watch a feature film. This was my experience when I saw the documentary *Near Death*, an impressive film by the American documentary-maker Frederick Wiseman, made on the intensive care ward for terminally ill patients in an American hospital. NEAR DEATH is an extremely long (6 hours) black and white account of a last struggle with death, in which Wiseman wants above all to convey a candid, true-to-life sensitivity towards all the parties involved. On several occasions the image quality suffers from a lack of light or space and that is understandable: the filmmaker was entering a real world and was not in a position to make demands. In other words, everything points to the fact that this is about reality. But in the cinema, where I saw NEAR DEATH, on several occasions I caught myself following the fate of the doctors, patients and nursing staff as if they were fictional characters. These very elderly men and women, their bodies frail and fatigued, their cheeks hollow, took on a rather quaint aspect in the twilight stage between no longer being alive and not yet being dead. A doctor, his face racked with doubt, became the role of some majestic, unjustly uncelebrated actor. Shortly afterwards NEAR DEATH was shown in its entirety on Dutch television. I watched it again and was this time even more impressed, because this time round I never had the feeling that I was watching some harrowing fictional account.

Why was this? It may have something to do with the fact that in the cinema you're sitting in a dark room and experiencing something, without having the chance to give a running commentary: Anything more than a quiet laugh or a silent tear is frowned upon. Things are very different when it comes to television, where direct reactions are not only very possible, but even desirable. The film screen invites us to enter a dream world; the television screen demands our active participation. And that is something many documentaries count on.

Nevertheless the documentary-maker is made to feel that his film only counts for something if it's exhibited in the cinema. This persecution of television is dictated by a kind of nihilism which I find incomprehensible: 'On the television nobody watches your film all the way through, everybody switches channels when a documentary comes on.' This isn't something I invented: such comments are regulaly to be heard and read, and usually come from the mouths or pens of documentary filmmakers and their producers, although never of feature filmmakers.

Have they taken leave of their senses? Filmmakers are supposed to be so convinced of the value of their work that the idea of switching channels would never even enter their heads. Of course, I'm taking it as read that every film represents the best that the filmmaker had to offer at the moment of making it. And how can these same documentary-makers bring themselves to be so optimistic about a cinema release? Why do they not think: there is no point in releasing it; after all, who goes to the cinema these days anyway?

Films are made for the people who watch them. Not people who are too lazy to go to a film theatre, and not the pathological zapper. Documentary filmmakers also shrink from television transmission, afraid that their films might be confused with the reportage spots made by television companies

37) Joyce Roodnat sharing Eleanor Coppola's point of view as she interrogates her husband in HEARTS OF DARKNESS *(1979), the documentary about the making of* APOCALYPSE NOW *(1979).*

who like to give the latter the chic label 'documentary'. But the fear is un-
founded. A screening in front of a cinema audience couldn't save a piece of
reportage, however cleverly it may be disguised as a documentary. Neither
does a documentary take on the appearance of reportage through being
shown on television. Documentary filmmakers aim at a depth which goes
far beyond the mere recounting of an event. Reportage demonstrates, a
documentary reflects. Reportage makes a report and informs. In reportage
the filmmaker has to show us the subject, in the documentary he has to
show us himself.

The fact that so much importance is attached to cinema exhibition is
partly the fault of film journalism. Together, filmmakers and journalists foster a circular argument, a simple case of a self-fulfilling prophecy. Four
documentaries which recently appeared in Dutch film houses – OSWALD,
BRAM, AMOR NO! and HET BACHVIRUS – all received attention on the film
pages of the daily newspapers. Not that someone deigned to shower these
films with a host of favourable comments – no, once again they were unani-
mously consigned to the scrapheap. But they were afforded disproportion-
ately lengthy articles, because they had been released in the cinema. Had
they been shown on television we wouldn't have given them a fraction of
the attention.

Heddy Honigmann's documentary METAAL EN MELANCHOLIE, however,
was shown last month – exclusively on television. But Honigmann's film
earned only short articles in the press, however beautiful we may have
found it. Praise, then, but in a handful of words and often with no illustration either. The film blew silently over.

I have never had any inclination to fathom that cinematographic dogma
dreamed up by the Americans and crystallised over here: *show them, don't
tell them*. When it comes to the documentary this dogma is just codswallop.
Telling and showing should both be weighed up and it is up to the filmmaker to bring them into balance. This balance can be seriously upset by
showing them on the big screen. Because size captures the eye and blinds
the ear. That was my experience when I watched HEARTS OF DARKNESS, the
documentary that came about on the basis of the material that Francis Ford
Coppola's wife collected during the shooting of his legendary war film
APOCALYPSE NOW. There are plenty of arguments for showing it in the cinema: the film is made up of fragments of APOCALYPSE NOW and these are best
seen on the big screen. But the audience for this film will almost certainly
have already seen APOCALYPSE NOW and this was Eleanor Coppola's premise in making the film. In her wish to document the remarkable evolution of
this film she creates a sort of war epic around the genial madman to whom
she happened to be married at the time. She uses film and sound footage

that she recorded, sometimes secretly, of conversations with him. And then there are the interviews she made, at the time and in the present day, with those people who played a main role, in whatever way, in what she depicts as a trench-war tragedy. Sitting in the cinema, you are forced to listen while your look is directed towards the towering faces of the figures on the screen. The filmmaker is more concerned with what is being told than how the audience watches the film. And however important the mimicry may be, this is much better suited to the television, where it is reduced from a giant-sized to a normal format.

I encountered similar problems during the screening of DE ONTKENNING (The Denial), a documentary by Tom Verheul based on the life of a woman suffering from MPS (Multiple Personality Syndrome). The film is exceptional for many reasons, but particularly in the clever way that Verheul interviews the various personalities hidden inside this woman. Watching the film brought me out in a sweat: the big screen brought her and her misery indecently close-to and the whole thing culminated in a kind of psychiatric group therapy session. In the larger-than-life format of the big screen it became tasteless. Because this was not a game, not an actress playing a dramatic role, this was pure, unadulterated distress. Blown up into feature film format it became merely sensation. In the intimate setting of the living room, however, it gains a measure of attention and involvement which does not leave you feeling embarrassed, but which is kept in balance by a certain distance.

Cinemas have their own very special atmosphere, and sitting silently in the dark in a big group of people certainly has a magic all its own. It would be crazy to stop screening documentaries in the cinema. Sometimes, like in the case of Jos de Putter's HET IS EEN SCHONE DAG GEWEEST, which was being shown to great acclaim, documentaries belong in the cinema and nowhere else. Like Johan van der Keuken he places the emphasis on visual conjecture, in this case in an atmosphere of nostalgia, remorse and love. His film is intended to fall somewhere between documentary and feature film. But that is no reason to undervalue the television screen, or to write it off as a medium for screening documentaries.

In a practical sense this disdain for television is actually rather short-sighted because it's playing into the hands of the broadcasters. Whereas broadcasters used to be happy to pride themselves on producing and showing a documentary, nowadays they find it too expensive and in other ways are rather loath to do so: viewing figures have become more important than scoring points for esteem. If broadcasters are also faced with the fact that cinema screening rather than television broadcast is seen as the hallmark of a film, a guarantee of quality, they will feel released from the duty to finance documentaries and to treat them with reverence. Why should they stick their necks out in the certainty that they will only ever be treated as second best? Documentaries and television need each other desperately. Anyone who saw Netty Rosenfeld's film IK HEB MIJN OOG AAN HET BED GESLAGEN, about the life of a GP in Amsterdam will know what I mean. Films like this, and documentaries by people like Cherry Duyns, certainly deserve to be shown in the cinema. But they are better suited to the television screen, and they confirm just what an important medium television is.

From Butterflies and Bees to ROGER AND ME

Stan Lapinski and René van Uffelen

In 1946 the Dutch documentary maker, Herman van der Horst sent his first film to the Cannes festival. METAMORPHOSE lasted for around twenty minutes and showed the life of caterpillars and butterflies. The maker had spent two years completing it. The jury was enthusiastic and van der Horst would have won the highest distinction, if a Russian colleague had not made an even more beautiful documentary – about the life of bees.

This happened only fifty years ago, and yet it seems unrecognisably strange. 'Every country, every culture, knows its own merry England', Orson Welles once remarked, 'its own period of innocence, its own dewy morning': it was a 'merry' Cannes where the battle for gold and silver was fought between bees and caterpillars, a battle now unthinkable. Films about the lives of insects are not normally shown in the cinema and certainly not at prestigious film festivals such as Cannes, Berlin or Venice, but they may find their way onto television outside prime-time slots.[1]

Much else has changed in European cinema since 1946: currently no European country, with the possible exception of France, has a film industry that can compete with Hollywood. However, most possess a reasonable or even flourishing television industry. In the Netherlands, for example, there is little enthusiasm for the quota laws such as proposed during GATT that aim to keep the American product at bay. Why bother if in its home market the Dutch product can easily outstrip the Hollywood-television-counterpart?

Meanwhile, this television industry weighs heavily on national film production, and not only in the Netherlands. In contrast to America, the revolutionary rise of television in Europe was not challenged by the principle of competition ('we'll give them something television cannot'), but with protective measures. Special funds were created to subsidise the industry, and television networks had to make a contribution. It is now almost impossible to produce a European film, be it fiction or documentary, without a substantial contribution from television: European film production has been made dependent on television. That this would have aesthetic consequences in the long run may not have been foreseen, but it is painfully obvious that this is the case: how many current European films would be perfect as the movie-of-the-week, on television? There are exceptions; someone like the German producer Bernd Eichinger once in a while makes a blockbuster such as THE NEVERENDING STORY (Wolfgang Petersen); the Frenchman Luc Besson (NIKITA, LEON, THE FIFTH ELEMENT) continues to refuse subsidies and television money, and the Pole Krzysztof Kieslowski, with DECALOGUE, gave us ten cinema jewels, funded with television money. Of course, these are and remain individual filmmakers.

What goes for the fiction film is even more true of the documentary. The Netherlands has a strong documentary tradition that dates back to the 1930s. Many documentaries, also those made for television, are filmed on 16mm film, sometimes on super-16mm that allows for a blow-up to 35mm. The choice of film stock does not only emphasise the stylistic characteristics of these documentaries, but also makes the step to showing them in the movie theatres smaller. Moreover, the Dutch situation of film subsidy prescribes that documentaries should be shown or receive circulation in the cinema. There, in the theatre, the documentary should not only (and certainly not primarily) compete with Hollywood, but also (and above all) with the national film supply. If a documentary is to have even the slightest chance, it has to conform to a number of basic conditions: the theme, the story, has to have a certain dramatic force; the camera work and the editing must be of the quality of a feature film.[2] In the last couple of years a number of Dutch documentaries have been successfully shown in the cinemas, before appearing on television: HANS, HET LEVEN VOOR DE DOOD by Louis van Gasteren, ROMANCE DE VALENTIA by Sonia Herman Dolz, HET IS EEN SCHONE DAG by Jos de Putter, METAAL EN MELANCHOLIE by Heddy Honigmann, MOEDER DAO, DE SCHILDPADGELIJKENDE by Vincent Monnikendam, AMSTERDAM, GLOBAL VILLAGE by Johan van der Keuken, DE SLAG IN DE JAVA ZEE by Niek Koppen, DE GROOTE POSTWEG, by Bernie IJdis. It may help if the name of the director is surrounded by an 'author's aura', like that of Johan van der Keuken. Unfortunately, just as many documentaries have proven to be misplaced in the cinema theatre.

Precisely because its position in the film theatre is precarious (if only because the question: 'why not just on television' comes to mind more readily than with a feature film), it is interesting to take a closer look at the phenomenon of the documentary, especially concerning the interaction of film and television. A few telling examples can be found in recent film history. The first is LE CHAGRIN ET LA PITIÉ by Marcel Ophuls, a documentary from 1969 that has attained the status of a film classic: it was made for television, but it was the cinema theatres that turned it into a classic. In a number of interviews Ophuls revealed which factors contributed to the success of the film, and he immediately points to the fierce opposition of the ORTF, the French national television. As mentioned, the film was primarily produced for television as a German-Swiss co-production. This seems strange as the subject is French. One explanation is that it was 1968 and therefore the ORTF was on strike, but there must have been more going on and there was. LE CHAGRIN endeavoured to bring into perspective, and even destroy, the myth of the heroic French resistance against the German occupier. The ORTF felt something was up, and the reason that the film could still be made with a French crew was because a number of French journalists had rallied together and had agreed to act as co-producer. When it was finished the ORTF refused to broadcast it. According to Ophuls, the reason given was that the film could not claim to narrate something that was previously unknown: 'there were books on the subject, although not many. It was because film and television are mass media.' The film caused a scandal, even before anyone in France had seen it. Left-wing intellectuals used the word 'censorship' and questioned the 'ruling classes" decision to ban the film. Others accused Ophuls of 'dirtying one's own nest'. In the end a group close to *Cahiers du Cinéma*, and led by François Truffaut, took the film under their wing. Louis Malle and his brother offered the use of their small cinema on the left bank, at first only for a week, considering that LE CHAGRIN ET LA PITIÉ is a good four and a half hours long. Seventeen months later the Malle's cinema was still sold out every weekend.

Was the ORTF guilty of censorship? Ophuls thinks not, not in the usual sense of the word: they simply did not want to buy the film, and considering that it was a German-Swiss co-production, they did not have to. Still, one can wonder aloud if there was a question of self-censorship, given what one knows about the nature of television in general and French television in particular. Public television, like the gas and water supply, reaches everywhere, even the darkest reactionary outpost. These audiences out there could cause trouble, something national television rarely thinks it can afford. The ORTF found itself in a double-bind situation: since it represented public television it also cannot afford to get into trouble with the government. Ophuls is right: if the government had prevented the release of the film, then there would have been a question of censorship. As it was, the ORTF chose to go for cover.

However, a cinema is much like a temple. Compared to public television, every film theatre at the time was a temple of freedom of opinion; one does not place such a temple in the dark reactionary outback. The analogy can be drawn further: a film shown in a theatre obtains an aura that television could never bestow. It was thanks to the success of LE CHAGRIN ET LA PITIÉ in a respected Paris cinema that Ophuls recieved his status as author, helped along by the dedicated support of other *auteurs* such as Truffaut and Malle. In the background, of course, Ophuls' prestige was further influenced by another author, his famous father Max. To what extent he reached beyond his grave to help his son one cannot be sure, but the family name surely did Marcel no harm.[3]

Another example is SCUM produced by the BBC in 1977, a single play about the subhuman conditions in an English juvenile prison. Director Alan Clarke used a raw, realistic style to shoot this film, with camera work reminiscent of the documentary. It was precisely this realistic , 'documentary' style that prevented the BBC from broadcasting it. Although it is fiction, SCUM leans too much towards documentary realism to be recognisable as such when shown to a television audience. This is not helped by its black, pessimistic ending. Consequently, Clarke remade the entire film for release in the cinema and SCUM was released as a feature film in 1979 without diffculty. Following Clarke's death in 1991 the BBC ran a retrospective on the headstrong television-director. Once again, SCUM caused a stir. It was only after lengthy negotiations that the BBC agreed to air the original single play-version, and SCUM finally received its belated television première.[4]

Like LE CHAGRIN ET LA PITIÉ, SCUM was eventually shown on television within an 'author's context' where it had formerly been ignored by national television for fear of profaning its reputation. Yet, whereas with LE CHAGRIN it was the controversial nature of the content that was the stumbling block, with SCUM the BBC also objected to a television viewing for formal reasons. In 1977 the BBC was still of the opinion that if it was difficult to distinguish fiction from reality, then this would be a valid enough reason to prevent a showing on television. Naturally, objections of this kind carry less weight with a staged nature-documentary about the life of caterpillars and bees than with a politically sensitive theme such as violence and inequalities in a juvenile prison, but still, one can understand the BBC's point of view.

In 1938, when Orson Welles aired his famous *War of the Worlds* series on the radio, he 'misused' the documentary form in order to tell H.G. Wells' story about the little men from Mars. It caused panic. In the Netherlands, during the 1970s, the VPRO started showing fictional documentaries. One of these, RUDI SCHOKKER HUILT NIET MEER (Pieter Verhoeff), was about a baby that, as a consequence of the excessive noise from a neighbouring airport, cried making the sound of a jet plane. Unbelievable as it may sound, it caused havoc throughout the country.[5] Apparently a certain clarity of method is expected of a radio or television production, a clarity that is not necessary for the making of a film shown in the cinema. There, this combination of fiction and documentary does not present a problem, presumably because the situation within the cinema provides a mythical aspect that undermines the realism of that which is seen. Critics have not failed to point out, for instance, that documentaries like ROGER AND ME or THE ATOMIC

CAFE were succesfully released in the cinema primarily because of their ironic tone and parodic style.[6]

While the cinema is a temple, where, to take up Joyce Roodnat's phrase 'every doctor becomes an actor,'[7] television is the water supply. As long as what comes out is clear, all is well. If it is cloudy, then there are problems. When one of the documentaries from the series *30 minuten* (*geboren in een verkeerd lichaam* [born into the wrong body] by Pieter Kramer and Arjan Ederveen, which tells the story of a farmer who has a surgical operation to become an African cattle-shepherd) was recently shown at a festival abroad, apparently without a 'fake' warning, those present showed irritation about this absurd country Holland where anything is possible.[8] Evidently, by 1997 the unspoilt morning dew of Herman van der Horst's 'merry Holland' of METAMORPHOSE has evaporated once and for all.

Nowadays, television features more and more programmes in which documentary stories are portrayed with stylistic means borrowed from the cinema. In reality television programmes, which can be seen as a form of sensationalism (*Rescue 911, Top Cops*), interviews with actual rescuers or victims are combined with reconstructed images of the accident as if the camera was there when it happened. News programmes also tend to make more use of staged reconstructions to enliven their topics. In these cases the images are still carefully classified and the words 'recorded earlier' or 'reconstruction' appear on the screen. A tradition started by CNN ('Live') is thus continued by others, to the point where it appears to become the norm. Another aspect of this phenomenon are the computer animations that have appeared in news reports, whereby complex processes such as the changes in weather, moving earth plates, landings on far away planets and other scientific subjects are visualised. By using simple, visual models complicated subjects can be presented in a dynamic manner. Few viewers will ask themselves how 'accurate' these representations are, from a science point of view.

Naturally these programmes are far removed from the documentary tradition where all action is placed in a context, one that tries to go beyond the mere imparting of 'facts'. A good documentary is not a long news report or factual item, but an essay that analyses and interprets the filmed events. Whereas reality television (a better word would be 'experience television', a term once introduced by the Dutch channel RTL5) emphasises the live-idea of television by using methods borrowed from film, and whereas news reports are bound by formats and brisk, easily accessible and dynamic presentation, the strength of the documentary lies in the possibility of depth and reflection, and sometimes even poetry. A documentary demands a patient and concentrated audience. The success of the documentary form on televi-

sion remains incontestable, and the economic argument of funding is difficult to quarrel with; nevertheless, one does not have to be a 'fundamentalist'
to believe that the cinema, with its inescapable, forced concentration (dark
room, no remote control) and its temple-like aura, still seems the place
where the documentary comes to its full right. Even ROGER AND ME takes
time out to show the audience how to skin a hare....

To Lie and to Act: Cinema and Telepresence

Lev Manovich

Throughout human history, representational technologies have served two main functions: to deceive the viewer and to enable action, i.e. to allow the viewer to manipulate reality through representations. Fashion and make up, paintings, dioramas, decoys and virtual reality fall into the first category. Maps, architectural drawings, x-rays, and telepresence fall into the second. To deceive the viewer or to enable action: these are the two axes which structure the history of visual representations. What are the new possibilities for deception and action offered by recently developed technologies of computer imaging and telepresence in contrast to older technologies of architecture, cinema and video? If we are to construct a history which will connect all these technologies, where shall we locate key historical breaks? This essay will reflect on these questions.

1. To Lie

Cinema

I will start with Potemkin's Villages. According to the historical myth, at the end of the eighteenth century, Russian ruler Catherine the Great decided to travel around Russia in order to observe first-hand how the peasants lived. The first minister and Catherine's lover, Potemkin, had ordered the construction of special fake villages along her projected route. Each village consisted of a row of pretty façades. The façades faced the road; at the same time, to conceal their artifice, they were positioned at a considerable distance. Since Catherine the Great never left her carriage, she returned from her journey convinced that all peasants lived in happiness and prosperity.

This extraordinary arrangement can be seen as a metaphor for life in the Soviet Union. There, the experience of all citizens was split between the ugly reality of their lives and the official shining façades of ideological pretense. However, the split took place not only on a metaphorical but also on a literal level, particularly in Moscow — the showcase Communist city. When prestigious foreign guests visited Moscow, they, like Catherine the Great, were taken around in limousines which always followed few special routes. Along these routes, every building was freshly painted, the shop windows displayed consumer goods, the drunks were removed, having been picked up by the militia early in the morning. The monochrome, rusty, half-broken, amorphous Soviet reality was carefully hidden from the view of the passengers.

In turning selected streets into fake façades, Soviet rulers adopted an eighteenth century technique of creating fake reality. But, of course, the twentieth century brought with it a much more effective technology: cinema. By substituting a window of a carriage or a car with a screen showing projected images, cinema opened up new possibilities for deception.

Fictional cinema, as we know it, is based upon lying to a viewer. A perfect example is the construction of a cinematic space. Traditional fiction film transports us into a space: a room, a house, a city. Usually, none of these exist in reality. What exists are the few fragments carefully constructed in a studio. Out of these disjointed fragments, a film synthesizes the illusion of a coherent space.

The development of the techniques to accomplish this synthesis coincides with the shift in American cinema between approximately 1907 and 1917 from a so-called 'primitive' to a 'classical' film style. Before the classical period, the space of film theater and the screen space were clearly separated much like in theater or vaudeville. The viewers were free to interact, come and go, and maintain a psychological distance from the cinematic diegesis. Correspondingly, the early cinema's system of representation was *presentational*: actors played to the audience, and the style was strictly frontal.[1] The composition of the shots also emphasized frontality.

In contrast, classical Hollywood film positions each viewer inside the diegetic space. The viewer is asked to identify with the characters and to experience the story from their points of view. Accordingly, the space no longer acts as a theatrical backdrop. Instead, through new compositional principles, staging, set design, deep focus cinematography, lighting and camera movement, the viewer is situated at the optimum viewpoint of each shot. The viewer is 'present' inside a space which does not really exist. A fake space.

In general, Hollywood cinema always carefully hides the artificial nature of its space, but there is one exception: rear screen projection shots. A typical shot shows actors sitting inside a stationary vehicle: a film of a moving landscape is projected on the screen behind the car's windows. The artificiality of rear screen projection shots stands in striking contrast against the smooth fabric of Hollywood cinematic style in general.

The synthesis of a coherent space out of distinct fragments is only one example of how fictional cinema deceives a viewer. A film in general is composed from separate image sequences. These sequences can come from different physical locations. Two consecutive shots of what looks like one room may correspond to two places inside one studio. They can also correspond to locations in Moscow and Linz, or Linz and New York. The viewer will never know.

This is the key advantage of cinema over older fake reality technologies, be it eighteenth century Potemkin Villages or nineteenth century panoramas and dioramas. Before cinema, the deception was limited to the construction of a fake space inside a real space visible to the viewer. Examples include theater decorations and military decoys. In the nineteenth century, panoramas offered a small improvement: by enclosing a viewer within a 360-degree view, the area of fake space was expanded. Louis-Jacques Daguerre introduced another innovation by having viewers move from one set to another in his London Diorama. As described by Paul Johnson, its 'amphitheater, seating 200, pivoted through a 73-degree arc, from one 'picture' to another. Each picture was seen through a 2,800 square-foot window.'[2] But, already in the eighteenth century, Potemkin had pushed this technique to its limit: he created a giant façade – a diorama stretching for hundreds of miles – along which the viewer (Catherine the Great) passed. In cinema a viewer remains stationary: what is moving is the film itself.

Therefore, if the older technologies were limited by the materiality of a viewer's body, existing in a particular point in space and time, film overcomes these spatial and temporal limitations. It achieves this by substituting recorded images for unmediated human sight and by editing these images together. Through editing, images that could have been shot in different geographic locations or in different times create an illusion of a contiguous space and time.

Editing, or montage, is the key twentieth technology for creating fake realities. Theoreticians of cinema have distinguished between many kinds of montage but, for the purposes of sketching the archeology of the technologies of deception, I will distinguish between two basic techniques. The first is so-called montage within a shot: separate realities form contingent parts of a single image. (One example of this is a rear screen projection shot.) The second technique is the opposite of the first: separate realities form consecutive moments in time. This second technique of temporal montage is much more common; this is what we usually mean by montage in film.

In a fiction film temporal montage serves a number of functions. As already pointed out, it creates a sense of presence in a virtual space. It is also utilized to change the meanings of individual shots (recall the Kuleshov effect), or, rather, to construct a meaning from separate pieces of pro-filmic reality.

However, the use of temporal montage extends beyond the construction of an artistic fiction. Montage also becomes a key technology for ideological manipulation, through its employment in propaganda films, documentaries, news, commercials and so on.

The pioneer of this ideological montage is Dziga Vertov. In 1923 Vertov analyzed how he put together episodes of his news program KINO-PRAVDA (Cinema-Truth) out of shots filmed at different locations and in different times. This is one example of his montage: 'the bodies of people's heroes are being lowered into the graves (filmed in Astrakhan in 1918); the graves are being covered with earth (Kronstad, 1921); gun salute (Petrograd, 1920); eternal memory, people take down their hats (Moscow, 1922).' Here is another example: 'montage of the greetings by the crowd and montage of the greetings by the machines to the comrade Lenin, filmed at different times.'[3] As theorized by Vertov, through montage, film can overcome its indexical nature, presenting a viewer with objects which never existed in reality.

Video

Outside of cinema, montage within a shot becomes a standard technique of modern photography and design (photomontages of Alexander Rodchenko, El Lissitsky, Hannah Höch, John Heartfield and countless other lesser-known twentieth century designers). However, in the realm of a moving image, temporal montage dominates. Temporal montage is cinema's main means of creating fake realities.

After World War II a gradual shift takes place from film-based to electronic image recording. This shift brings with it a new technique: keying. One of the most basic techniques used today in any video and television production, keying refers to combining two different image sources together. Any area of uniform color in one video image can be cut out and substituted with another source. Significantly, this new source can be a live video camera positioned somewhere, a pre-recorded tape, or computer generated graphics. The possibilities for creating fake realities are multiplied once again.

With electronic keying becoming a part of standard television practice in the 1970s, not just still but also time-based images finally begin to routinely rely on montage within a shot. In fact, rear projection and other special effects shots, which had occupied a marginal presence in a classical film, became the norm: a weather man in front of a weather map, an announcer in front of footage of a news event, a singer in front of an animation in a music video.

An image created through keying presents a hybrid reality, composed of two different spaces. Television normally relates these spaces thematically, but not visually. To take a typical example, we may be shown an image of an announcer sitting in a studio; behind her, in a cut out, we see news footage of a city street. If classical cinematic montage creates an illusion of a coherent space and hides its own work, electronic montage openly presents the viewer with an apparent clash of different spaces.

What will happen if the two spaces seamlessly merge? This operation forms the basis of a remarkable video STEPS directed by Zbigniew Rybczynski in 1987. STEPS is shot on videotape and uses keying; it also utilizes film footage and makes an inadvertent reference to virtual reality. In this way, Rybczynski connects three generations of fake reality technologies: analogue, electronic and digital. He also reminds us that it was the 1920s Soviet filmmakers who first fully realized the possibilities of montage which continue to be explored and expanded by electronic and digital media.

In the video, a group of American tourists is invited into a sophisticated video studio to participate in a kind of virtual reality / time machine experiment. The group is positioned in front of a blue screen. Next, the tourists find themselves literally inside the famous Odessa steps sequence from Eisenstein's BATTLESHIP POTEMKIN. Rybczynski skillfully keys the shots of the people in the studio into the shots from POTEMKIN, creating a single coherent space. At the same time, he emphasizes the artificiality of this space by contrasting the color video images of the tourists with the original grainy black and white Eisenstein footage. The tourists walk up and down the steps, snap pictures at the attacking soldiers, play with a baby in a crib. Gradually, the two realities begin to interact and mix together: some Americans fall down the steps after being shot by the soldiers from Eisenstein's sequence; a tourist drops an apple which is picked up by a soldier.

The Odessa steps sequence, already a famous example of cinematic montage, becomes just one element in a new ironic re-mix by Rybczynski. The original shots which were already edited by Eisenstein are now edited again with video images of the tourists, using both temporal montage and montage within a shot, the latter done through video keying. A 'film look' is juxtaposed with 'video look,' color is juxtaposed with black and white, the 'presentness' of video is juxtaposed with the 'always already' of film.

In STEPS Eisenstein's sequence becomes a generator for numerous kinds of juxtapositions, super-impositions, mixes and re-mixes. But Rybczynski treats this sequence not only as a single element of his own montage but also as a singular, physically existing space. In other words, the Odessa steps sequence is read as a single shot corresponding to a real space, a space which could be visited like any other tourist attraction.

Computer Imaging

The next generation in fake reality technologies is digital media. Digital media does not bring any conceptually new techniques. It simply expands the possibilities of joining together different image sources within one shot. Rather than *keying* together images from two video sources, we can now *composite* an unlimited number of image layers. A shot may consist of dozens or even hundreds of layers, all having different origins: film shot on location, computer-generated sets or actors, digital matte paintings, archival footage and so on. Most current Hollywood films contain such shots.

Historically, a digitally composited image, like an electronically keyed image, can be seen as a continuation of montage within a shot. But while electronic keying creates disjoined spaces reminding us of the avant-garde collages of Rodchenko or Moholy-Nagy from the 1920s, digital compositing brings back the nineteenth century techniques of creating smooth 'combination prints' like those of Henry Peach Robinson and Oscar G. Reijlander. However, what in the nineteenth century was only a still image can now become a moving one. A moving nineteenth century 'combination print': this is the current state of the art in the technologies of visual deception.

2. To Act

Telepresence
So far, I have considered the historical connections between some of the technologies of deception: fake architectural spaces, montage, video keying. I will now consider the second axis which structures the history of visual representations: action.

Imagine a person sitting in an automobile simulator, and wearing a head-mounted display. The display allows the driver to see an image transmitted from a remote location, thus making it possible to remotely operate another vehicle. In short, the driver becomes 'telepresent.'

If we look at the word itself, the meaning of the term *telepresence* is presence over distance. But presence where? Brenda Laurel defines telepresence as 'a medium that allows you to take your body with you into some other environment... you get to take some subset of your senses with you into another environment. And that environment may be a computer-generated environment, it may be a camera-originated environment, or it may be a combination of the two.'[4] In this definition, telepresence encompasses two different situations: being 'present' in a synthetic computer-generated environment (what is commonly referred to as *virtual reality*) and being 'present' in a real remote physical location via a live video image. Scott Fisher, one of the developers of NASA Ames Virtual Environment Workstation, similarly does not distinguish between being 'present' in a computer-generated or a real remote physical location. Describing Ames system, he writes: 'Virtual environments at the Ames system are synthesized with 3-D computer-

38) Revolution in the movies: BATTLESHIP POTEMKIN *by Sergei Eisenstein (1925). Eisenstein's restaging (the 'lie'?) of the brutal Tsarist regime's military 'action' at a remote location: the Odessa Steps.*

39) Revolution on television: live images from the 'revolution' in Romania in December 1989 simulated popular action which turned out to have mostly been stage managed by those in control of state broadcasting: Potemkin's villages for an all to credulous world audience. From Harun Farocki and Andrei Ujica's VIDEOGRAM OF A REVOLUTION *(1993).*

generated imagery, *or* are remotely sensed by user-controlled, stereoscopic video camera configurations.'[5] Fisher uses 'virtual environments' as an all-encompassing term, reserving 'telepresence' for the second situation: 'presence' in a remote physical location.[6] I will follow his usage here.

Both popular media and the critics have downplayed the concept of telepresence in favor of virtual reality. The photographs of the Ames system, for instance, have been often featured to illustrate the idea of an escape from any physical space into a computer-generated world. The fact that a head-mounted display can also show a televised image of a remote physical location was hardly ever mentioned.

And yet, from the point of view of the history of the technologies of deception and action, telepresence is a much more radical technology than virtual reality, or computer simulations in general. Let us consider the difference between the two.

Like fake reality technologies which preceded it, virtual reality provides the subject with the illusion of being present in a simulated world. Virtual reality goes beyond this tradition by allowing the subject to actively change this world. In other words, the subject is given control over a fake reality. For instance, an architect can modify an architectural model, a chemist can try different molecule configurations, a tank driver can shoot at a model of a tank, and so on. But, what is modified in each case is nothing but data stored in a computer's memory! The user of any computer simulation has power over the virtual world which only exists inside a computer.

Telepresence allows the subject to control not just the simulation but reality itself. Telepresence provides the ability to *remotely manipulate physical reality in real time through its image*. The body of a teleoperator is transmitted, in real time, to another location where it can act on the subject's behalf: repairing a space station, doing underwater excavation or bombing a military base in Baghdad.

Thus, the essence of telepresence is that it is anti-presence. I don't have to be physically present in a location to affect reality at this location. A better term would be *teleaction*. Acting over distance. In real time. Catherine the Great was fooled into mistaking painted façades for real villages. Today, from thousands of miles away (as was demonstrated during the Gulf War) we can send a missile equipped with a television camera close enough to tell the difference between a target and a decoy. Using the image transmitted back by the missile's camera, we can carefully direct its flight towards the target. And, using the same image, we blow the target away. All that is needed is to position the computer cursor over the right place in the image and to press a button.

Image-Instruments

How new is this use of images? Does it originate with telepresence? Since we are accustomed to consider the history of visual representations in the West in terms of illusion, it may seem that to use images to enable action is a completely new phenomenon. However, French philosopher and sociologist Bruno Latour proposes that certain kinds of images have always functioned as instruments of control and power, power being defined as the ability to mobilize and manipulate resources across space and time.

One example of such image-instruments analyzed by Latour are perspectival images. Perspective establishes the precise and reciprocal relationship between objects and their signs. We can go from objects to signs (two-dimensional representations); but we can also go from such signs to three-dimensional objects. This reciprocal relationship allows us not only to represent reality but also to control it.[7] For instance, we cannot measure the sun in space directly, but we only need a small ruler to measure it on a photograph (the perspectival image par excellence).[8] And even if we could fly around the sun, we would still be better off studying the sun through its representations which we can bring back from the trip – because now we have unlimited *time* to measure, analyze, and catalog them. We can move objects from one place to another by simply moving their representations: 'You can see a church in Rome, and carry it with you in London in such a way as to reconstruct it in London, or you can go back to Rome and amend the picture.' Finally, we can also represent absent things and plan our movement through space by working on representations: 'One cannot smell or hear or touch Sakhalin Island, but you can look at the map and determine at which bearing you will see the land when you send the next fleet.'[9] All in all, perspective is more than just a sign system, reflecting reality – it makes possible the manipulation of reality through the manipulation of its signs.

Perspective is only one example of image-instruments. Any representation which systematically captures some features of reality can be used as an instrument. In fact, most types of representations which do not fit into the history of illusionism – diagrams and charts, maps and X-rays, infrared and radar images – belong to the second history: that of representations as instruments for action.

Telecommunication

Given that images have always been used to affect reality, does telepresence bring anything new? A map, for instance, already allows for a kind of teleaction: it can be used to predict the future and therefore to change it. To quote Latour again, 'one cannot smell or hear or touch Sakhalin Island, but you can look at the map and determine at which bearing you will see the land when you send the next fleet.'

In my view, there are two fundamental differences. Because telepresence involves electronic transmission of video images, the constructions of representations takes place instantaneously. Making a perspectival drawing or a chart, taking a photograph or shooting film takes time. Now I can use a remote video camera which captures images in real-time, sending these images back to me without any delay. This allows me to monitor any visible changes in a remote location (weather conditions, movements of troops, and so on), adjusting my actions accordingly.

The second difference is directly related to the first. The ability to receive visual information about a remote place in real time allows us to manipulate physical reality in this place, also in real-time. If power, according to Latour, includes the ability to manipulate resources at a distance, then teleaction provides a new and unique kind of power: *real-time remote control*. I can drive a toy vehicle, repair a space station, do underwater excavation, operate on a patient or kill – all from a distance.

What technology is responsible for this new power? Since the teleoperator acts with the help of a live video image, we may think at first that it is the technology of video, or, more precisely, of television, if we recall the original nineteenth century meaning of television: vision over distance. Only after the 1920s, when television was equated with broadcasting, does this meaning fade away. However, during the preceding half a century (television research begins in the 1870s), television engineers were mostly concerned with the problem of how to transmit consecutive images of a remote location to enable 'remote seeing.'

If images are transmitted at regular intervals and these intervals are short enough, the viewer will have enough reliable information about the remote location for teleaction. Modern television images are based on scanning reality at a resolution of a few hundred lines sixty times a second (the early television systems used slow mechanical scanning and a resolution as low as thirty lines). Radar images are based on scanning reality once every few seconds reducing the visible to a single point. A radar image does not contain any indications about shapes, textures or colors present in a television image – it only records the position of an object. Yet this information is quite sufficient for the most basic teleaction: to destroy an object.

So the technology which makes teleaction possible turns out to be electronic transmission of signals, in other words, electronic telecommunication. Electricity and electromagnetism, these discoveries of the nineteenth century, are what allows for the new and unprecedented relationship between objects and their signs in teleaction. *Electronic telecommunication makes instantaneous not only the process by which objects are turned into signs but also the reverse process – manipulation of objects through these signs.*

Umberto Eco once defined a sign as something which can be used to tell a lie. This definition correctly describes one function of visual representations – to deceive. But in the age of electronic telecommunication we need a new definition: a sign is something which can be used to teleact.

Digital Cinema: Delivery, Event, Time

Thomas Elsaesser

Deconstructing the Digital

The 'Digital Revolution', I argued in the introduction, is the 'flag-pole' around which many different parties and positions have rallied. The pace of change has been such that we instinctively feel the need for a common denominator. But the upheavals in our media landscape, seemingly coming together in this single term, are finally too important to find themselves thus pigeon-holed. Our current uses of information technology and commerce with images does not always depend on digitization. They often pre-date it, or in any event require a wider context, in which digitization is itself merely one factor, however crucial. The 'convergence' argument around the digital media as the 'motor', by overstating the case, is in danger of losing credibility. It gives a false impression of destiny, and with it, a sense of disempowerment that overlooks a number of salient forces also shaping the current situation. For instance:

- it obscures the processes of economic concentration on a global scale, which started before the digital revolution, and involve major innovations in technologies as different as jet propulsion and satellite technology, fibre-optic cables and the transistor
- it ignores the geo-political realignments of the recent decades since the oil-crises and the collapse of Communism, with the move from ideologically opposed power blocks to neo-liberal, capitalist trading blocks, leading to the emerging markets of Asia and Latin America
- it does not take into account deregulation (ie legal and institutional changes) as it has affected national television industries and state-controlled or corporate telecommunication monopolies in the developed countries.

When we use the computer to generate letters of the alphabet, few of us seem particularly vexed. When we listen to digital music and sound, again, there is a large degree of acceptance; it is only when digitization generates images that something akin to a cultural crisis appears to have occurred, with exaggerated claims being made by some, while huge anxieties are being voiced by others.[1] This is the more surprising, considering that the majority of cinematic digital techniques are modelled on tricking the eye with special effects, something that has been practised since Georges Méliès, Fritz Lang's DIE NIBELUNGEN, Walt Disney and KING KONG. Are we simply witnessing a new round in the bout between the advocates of 'realism' and the perfectors of 'illusionism'? Or is something more at stake, to do with a major change of cultural metaphor, away from 'representation' to 'simultaneity', 'telepresence', 'interactivity' and 'tele-action'? Media gurus even speak about 'preparing mankind to accept its own obsolescence', as homo sapiens leaves the planet to artificial intelligence organisms. At which point digitization starts lending support to wild evolutionary speculations, but also to a skewed history of the media.

To briefly illustrate the dilemma confronting media historians. Research into early cinema as well as early television has largely questioned the old genealogy in which devices such as camera obscura, magic lantern, photography, inevitably lead to the cinematograph and television. This cautions us against looking for a new teleology (along the lines of the 'evolution of cinematic language' or the 'fulfilment of mankind's age-old dream'), in order to make room for the digital multimedia. Nor can we make technological specificity the criterion that defines a medium, its *apparatus* or *dispositif*.[2] On the other hand, common sense suggests that these devices nonetheless belong together (for example, as instances of 'mechanical mimesis'), because only the family resemblance with the various modes of the photographic makes the changes brought on by the digital revolution seem so dramatic. The answer must lie in a more conjunctural history of the technical media, respecting uneven developments and discontinuities, while reminding oneself that one is constructing an archaeology,[3] in which concerns pressing on the present formulate the questions one puts to the past, as a way of coping with the future.

This observation does not make irrelevant, indeed makes more urgent, the debate which the digitization of images has given rise to, a debate involving a change in the status of the moving image, or at any rate, in the long held assumption that visual images, when mechanically produced, are in some fundamental sense 'indexical' (from which derive some of the truth claims of the visual). Any technology that materially affects this status, and digitization would seem to be such a technology, thus puts in crisis deeply-held beliefs about representation and visualization, and many of the discourses – critical, scientific or aesthetic – based on, or formulated in the name of the indexical in our culture need to be re-examined. It is in this last respect, I would argue, that the digital has come to function less as a technology than as a 'cultural metaphor' of crisis and transition.

Digital Delivery and Film Production

An example of such a conjunctural approach to the history and thus the future of the cinema would be to look at an apparently odd phenomenon, namely that much of the digital revolution around the cinema has at its heart a familiar commodity, the narrative feature film, mainly identified with Hollywood. It is still the one 'killer application' for many of the new developments, whether directly (on pay-tv, cable-tv, home video, the cinema multiplexes) or indirectly (for video-games, theme park rides and CD-ROMs). For this remarkably stable product, digitization is a contradictory factor, at once an ingenious technical process of translation, generation and storage, and the totem-notion around which a notoriously conservative industry is in the process of reorganizing – and this usually means reinventing – itself, in order to do much the same as it has always done.

If change there is, it is above all in the form of new distribution and circulation opportunities, where digital cinema is basically a new delivery system, adding 'value' to the product as it percolates through the entertainment industries, but where digital transmission seems so far to have had relatively little effect on the product itself: we are still dealing with the big picture, the blockbuster movie (and its 'moons and satellites').[4] The blockbuster movie is among other things, as we know, a marketing concept, generating attention, high recognition value, and involving shorter exploitation spans by implementing in the audiovisual market a principle perhaps better known from publishing and the music business: the 'best-seller' and the promotion of a 'top ten' or 'popularity chart'.[5]

One can think of such a marketing principle as one likes, but it is not only crucial for the secondary markets (recognition value is what television buys from the film industry, because it in turn is what advertisers are buying time for on television).[6] In the primary market, on the other hand, the best-seller or blockbuster, because of the size of its budget, also acts as a starter engine, pulling along other productions, as well as often providing the funds to finance changes in the infrastructure of the industry, such as updating equipment and investment in the plant. It can also provide training-sites for new skills, talent and services, as well as occasioning other kinds of spin-offs.[7] The principle or model would be that of the 'prototype', as it features in other industries, such as the car industry, which develops and tests its prototypes in-house, or in the aircraft or armament industries, where fighter planes and advanced weapon systems often function as prototypes also for civilian applications, but which are tested by the military.[8] Finally, the blockbuster as prototype helps set standards also on the service side, for the exhibition sector: for instance, it may demand the installation of better sound and projection equipment in cinemas. In each case, digitization is 'somewhere', but it is not what regulates or disrupts the system, whose logic is commercial, entrepreneurial or capitalist-industrial.

Thus, despite the fact that the narrative feature film is still at the centre of the system, we must be careful not to underestimate either the multiple types of input that are invested in this single, apparently unified commodity which is the Hollywood movie, nor can we ignore the mesh of connexions tying such a smoothly coherent feature of the media-scape into its economic and technological surroundings. Perhaps the most appropriate way to put it is to remember that when we speak of the cinema today, we speak of a cinema *after* television and *after* the video game, *after* the CD-ROM and the theme park. What does this mean in practice? From the point of view of production, cinema has always been a composite business, with a multitude of skills and very different techniques and technologies coming together in the finished product. The difference digitization has brought to this division of labour is to have shifted the balance between pre-production and post-production towards the latter, but even so, the completed film is still likely to combine live action in real settings; live action in studio settings; live action in painted sets; live action and animation combined; mechanical special effects, robotics and animatronics combined with digital visual effects; and all of the above combined with digital sound effects. In this respect, digital cinema is not new in itself, but a possibly more efficient and maybe in the long run even cheaper way of continuing the long-standing practice of illusionism in the cinema, while adding another element to the mixed-media, multi-media hybrid that is commercial filmmaking.

In the light of this, and given the central importance of the narrative, star-cast feature film for the economic system that is the international film industry, it is fair to assume that traditional ways of making films will, for the foreseeable future, continue. We know that the revolution announced by Francis Ford Coppola in the late 1970s, which he hoped to implement with his Zoetrope Studio and all-digital filmmaking, has so far not materialized, while another guru of digital cinema, the inventor and owner of 'Industrial Light & Magic' George Lucas has voiced, as recently as February 1997, a certain scepticism,[9] and this not after a commercial failure, as Coppola's ONE FROM THE HEART proved to be, but flushed with success after the tremendously lucrative re-launch of the first part of his STAR WARS trilogy, and his digital empire, working to full capacity, evidently also having 'the Force' on its side.

It would appear that I am arguing that the cinema in the age of the digital will basically remain the same. Yes, it will remain the same, *and* it will be utterly different, it is already utterly different. For, as suggested above, the digital is not only a new technique of post-production work and a new delivery system or storage medium, it is the new horizon of thinking about cinema, which also means that it gives a vantage point from beyond the horizon, so that we can, as it were, try and look back to where we actually are, and how we arrived there. The digital can thus function as a time machine, a conceptual boundary, as well as its threshold. Therefore, if one extrapolates from the present, but with this border-limit in mind, one comes to something like the following considerations:

Faced with the increase in special effects, but also the use of digital visuals in all kinds of other fields, one can speculate whether this 'norm' that we have so far referred to, namely the Hollywood-type feature film will one day be seen as what Lev Manovich has called merely the 'default value' of the cinematic system.[10] According to him, it is now possible to conceive of so many ways of generating moving or animated images, all of which fulfil the perceptual criteria of photographic presence (Manovich calls it 'perfect photographic credibility'), that the most common use today, the live action film, will seem but one variant among others, a historically and culturally specific type, with no further claim to dominance, either in the market place or conceptually. In fact, the 'photographic' mode may come to be seen as a left-over from the nineteenth century, part of a curious obsession with 'footprints'.[11] At the present time, then, we would be witnessing a transition from what one could call the optical (or the photographic) to the digital (the post-photographic) mode of image production.

Manovich goes even further in reversing the traditional hierarchy, arguing that we need to see the digital not as a post-photographic, but a graphic mode, one of whose many possibilities is the photographic effect, and by extension, the live action cinematic effect. Considered as a graphic mode, the digital presents itself with a long history, which not only predates the cinema and accompanies its history throughout, but which also makes crucial reference to a history that, in the modern period, has often been seen in contrast and opposition to the cinema, namely the history of painting.

This has two implications: firstly, the rise of photographic cinema appeared to marginalize graphic cinema, relegating animation to a minor genre, to this day confined either to avant-garde forms, such as abstract cinema and video, or more frequently associated with cartoons, which is to say, with cinema (and television) made for children. The reversal of priorities makes animation the general, higher-order category for the cinema, of which live action, photographic-effect filmmaking is a specialized subsection within the overall possibilities of the graphic mode, especially when 3-D graphics, simulated environments and other kinds of virtual reality spaces are added.[12]

The second point is that, as a graphic mode, digital cinema joins painting also in another respect: it requires a new kind of individual input, indeed manual application of craft and skill, which is to say, it marks the return of the 'artist' as source and origin of the image. In this respect, the digital image should be regarded as an expressive, rather than reproductive medium, with both the software and the 'effects' it produces bearing the imprint and signature of the creator.[13] This is reminiscent of the way George Lucas describes digital filmmaking as 'the process of a painter or sculptor. You work on it for a bit, then you stand back and look at it and add some more onto it, then stand back and look at it and add some more. You basically end up layering the whole thing.'[14]

Lucas' and Manovich's drastic perspective corrections are very welcome. Declaring the photographic a graphic mode elegantly disposes of the semiotic conundrum of the 'indexical', and the analogy with sculpture introduces important new aspects of 'embodiment' into our speculations about the future of cinema.[15] At the same time, their new archaeologies of digital cinema are not unique: they echo other 'alternative' histories of the cinema and the audiovisual media, propounded even before digitization entered into the debate. The classical narrative film, for instance, has in recent years often been seen as an 'intermediary', an 'intermezzo', a 'mere episode' in a historical account centred elsewhere; for instance, in the 'cinema of attractions'; in 'simultaneity', in 'interactivity'. In each case, the centre chosen depended on whether the vanishing point was the post-classical cinema of 'roller coaster rides',[16] video in the form of television as both the storage medium of record as well as the mass-medium of choice,[17] or the internet as the real-time multi-directional communication and interaction mode.[18] Today's media historians need to keep these different entry- and exit-points in mind, while not forgetting what has been argued so far: that economically, the feature film is still a key element; that socially and politically, television is still a very powerful medium; and that our culture is evidently more than a little reluctant to leave the episteme of the trace and the imprint, that is to say, give up the concept of record and evidence, of truth and authenticity.

Cinema: The Art and Act of Record?

In other words, the graphic mode argument disposes perhaps too neatly of the problem of the indexical, and by extension, of issues of representation, by treating the digital either as a matter of terminology and definition, or considering it mainly as a new 'poetics' of cinematic technique and practice. What is not addressed are the consequences that follow from the breakdown of belief in 'evidence' or 'truth' habitually invested in photographic images. A second example of a conjunctural history of the cinema would therefore be to ask how we can best understand this cultural crisis of ocular verification arising in the change from the photographic to the post-photographic in cinema.

The analogue audiovisual media this century possess a certain cultural prestige. Although not as great as that enjoyed by print, the value given to the moving image in the public sphere has steadily grown: paradoxically, one might say, given that its use for propaganda and persuasion has also made it more suspect. By contrast, the cultural value of an expressive mode such as painting has also grown, but in quite different domains, in the art-world, for instance, or at the museum.

The sound and image media derive this new self-confidence to a large extent from television, a medium that calls upon and consumes vast quantities of 'historical footage'. No subject is too remote, too personal, too secret, too shameful for there not to have been photographs taken, voices recorded and films made. Equally remarkable, an extraordinary quantity of this material has survived, in public archives and commercial picture libraries, in film, radio and television studios, in private possession, photo-albums, family collections, local and regional museums. Nothing – or so it seems – has happened in the twentieth century, without a camera recording it. Brought back to life, it can speak for itself, give itself away or accuse itself: an illusion, of course, and possibly a dangerously naive one. But this does not diminish the fact that photographs and films, both fictional and factual, have left us with the most extraordinary 'art of record' for the last 150 years, a most extensive 'archive' of what, for instance, cities looked like or buildings, how people dressed or gestured, how they lived indoors and out, how they saw themselves, were seen by others or wanted to be seen.

This mass of evidence derives its truth-claim from the idea of material traces, the dominant model in our culture for identifying 'pastness' in such fields as history or archaeology: an event has left a material residue, which the historian verifies to be 'authentic' and then proceeds to interpret as a 'document'. The photographic as imprint, mechanically and thus objectively recording an event of which it is the trace, would seem to fit rather well into this general matrix of historical knowledge. Yet especially in the moving image, the indexicality of the trace is so bound up with the iconicity of the likeness that it has, in some ways, confused the categories. At one extreme it has led to a 'naturalization' of the audio-visual illusion, crediting the moving image with the status of proof, and at the other end, to sceptical caution, with most professional historians reluctant to grant to cinematographic records much value as evidence whatsoever.

Yet what if we were to turn the argument around, by claiming that the status of authenticity and proof of a photograph or moving image does not reside in its indexical relation at all, but is a function of the institutions in charge of its verification and dissemination? For instance, most photo-graphs we find on the front-pages of our newspapers are either stills taken from video, or photographs transmitted digitally: in both cases, they have been manipulated in all kinds of ways before they are printed. But since we still accept our daily paper – tabloids perhaps excepted – as a medium of record, its digital mode of reproduction is secondary compared to the con-tract we expect the newspaper to honour with its readers, a contract of ve-racity and accuracy, extending from the text in a newspaper to its pictures and vice versa.

In which case, it would seem that any threat to the 'authentic', to the truth status of the moving image, too, does not come from digitization per se, but might well come from, say, deregulation. If television, for instance, is no longer trusted as a public medium of record, it may be because in the com-mercial environment it finds itself in when competing for ratings, it no longer enjoys the same political or social legitimation as an institution which 'polices' or self-regulates the veracity of its messages and representa-tions. By the same token, in East European countries, we may see the in-verse: the media were distrusted because the state controlling them lacked legitimacy, so that it is the commercial press and the newly privatized audiovisual media that are now endowed with the expectation of providing reliable evidence. The question of truth arising from the photographic and post-photographic would thus not divide along the lines of the trace and the indexical at all, but rather flow from a complex set of discursive conven-tions, political changes and institutional claims which safeguard (or sus-pend) what we might call the 'trust' or 'good faith' we are prepared to invest in a given regime of representation.

Yet something else supports the impression or illusion of 'truth' emanat-ing from the moving image almost as decisively as the contract of trust we have with the institution. Roland Barthes, in *Camera Lucida*, speaks of the way a photograph involves the viewer in a peculiar kind of presence and absence, what he named the sense of 'having been there'. This sense, as he analyzes it, is also a tense, joining a perfectum with a present, in a conjunc-tion of a place and a time. And with its 'thereness' it also embeds a deictic mark, that is, a speaking position and the trace of a subject in discourse: a photograph addresses us by the very act of placing us before it in relation to our existence in time and language. The moving image, by extension, de-rives its reality-effect similarly not only from its iconic features, but also from the tense-structure within which it holds the viewer, a 'here and now' which is, however, always already a 'there and then'. To this temporality thus correspond distinct spaces, so that the audiovisual experience always involves several space-times, related to each other and yet distinct from each other, a then/here space, and a now/there space, which, by at once doubling and displacing the viewer's own now/here space-time make possible the subject-effects of audiovisual experience as an affective engagement. We might say that vision is only part of what makes the moving image 'real' to a viewer, so that the question one needs to ask is not so much whether the digitized image severs the link between the material trace of the real in the photograph and its power to resemble the real, but how digitization might affect the time-space relations for the viewer, and thereby the 'tense' of the image.

Television and the Media Event
There are several ways of approaching this issue, which will eventually lead us to a consideration of the time-space coordinates in video-games and interactive narratives. One necessary intermediary step is to look at television, and to briefly outline the conjunctural argument that would put the digital 'in perspective' for the televisual image, which in the form of video, has also broken with the indexicality of the photographic image, without however provoking a similar crisis. More directly put, how would one go about defining the 'ontology' of television and the video image? Television, rather than being examined around essentialist assumptions derived from its 'apparatus' (e.g. the cathode-ray tube or the video-camera), is mostly understood according to the ideology of its institutional structures, by studying the uses people make of programmes in their everyday lives or how the television-set figures in the 'gender politics' of the living room.[19] However, there have been two classic attempts to outline an ontology specific to television and video, one by Jane Feuer, focusing on 'liveness' in television, and one by Fredric Jameson, defining the ontology of video around the concept of 'empty time' and 'boredom'.[20] Both thus involve temporality and space, and they are my lead for identifying two typical 'tenses' of television's mode of address. One seems to mark television's limits: I have called it the 'stand-by' mode of schedule-busting, when television interrupts itself, as it were, to bring into the domestic sphere wars (e.g. Bosnia), revolutions (e.g. the fall of Communism), assassinations, genocide, natural or human disasters, such as hurricanes, the explosion of the Challenger shuttle or the death of Diana, Princess of Wales.[21] The other mode is the segmented flow, the 'stand-for' mode of schedule-programming: the day-to-day business of consensus-building and agenda-setting on television, by a process of attrition and negotiation, as witnessed by the inexhaustible 'talk' of news interviews, chat-shows, soap-operas.[22] The latter, with its 'therapeutic' discourse as the dominant form of personal interaction and the resolution of conflict is what one might call the simulation of the social, and to this extent a 'virtual'

mode without it being based on digital technology. The former mode, on the other hand, actualizes (or rehearses?) the red-alert of critical emergency and catastrophe (and thus connotes the return of – political, ideological – contradiction, albeit disavowed). Neither, I would argue, has any privileged relation to the real, and instead, engages us on the time-axis.

While the stand-for strategies generate the imagined communities typical of television (from the fan community all the way to 'the nation'), the stand-by mode breaks through this staging of national self-identity and social role play towards the universally human(itarian). But it is always also a self-staging of televisual technology and power, as the whole hardware infrastructure of satellite hook-ups, equipment-laden camera crews, frontline reporters in Land Rovers, and telephone links via laptops becomes visible and audible, making time palpable, and distance opaque – together signifying the proper 'materiality' of media-disasters. Yet this self-staging of technology and manpower has also a fetish or totem function in another sense: as it demonstrates its ability to bring us the signal, to assure us that it won't fail, fade or break down, it also invokes this very spectre of failure.[23] With it, the viewer enters a world that is at once unreal and hyperreal, grounded in a space-and-time location and yet also a simulation: the world of the media event.[24]

The stand-by mode may seem to be the exception, but on reflection, it is clearly the more 'fundamental' of the two: the very fact that by definition it has the power to override the schedule indicates its primacy. Perhaps one way to put is to say that it, too, is one of television's 'virtual' modes, permanently threatening to become actualized behind the regular programmes. Among the channels with a global reach, CNN International ('CNN Live') is the one most often – and most literally – on stand-by mode. The network can in some sense claim to be television's model for how to put media events into circulation, and it has made an art of managing both sides of this mode, the moments of boredom when nothing happens, as well as those of high tension, when anything can happen (hence the term stand-by: waiting, and being ready when the story 'breaks'). Intriguingly, CNN often gives its longer-running 'event stories' titles that are or could be borrowed from the cinema (as does the US military to its operations and initiatives, e.g. Star Wars or Desert Storm): for instance, 'The Siege of Baghdad' (in analogy to 'The Thief of Baghdad', also used, incidentally, as a nickname for Saddam Hussein when he invaded Kuwait), or 'The Waco Stand-Off' (played at first according to the Spaghetti Western-Clint Eastwood scenario of 'The Three-Way Mexican Stand-Off').[25]

While television on these occasions seems to be attempting to 'narrate' disaster and catastrophe, it is dramatizing a fundamental contradiction constitutive of television.[26] On the one hand, television sees itself as a medium of record, but on the other, event for television is a pure time category, but a time category in the state of both scarcity and loss: time is always running out on television, even though it has so much of it to fill. This is because its 'material' substance and trace is information, whose value is the moment, making 'news' a commodity always on the verge of attrition and effriction, in other words, it is a transaction that has a meter ticking to oblivion, as it were, from the moment it is 'aired' or 'broken'.

The media event could thus be seen as the drama of television itself: trying to turn information into narrative (which is to say, turning something that is constantly perishing into something that 'keeps': a narrative, a story). The media-event becomes the embodiment of televisual time in its purest form, modulated into its different aggregate states.[27] The stand-by mode (catastrophe) while situated at the margins of television, would thus be my 'ontology' of television, while the stand-for mode (consensus), usually seen as the 'representation of the real', becomes the fragile in-between state, always threatened by the other mode's sudden and necessarily sudden i(nte)rruption.

This ontology produces some powerful subject effects, and once again, these are characterized by a peculiar conjunction of space and time. I am referring to the classic 'media event' situation, encapsulated in the question 'where were you, when President Kennedy was shot' (or: '... when the Challenger Mission exploded', or: '... when you first heard of Diana's death'): in each case the question 'where were you...' also implies '... when television brought it, showed it and replayed it all day/all week?'.[28] A conjunction of temporalities and spaces (now/here, now/there) would be the ground on which identification takes hold, rather than a specular relation to a sight, image or view. Time-shifting would constitute the mode of 'subjectivation' typical of a 'media event'.

Cinema as Social Event and Site

What is it that the cinema can set against this, how does it compensate for its rival medium's recursiveness, this sense of 'being there', in order to have been there, or the peculiar eyewitness-as-viewer effect of the typical media event, sustained by the double temporality of 'live' and 'replay', 'real-time' and its repetition? We might begin by differentiating between cinema as ritual and cinema as spectacle, as social event, site, and audiovisual experience. Evidently, a certain event-character is the cinema's 'external' organizing principle: going to the movies is to entertain a set of expectations, with which we are all familiar, but which vary crucially from culture to culture: it is not the same in The Netherlands, where there is a break for drinks and a smoke in the middle of the film, from what it is in the United States, where the (smell of) popcorn is mandatory. In some cinemas, the audience talks through the film and behaves as if in front of the television set, in others there is more hushed seriousness than in a church on Sunday. The contemporary film experience is socially and culturally multi-coded, for some it ranges alongside shopping or eating out, and for others, it is comparable to an exhibition or gallery opening. In each case, the occasion is to some extent also doubled by self-reference, implying an element of seeing and being seen: not only the cinematic spectacle itself, but added to it the recursive effect of 'ritual' and community, being there and being seen to be there.

But the cinema experience has an event-scenario as its organizing principle also in a different sense. One could propose a definition of cinema in the television age, ie *after* television, which, however, merely highlights a general feature of cinema since its beginnings, namely that a film *requires a performance for its completion, and an event for its actualization*. The combination of performance and event has – over the past hundred years – taken very diverse forms.[29] For instance, if the performance character of silent cinema required an orchestra in the pit, the event character in the 1930s and 1940s was defined around the family audience; in the 1970s and 1980s the event modelled itself on the leisure habits of its predominantly youthful, male audience, while in the 1990s is said to cater increasingly again for a family audience, its performance character now requiring dolby and digital sound. The success of cinema as social and performance event is for the exhibitor a critical factor economically, since his income from concessions and amenities can often exceed that from admissions.

Another index that the cinema has had an event-scenario built into its commercial exploitation almost from the very beginning is the fact that, since the 1910s, spectators have been charged according to a time advantage and a location advantage: the principle of 'first run' or 'première exclusivité' or 'West-End release' by which cinemas and admission prices are classified mean that in effect, audiences pay a premium for seeing a film during its initial release period, when it has the attention of the press and the general public. Its commodity value resides in its temporality, here expressed as the time advantage: we are prepared to pay extra for a film while it is still an 'event'. The emergence of the pre-recorded video cassette and its proliferation, at costs barely above the admission-price of a cinema ticket may have shortened the period in which the cinema film is an 'event', but it has, of course, given films a substantial secondary market, in which its event character can and does reverberate as pre-publicity.[30]

40) The triumph of the will to illusionism: spectacular special effects astonished audiences in Fritz Lang's THE NIBELUNGEN *(1924)....*

41) ... much the same as they did seventy years later in Steven Spielberg's JURASSIC PARK *(1993).*

The 'event-driven' nature of cinema today also reflects the changing function of public spaces in the wake of 'urban renewal' schemes for inner cities, where crowds no longer gather for political action or to go to work. Since the ubiquity of television and the motor car, a whole range of other activities compete for the population's free time. But these domestic appliances also mean that those who now populate the streets of city centres do so almost wholly for the purposes of shopping, leisure and entertainment: activities connected again with seeing and being seen, in which 'going to the movies' is both part of a continuum of spectatorship, ranging from window-shopping, meeting friends at a cafe or eating out, but also marks a liminal space, at once a physical focus and social site, defined in relation to its opposite: home. As Edgar Reitz has put it: 'cinema is a sort of consensus about going out, it gives a name and an address to the desire of leaving the house for an evening'.[31]

A further effect of the blockbuster as the main attraction of theatrical release is that it makes 'cinema', too, partake in the meta-genre 'media-event' as sketched above. We come across the cinema everywhere, but in a peculiar temporal modulation. A new film, more likely than not, first hits us in the form of movie trailers, posters, billboards, behind-the-scenes features on television and star interviews. In fact, in this respect the blockbuster's carefully orchestrated marketing campaign involves a build up and an intensification, followed by a media-blitz whose nearest analogy is the weather. It is much like a hurricane gathering force in mid-Atlantic, as it were, showing first signs of turbulence in toy shops or on MTV, before moving inland to the capital for its big release, and then finally sweeping the rest of the country's screens before gently subsiding in the videotheques. The event-movie par excellence, such a blockbuster is characterized by the fact that it takes place in a kind of count-down time and that it occupies all manner of urban, mental and media spaces. On the other hand, it also 'devastates' the cinema landscape for the more modest films, usually of domestic or European origin.

The effect of the onslaught and its peculiar event logic is also reflected in cinema architecture and cinema siting, notably symbolized in the move from urban multiplexes to suburban cineplexes. These new structures, attached to or integral part of shopping malls, leisure parks and amusement arcades, suitable for daytime family outings as well as evening entertainment, have begun to transform the physical identity of cinema, doing away, for instance, with the unsightly, undignified and often extremely unappealing back-alley rear exits through which the traditional inner-city cinema used to dismiss its audiences at the end of the show, as if to express graphically its contempt, after having relieved them of their money. The new cinemas, by becoming absorbed into a different dimension (be it the theme-park atmosphere of the cineplex or the art-house ambience modelled on museums, or the lobby areas of other high-profile high-tech public or corporate buildings), are part of an urbanism in which they figure as 'cathedrals of another faith', to use a memorable phrase coined by the architect Hans Hollein for the kind of prestige buildings that today make up a metropolitan skyline. If this seems a little too metaphoric and hyperbolic, it is worth remembering that the contemporary cinema's most 'architectural' features are in fact the films themselves: in their action-, sci-fi- and adventure genres especially, their spectacles represent mega-structures of image volume and sound space.

But here also lies the chance for non-Hollywood films: a more attractive physical environment, thanks to multi-screen luxury theatres, with sound and projection equipment that does justice to the new technologies of the image, is like an event waiting to happen. It provides the physical conditions for even 'small' films to partake in what John Ellis calls the 'sacred' quality of the event. For him, it is the possibility of 'epiphanies' that justify the cinema's main claim to be different from television:

> A cinema is a special space, one to which we are permitted a limited access. It is not *our* space, it is a controlled public space which we enter according to set rules – the payment of money, arrival at an appointed hour – and agree to behave according to still further established rules. These rules certainly vary according to the particular culture in which the screening is taking place, but in Europe our established convention is that we sit, we do not talk, and we attend to the spectacle. We submit – and, having submitted, we can enter into a different modality of existence, into a realm of fantasy. This process is essentially a *sacred* one. [...] Collective submission to rules and rituals allows the individual a degree of epiphany. [...] Television, on the other hand, occupies a different space entirely, one that has no sacred dimension to speak of. We have television of right in our society. It is a social necessity in the same way that indoor plumbing is a social necessity.[32]

Compared to the old stand-alone cinemas, but especially the shoe box cinemas of the 1970s, the new cineplexes of the 1990s offer not only a difference of kind and level in the amenities but a different encoding of space itself. The old cinema space is all about 'drawing boundaries', inviting the audience by a palatial foyer, but at the rear, separating the cinema from the street. By contrast, the new ones are about integration, making the cinema space merge with a café, a bar or restaurant space: reflection of a different policy not only of services inside the cinema, but of how contemporary public spaces relate, communicate and connect with each other, and what experiences are being offered across these spaces. In contrast to Ellis' sacred space, which is essentially a homogeneous and threshold space, the auditorium can also be a participatory space, linked to other participatory spaces, in which case, the function of the screen space may become quite different: one recalls the phenomenon of cult films like THE ROCKY HORROR PICTURE SHOW or THE BLUES BROTHERS, where the narrative action has become secondary (and with it the temporality of suspense or other narrational devices). The fans' familiarity not only favours participation, but turns the film into a cue sheet for a performance. One might call the film – in anticipation of what I shall discuss below – a map to be navigated, an environment to be entered, rather than a window to be viewed or a text to be read. The Italian director Gianni Amelio summarized this reversal of hierarchies between the auditorium space and the screen space, when he remarked in 1987 (possibly on a note of regret) that today's audiences 'consume cinema collectively. They go in groups of up to twenty, and they want the kind of film which is prepared to become the accomplice of their group behaviour, with regular gags, where you can nudge your neighbour and slap him on the shoulder. This sort of cinema functions a bit like a discotheque; you go to the cinema, not to watch a film but to enjoy being together *at the expense* of the movie.'[33]

The Digital Media as Event

This example of interactive non-digital cinema finally brings me to 'digital cinema', understood as the use of digital technology to construct either virtual environments or to tell stories interactively. Here, we right away encounter a paradox: one widely held view is that, basically, there is no such thing as an interactive narrative. The reasons may partly be terminological: what commonly passes for interactivity in narratives is strictly speaking hyperselectivity. The aim is to programme an architecture of multiple choices presented from a pre-arranged menu, and leading to different paths, which among themselves have certain nodal points. When these are carefully or cunningly devised, they can give the illusion of freedom of response: 'creating a better kind of mousetrap' as it has been called.[34] Yet even if the menu could be extended indefinitely (and with it, the options arising from the nodal points correspondingly multiplied) another, perhaps even graver difficulty would arise. This difficulty has to do with a story's 'point of view': who tells what to whom, or put differently, who controls the relation between information and inference for the viewer in the process of narration, and organizes the levels and perspectives of narration. In other words, even if cinema were to be totally 'digital' in sound and image, this would not make the films interactive, for the latter implies that the viewer could intervene actively in the progress of the narrative or take over the function of the narrator.[35]

While the ideology of a self-selected narrative and open-ended storyline suggests freedom and choice, this is precisely what interactive cinema strives to conceal. The user colludes with being a 'player', whose freedom can be summed up as: 'you can go wherever you like, so long as I was there before you' – which is of course precisely also the strategy of the 'conventional' story-teller (or narrational agency) whose skill lies in the ability to suggest an open future at every point of the narrative, while having, of course, planned or 'programmed' the progress and the resolution in advance. This casts doubt also on an argument sometimes advanced in favour of the absence of a narrator, of point of view, of a central perspective: might it not 'free' the narrative image from its 'bourgeois-patriarchal' symbolic which film theory in the 1970s always protested against? Reviving Roland Barthes' term of the 'writerly text', theorists such as George Landow and others have argued that Barthes' and Derrida's literary theories 'anticipate' hypertext and interactivity and thus provide these practices with philosophical foundations. But this would be attributing an excessive literalness to a theory of excess and indeterminacy![36]

The problem can also more humbly be phrased as one between 'narration' and 'navigation': there is a category shift between random access in media that offer some resistance in the form of an irreversible temporal flow, like the novel or a narrative film, and those that do not.[37] If a medium does not offer this resistance – such as, for instance, an ordinary electronic database – what exactly does random access represent or add, in respect of this dialectic of freedom and constraint? To what extent does navigating rely on a 'map', and what would a map in the case of such a narrative look like? No longer would a story be the exploration of a world thanks to narrative. The CD-ROM or interactive video game is more like the exploration of a narrative thanks to a 'world'. The setting or set, the fiction, the collection of information functions then as background to a new kind of (serial) activity: a sampling or sorting information, making connections in the form of montage, or more likely, following the connexions laid by others. In other words, with an interactive story on CD-ROM or the Internet we may be invited to 'enter a world', but rather than begin to explore it, we explore its narrative architecture: its paths and its detours, its branching and its multiple choices. We enter a territory in order to explore its map, rather than use a map to explore a territory. What we have as our mode of transport – to move, surf, connect – is the mouse, a static vehicle par excellence. Shooting an enemy, ascending a tower or descending into a dungeon are actions translated into clicks, which in turn initiate a movement at one remove, while the locations we thus reach conceal their own motion vehicles: the hyper-links and hot-spots, transporting us elsewhere. It is the point at which narrative becomes, in Manovich's words 'tele-action' and we are in what would seem related but nonetheless distinct paradigms (of action, rather than representation).[38] The digital is in this case the more convenient or efficient means to this end, though not the end itself. The end has to do with spatialization of time: providing mobility, conveyance, 'transport', action. The 'motion picture' narrative as 'static vehicle'.

Alternatively, the space-time coordinates of interactive cinema have to be constructed in order to convey an impression of movement while allowing for the 'illusion' of freedom and choice to arise. Grahame Weinbren seems to have pondered these questions harder than most, partly by commenting on his own interactive cinema. Once again, the issues arise, irrespective of digitization, and Weinbren conceived and developed his interactive films prior to the advent of digital images, since he initially used analogue laser discs, connected to a computer software programme.[39] His work is a most intriguing example of interactive/multiple choice cinema, and in its terms, extremely successful: with *The Erl King* and *Sonata* he has made film-installations which create a sort of multiple perspectivism by first of all telling the story from different vantage points or 'narrators' (à la RASHOMON or the films of Alain Resnais), all of which are accessible to the viewer in the form of hyperselectivity. But he also allows the viewer-as-user to 'enter' into and explore 'pockets' of the narrative world, which are not exactly parallel universes, yet have a high degree of autonomy, while nonetheless belonging thematically or in their visual or aural motifs to the underlying story world. What adds to the suspense, however, is that while one is 'inside' these pockets, the story 'elsewhere' is nonetheless progressing in linear fashion towards its predetermined conclusion. The viewer-user is therefore structurally split between his desire to explore the pockets, and his anxiety not to lose the thread of the narrative, which seems a rather intriguing compromise between (the 'laws' of) narrative and (the possibilities of) interactivity, making one 'police' the other, so to speak, while creating a number of unusual and unusually powerful subject-effects.

Weinbren's interactive cinema are installation pieces: not so much a prototype as a meta-type and senso-theoretical object. In the nature of such work, his interactive cinema may not have a mass-media future. Intriguingly enough, again, the obstacles in the way of interactive cinema are perhaps not primarily technological, nor in the order of a logical impossibility. What they highlight are the misunderstandings as to the social character of the cinema experience, that is the event status of cinema, and the temporalities it implies. Andy Cameron, for instance, has pointed out that the difficulties of 'interactivity' are too often euphemized by fine art circumlocutions, such as 'interactive media environment', 'interactive installation' or 'transformational space', where by rights the more obvious word 'game' should be used, though because of its low-culture associations it is avoided, even repressed: 'if the repressed reading of interactivity is that of the game, the preferred reading of interactivity is that of postmodernism'.[40] What is satisfying about Weinbren's pieces is that they are precisely neither 'games' nor 'postmodern' narratives, but instead, feel 'readerly', in the way they give a strong sense of an underlying, continuous time-management, in other words, suggest the presence of a super-narrator, a story-teller.

Granting that normally only games should be called 'interactive', these examples highlight differences between a narrative scenario (where the user/viewer confront a narrator as his Other) and a 'game' scenario (where the user/player confronts another player as antagonist, and the designer as the super-narrator). Important, again, is the time/space dimension. Games may seem to have a different way of representing time, but one can relate it to narrative devices: video games/interactive programmes usually create artificial time constraints which force decisions, choices. This means that the identificatory potential of film-narrative time (made up of suspense, surprise, the uneven distribution of knowledge and how to maintain it from one plot situation to the next) is replaced by the temporality of the countdown, by levels of difficulty (usually measured in the time it takes to complete tasks), or of branching points and the containment of hyper-selectivity or 'branching explosion'.

We seem to have come full circle, for this dilemma not only corresponds to the basic situation of hyperselectivity, it may actually 'rehearse' it and thus give us a broader framework for understanding the social function of the digital media, in the way Walter Benjamin understood the cinema as 'rehearsing' the distracted attention/perception of the metropolitan subject of 'modernity'.[41] In our consumer society, choice could be regarded as much a burden and an obligation as it is a right, but more crucially, perhaps, the way and frequency with which 'interaction' with the human-machine interface is required in the place of work as well as in situations of leisure, necessitating new skills of cognition, vision and embodied sensory coordination. If the digital in the realm of images breaks with the indexical, by the same token, though not primarily for technological reasons, it privileges a new cognitive coordination of 'seeing', 'believing', 'knowing': although, one might add – appropriating another famous phrase by Jean-Luc Godard –, 'not necessarily in that order'.

The Digital as Cultural Metaphor

The digital thus above all allows us to rethink cinema and television across the categories of space, time and subjectivity. Random access does not break with linear narrative per se, but only with single-strand narrative: a change which in itself is neither revolutionary – think of the nested narratives of German Expressionism or the multi-strand narratives of Luis Buñuel – nor a sufficient condition for interactivity. Similarly, computer-based stories do not eliminate the need for narration: automated story generation will simply pose new challenges to 'narrators' when deciding on the temporalities of information flow and distributing the contiguity of alternative options. Time warps, virtual worlds, parallel universes, just as much as multiple personalities, magical transformations, fantastical identities and disguises are nothing but more or less pleasingly metaphoric embodiments of contiguity, raising the same questions of identification, participation and suspense as single-strand narratives: in short, the subject-effects of fictional experience.

It is in respect to these subject-effects that the argument over the fundamental difference or likely convergence between narratives and games may have to be rethought. For instance, in some so-called interactive narratives,

42) The nineteenth century meets the twenty-first century, when even in traditional half-timber buildings, households are linked by satellite to the television-universe of unlimited access and bewildering choice: here a Stuttgart street enjoys a mixed architectural blessing.

13) *By contrast, the new cineplexes want to be architectural highlights and suburban magnets: the Cinedom in Cologne once more presents 'going to the movies' as a special event.*

the games principle of accumulating points is fictionalized into serial repetition of actions, with the higher score of points giving access to other story levels, thus simulating greater narrative complexity. Similarly, rewards and punishments can be narrativized into feedback loops, while magic worlds are needed to motivate the randomized appearance or disappearance of protagonists and antagonists. What is perhaps most useful about the games metaphor infiltrating into narrative theory is that it points once more to the 'contractual' nature of the intersubjective interaction in the digital media, rather than its dependence on truth and ontology.

'Cable' in the title of the collection signals our attempt to mark the vantage point for this re-thinking, and while it can draw us further and further into the internet and cyberspace, it might also bring us back to the cinema of trust, belief and the suspension of disbelief: the televisual and audiovisual event as the end of the face-to-face, but as our only hope of the face-to-face – eliminating the 'noise' of failed communication, but also creating its own 'interference' or felicity conditions: here again, the digital can stand as a metaphor, rather than the one-way street to the digital-as-destiny. Cain, Abel *and* Cable: Television, cinema and their transformation. The peculiar verbal contraction plays on this relationship between the two media or event modes, where the final term is neither a collapse of the two into one, nor their Hegelian sublation, but their refiguration as 'new media'. I started off with the metaphor of the enemy brothers and the family resemblance, with the feuding siblings perhaps about to be swallowed up by the digital. I want to conclude with another order of convergence altogether: that of a cultural shift, the consequences of which seem to be to leave everything the same while simultaneously altering everything. The digital in this view is not a new medium, but rather, for the here and now, for the time being, for film and television, first and foremost, a new medium of 'knowing' about these media.

The Television Screen: from Spoil-sport to Game-maker

Ed Tan

Today we should be talking less about television as a medium of communication, a cultural form, a producer of meanings. Instead, why do we not
look at television, as we did when we were small, as a box for seeing and
hearing films: television as a kind of cinema in the home. But we do not need
to go back as far as our childhood years to watch television in this way. A
significant part of what is shown on television is the fiction film: feature
films, television films, drama series. Another part can be watched with the
same attitude as the one we adopt when watching non-fiction in the cinema.
News, nature films, ethno-documentaries, sport and adverts offer us,
among other things, fascinating images and sounds, sights, and spectacle.
Television researchers have discovered that television viewers no longer
put 'spectacle' at the top of their list. It is now common knowledge that television sound serves mainly to drown out the cracking of peanuts and the
gurgling of beer at so-called 'important moments', but research in the last
few years has shown that viewers talk through the programmes and are
usually busy doing something other than just watching television. What is
more, television-watching seems to have become a rather rare phenomenon, having taken over from the incidental glance out of the window when
you are occupied with other things. Then there is the growing practice of
zapping, so that, even if we are not doing something else, what we see and
hear could be described as little more than a dazzling parade of minuscule
programme fragments.

The television researcher should, then, be surprised that things were ever
otherwise. Zapping, of course, is a new development, but whatever induced
the viewers to watch a programme anyway? Have we become so fickle in
the past ten or fifteen years? The number of channels has certainly gone up.
But then, these days only a relatively small fraction of the channels on offer
are actually viewed with any regularity. This fact, combined with the
broader selection available should, you might think, lead to more pro-
longed and intensive viewing of those channels which the customer has
been able to select. I tend to believe that we used to be well-behaved in the
old days. We were better at doing what the box asked of us: watch, watch
and watch some more. At home we would angrily 'shush' anyone foolish
enough to try to straighten a seam in their trousers when *The Avengers* was

on. The opponents of television had no trouble finding terms to describe this phenomenon: the terror of television resulted in enslavement to the box, destroying our creativity and our interpersonal relations, particularly within the family.

If we turn to the quality of the box it soon becomes clear that we would eventually be cured of our compliance. Even if the remote control had not made its appearance and we had grown more insubordinate at all levels of existence the box would have died a death. Because basically the box is pretty useless. Let us begin with the front of the box, the television screen. As a cinema-in-the-home it is a poor substitute for the big screen.[1] The resolution is hopeless due to the low number of image lines and the coarse scanning of the screen. The finer details are lost and so, therefore, is a great deal of formal information. Static depth cues are rendered ineffective. The screen and the small frame emphasize the flatness of the image and dominate those depth cues which still exist. The image therefore is flattened, cartoon-like, and accommodates a low level of spatial information. The scanning pattern, interacting with the set image point structure, leads to disturbing moiré patterns, twinkling images and alias effects. These effects cannot be eliminated entirely, they can at best be temporarily counteracted. But there is a price to pay. An excess of close-ups, for example, can become annoying and certainly does not help the image to look any less flat. The critics of television have an easy task: television aesthetics are not in the same league as film aesthetics. The television screen is not even capable of reproducing a beautiful film. It is a spoil-sport. If we compare the front side of the box with the cinema screen there is only one conclusion: do not watch television!

But there is hope. High Definition Television (HDTV) is on its way, preceded by the even more mixed blessing of wide-screen television. If the image can be sharpened and the resolution retained in the process of substantially enlarging the screen, then this could be the saviour of television as a box for instant viewing. The digital image is managing to achieve the quality of a cinema film and the end of the negative television aesthetic is in sight. Our obedience will no longer be required to glue us to the telly; the spectacle itself will be sufficient, just as it is in the cinema. That is a good thing. But we have been so busy following the developments at the front of the box that we have completely forgotten about the back. And it is here that the really fundamental changes could occur.

The fact that the television screen is a spoil-sport has a lot to do with the back of the box. Current television can only process signals which contain relatively little information. The signal is decoded and transformed into a scan. The set is unable to add anything to this rather scanty signal. It can be intensified or filtered here and there, but a signal of such poor quality remains poor when it is enlarged. The back of a television has about as much intelligence 'as the back of a pig' (as we say in Holland). But the back of the television set is constantly being added to in terms of computer technology.[2] The box is learning. It will soon be helping us to select titles from a large supply of about 50.000 films made since the invention of cinema. Your television will soon be cleverly compressing and then sifting signals intelligently, allowing more information to be sent along the same band width. The transmitter has an anticipatory function, sending out digital information during quiet scenes which belong to later, busier scenes. This technique allows an hour of video to be transmitted in less than five seconds on the cable. The digital information can be stored in the television set's files and played at any given time, but can also be edited in many different ways. The viewer can call up other, related files. This is how 'tell me more television' comes into being. The newsreader will be able to go into selected items in any depth of your choice. Clever compression techniques are expected to enable the signal to contain not only the information that is stored before the camera, but also an extensive mathematical 3-D model of the scene. The viewer could then select for him/herself a particular perspective at a football game and could, for example, even select a position behind the opposing team's goal-keeper. Personalised television, 'narrowcasting' as opposed to broadcasting becomes a reality. The box can be instructed to collect certain television programmes or even certain kinds of material, and to edit them into a manageable package. You do not even need to give it explicit instructions. Your television can learn what you want to see by storing this preference in its memory. If an hour-long programme can be compressed into a five-second transmission, the back of your set can watch and edit a seven-hour work-day's viewing, made up of 5.000 programme hours, and then, for example, scroll this before your eyes in the form of a ten-minute-long collage, with a 'tell me more' facility, of course. If the zapping is already being done for you, and more efficiently than you could do it, you will keep watching, and issuing orders. It is television's turn to be obedient.

But even in the absence of a spectacular broadening of the signal, with or without compression technology, the vast amount of information which is constantly reaching our screens can be stored in the back of the box. You only have to give it a quick signal and it will be sent to the front of the box. Just to take one example, discs containing information about 54,000 houses can be issued to potential property-buyers. The disc is loaded onto every client's set. The transmitted signal marks the houses which are available at the time of viewing. Or to take another example, every film contains people. In most films you see the houses, rooms, hall-ways, windows, doors, chairs, tables, telephones. You see the sky, trees, roads, squares, cars, street-lamps.

Every time you see one of these things on television it has already been recorded, edited, transmitted and received countless times. Of course, every
image of a person or an object differs from all its predecessors, but there is
one core of information which all these images share. Columbo's car driving
up the hill has something in common with Laurel and Hardy's car parked in
front of the house and being wrecked by the man next door. The common
feature in all these cases can be stored in the back of the set as a model and be
transformed on the instructions of a transmitted signal by an intelligent television into unique and living images. Nicolas Negroponte, whose article in
Scientific American (September 1991) forms the basis for much of the information above, estimates the extent of the gains in transmission. One frame
of a form of 3-D short animation film takes something like 50 million bytes
to cover all the dots on an HDTV screen. It would be possible to store models
of all the objects in the receiver, so that only instructions concerning their
movements would have to be transmitted.

So it looks as if the television set is capable of being more than just a
spoil-sport; all we have to do is provide what lies behind the screen with a
bit of computer intelligence. But as long as the back of the television set is
fed with a cable that links it to a transmitter somewhere 'out there', your
own television screen cannot yet perform the function of a game-maker.
However necessary the clever intervention of electronics in the box might
be, there is still the question of a certain determining control from 'out
there'. The next step can, technically speaking, already be made. We take
the lead-in cable out, and upgrade the back of the set to a powerful computer. Alluding to the well-known concept 'profilmic reality' we can say
that the screen now no longer reflects the 'protelevision-ic' reality of the studio or a given location, but paves the way for a world inside the box. So,
computer programming facilitates the screen becoming a game-maker.
Computer games, graphic simulations, virtual reality and artificial life are
just some examples. The world of comparisons and other formalisms which
is operating in the box only acquires a meaning at the point when it is 'output' as moving graphics on the screen. The screen invites the user to act, and
the user's actions influence, via the formal mechanics in the box, the image
that appears on the screen, and these changes in turn invite the user to act.
To a certain extent the world on the screen is autonomous. Not only is there
no link with an exterior transmitter, but what appears on the screen is not
predicted by the programmer, or at least cannot be predicted.[3] Programme
formalisms such as fuzzy logic and genetic algorithms can bring unpredictable images to our screens. What is more, the images are easily surveyable,
unlike most formalisms that generate the image. Read the euphoric report
by Richard Dawkins in *The Blind Watchmaker* about the mutations which his

44) The movies and the telephone have always had a fatal attraction for each other. France Telecom celebrated the 1996 centenary of the cinema with special edition phone cards: here Jeanne Moreau shares an intimate moment with an electronic chip.

45) The new synergy of television, personal computer and the telephone. Will a simple set-top box turn the domestic television set into a multi-media workstation? Technologically it is possible, yet the pundits are still divided over whether the great public really wants to play and work from the armchair and the couch.

primitive graphic insects underwent in subsequent generations. According to the author, these creatures are not created, but discovered. In the process of observing artificial life, the user experiences what appears on the screen as real, precisely because it is not provided by somebody, not thought out by somebody, but quite simply *is*. There is a Russian artificial life programme that generates unpredictable, moving fish in a sort of underwater world. The programme turns the box into an aquarium, a kind of 'telefishion'.

The emancipation of the computer screen goes even further. Data visualisation with the aid of moving images and sound is becoming an indispensable tool in providing an insight into complex processes, such as weather systems or ecosystems. I recently read an article with the arresting title 'The Death of Proof', which contained a description of how formal proof in mathematics was also being infiltrated by computer visualisation.[4] In mathematics, that bastion of formal truth *par excellence*, computer-aided experimental research has been going on for some time now. Fermat's famous last theorem was recently proven, and the proof covered two hundred pages. And this kind of proof is set to grow in the future, bringing about a decrease in the number of people to whom it is available. As a result, so-called 'video proofs' will play a much more central role and it does not seem impossible that they could replace formal proofs in some cases. In such cases the screen is not reproducing or transmitting something external. It has become a reality in itself, with a truth that cannot be traced back to something else – neither to a world in front of the camera nor to an accessible formal world behind the screen. The screen has become a game-maker.

Random Access Rules

Grahame Weinbren

It is 1981. They show me a videodisc. They explain what it is and how it works. And I realize that the language, the possibilities, the significance of cinema is forever changed. This is how it is: cinema communicates on the basis of one frame following another. First, frame sequence gives us the illusion of motion (because of 'the persistence of vision' or some such phenomenon), then the sequences of moving pictures demand sequencing themselves. Shot sequence; then a defined, determinable relationship of image to sound. And in the shrieks of Herrman's violins against Anthony Perkins' upraised knife/cut to the swinging lightbulb/cut to Janet Leigh's face ... we get cinema. Our stomachs tighten, we feel something, there in the dark, and everyone around us, to a greater or lesser degree, feels the same thing. The power of this medium! And they all agree, from David Bordwell to Stephen Heath to Siegfried Kracauer to Slavoij Zizek, from Thorold Dickinson to Sergei Eisenstein to Veselvod Pudovkin (not to mention the filmmakers), that a necessary condition of the power of cinema is ...

... montage.
What do all the great commercial filmmakers want? Do they insist on writing the script? Or even rewriting it? No. The final cut. Control over the edit. For in the edit is the language, the meaning, the music, the emotion, the expressivity of the medium.

Give up control of image sequence and you give up the cinema we know.
Videodisc is now an outdated, passé vinyl disc. It is too big for the late 1990s. Like an LP. It stores its data in analogue fashion (microscopic pits in the plastic surface), for one thing, and, for another, you cannot fit a videodisc player into the housing of a standard computer. Its light grey prismatic surface and 12 inch diameter even look old. Like those spinning tops that use hologram techniques to make patterns hover above them as they spin. But the digital media (at this point anyway ... we haven't seen DVD yet) offer limited motion, inferior little images in a fraction of the monitor screen. Images are already inferior on monitors compared with light projected through transparent celluloid. Not even fast enough (in frames per second) to give a real 'persistence of vision', the irony of the product name 'Quick Time' is lost in the babble of hype, the chatter of metaphors for leisure and

freedom and non-accountability that pepper the world of computer technology. Quick Time movies are slow and inferior. It is hard to imagine them
carrying the power of the cinematic in their stopwatch-sized rectangles.

The videodisc made it possible for the images embedded in its surface to
appear in sequences other than that in which they are recorded. Instead of
having to go through frames 1 to 100 to reach frame 101 – the serial access
imposed by videotape or film – with a videodisc we can first display frame
101, then frame 6, then frame 14, etc. The videodisc gives us, through the
computer control of a videodisc player, random access to each image in the
sequence. So the sequence of images can be determined at presentation
time, rather than during the process of production. Suddenly the viewer can
have some control over the montage.

Pathways through a landscape

If it is true that montage is at the center of cinematic meaning, this potential
shift in control has profound significance. The interactive filmmaker's task
becomes that of producing a set of film materials and plotting some pathways through it. The viewer then follows the pathways, deviating or continuing in a line as the mood takes him. The filmmaker becomes more the
designer of a pattern of trails through a landscape of images, less the tour
bus driver. And maybe, in the process, the filmmaker gives up controlling
what his work means – or, alternatively, the nature of cinematic meaning is
transformed in the process.

What can a system of pathways through a moving image landscape be
like? And what kind of image set can be mapped in this way? What kinds of
vehicle do the explorers of this landscape use? To what extent are the pathways paved and laid, to what extent are they tracks we cut with a virtual
machete, as opposed to open landscapes traversed by all-terrain vehicles?

For the last 15 years, I have attempted practical answers to these questions, in a series of what I call 'interactive cinema' installations. In my pieces,
the landscapes are composed of narrative and music, the pathways through
them montage sequences plotted before a viewer enters, and the vehicles of
exploration are touch screens, frames to point through, and surfaces to walk
on, while the windows into the depicted world are monitors or projection
screens. By far the most difficult issue I have taken on has been that of developing a structure or shape for the interactive narratives, a narrative architecture that requires that a viewer explore it rather than experience it from a
(literal and/or metaphorical) sitting position. *The question of who retains control over what the piece is saying comes up at every turn* – it is possible that as an
artist one might disagree with the overall sense of one's own work.

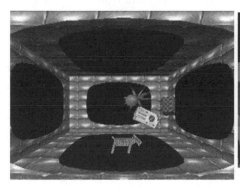 

The interactive filmmaker's task becomes that of producing a set of film materials and plot-ting some pathways through it. There can be very simple signs or very complex systems as the works of Perry Hoberman 'Bar Code Hotel' (this page), John F. Simon Jr. 'Thick and Thin' (p. 237; see also p. 239), Grahame Weinbren 'Sonata' (p. 233, top right) and Ken Feingold 'JCJ-Junkman' (p. 233, top left) are showing.

Though the breakthroughs in the use of computers in communication is often described as a 'digital' revolution, I believe that for cinema, if not for other communication forms, the more fundamental breakthrough is in random access to data. Digitization in the movies has brought about a remarkable series of changes in the production and manipulation of images, so that many things look photographic even though they are created without a lens anywhere in the production path. *But nothing achieved on the basis of digitization is different in kind from what was created before binary encoding of images and sound: the new material is simply better.*

The most important social effect of the digitization of images is in the photographic image's epistemological status. The fact that the photographic is indistinguishable from the non-photographic changes the status of photograph as evidence. Photographs are no longer indicators of the truth of what they depict, a change that we have yet to adjust to. To take an obvious example: the effect that the shifting truth status of the photograph will eventually have on the porn industry is mind boggling. When the consumer can no longer fantasize along the causal chain of photographic reproduction back to the events or physical relationships represented in the image, the erotic potential of pornographic images will fizzle. But the epistemological shift hasn't sunk in yet. Not even on the internet – though photographs where the digital manipulation is not subtle enough are quickly condemned.

Digitization has streamlined and automated production processes, ena-bling detailed and repetitive work that twentieth century human beings do not have the patience, the attention to microscopic detail, the ability to re-peat precise tasks, in a word: the time for. But the binary encoded image re-mains an image, produced by the same class of techniques, with the same look and the same way of representing reality; but with a shifted truth-status.

The film JUMANJI, for example, could not have beeen made without com-puter generated imagery, and the special effects in that film (of a wild ani-mal stampede, for example) are absolutely convincing. However, this represents no more than a difference in degree from what was achieved without computers: for example in STAR WARS in 1977 or KING KONG in 1936. Without doubt the effects in the STAR WARS remake are much more spec-tacular, as were the explosions of INDEPENDENCE DAY and the robots of TER-MINATOR 2. But it is better, not different. In contrast, *random access brings about a different cinema*: a cinema different in what it can say and how it says it, in the manner it represents reality and the aspects of reality it can repre-sent.

De-emphasizing the sequence of the images

To repeat: random access allows the sequence of images to be determined at the time of presentation, rather than fixed during the production process. This implies that the viewer, by some method or another, or other external factors (weather conditions, the time, the sound level in the viewing space ... the possibilities are endless), can determine the sequence. Obviously, a work that makes use of this potential needs a structure, a shape, an architec-ture, a content that can benefit from it.

The structure of a film is determined by the sequence of its elements. But if sequence is an aspect of the film no longer determined by the filmmaker, what kind of structure is available? If the author of a work is to retain his authority, sequence must be de-emphasized since it is an aspect of the expe-rience that the filmmaker, to a greater or lesser degree, is passing on to the viewer.

So the first structural issue is to find a cinematic or narrative form that de-emphasizes sequence. In an earlier paper,[1] I referred to the dream inter-pretations of Freud as examples of narrative structures that make the same sense and have the same narrative effect whatever the sequence in which they are recounted. In psychoanalysis, the analysand is deeply committed to the construction of narrative, but the order in which the elements of the narrative arrive in the psychoanalytic dialogue, though not random, is cer-tainly determined by factors extraneous to the story-structure. Freud insists

that the elements of the dream are present, all at once, and that the sequencing necessitated by the linearity of writing adds an imprecision to the description of the dream-analysis: '[The] task [of forming a synthesis from fragments that emerge in the analysis of a patient ...] finds a natural limit when it is a question of forcing a structure which is itself in many dimensions onto the two-dimensional descriptive plane. I must therefore content myself with bringing forward fragmentary portions, which the reader can then put together into a living whole.'[2]

A problem with a text already organized into a linear structure, especially when the writer is someone who handles prose as delicately as Freud, is that it is difficult, if not impossible, to 'put together a living whole' that diverges in sense or interpretation from the text presented. Freud's brilliant organization of his material into narrative blocks, replete with drama, suspense and surprise, presupposes a particular set of criteria as to what counts as successful dream analysis. Without Freud's 'reading', and subsequent writing of the associations produced by his patient, it is unlikely that a casual reader would place the sighting of parental copulation at the center of the analysis of the Wolf Man's gorgeous dream image of staring white wolves sitting in a walnut tree. The heuristic that Freud wishes to communicate in his analyses may easily be lost in a hypertextual version of the case history, where the weights accorded to the various elements of the interpretation would be equalized. So, in the spirit of the Freudian tradition, there is something of a split between what Freud says he wishes for and the putative results of his wish being fulfilled. On the other hand, there is much to be said for the idea of transferring to the reader the burden of coming to a general interpretation of a set of image/sound/textual material.

Another advantage secured by presenting the non-sequenced narrative as a tightly wound ball of data to be unwoven through interaction is that the sense of simultaneity is preserved. As viewer, the very fact that I have produced an element implies that its logical or expressive or evidentiary weight is equal to that of another element that I might have accessed. It is my action that pulled this piece of data out now, so its significance is no greater than the piece I pull out instead, the piece I pull out next. The burden of making relationships between the parts of a work has shifted from author to viewer.

An interactive Narrative?

But does eliminating fixed sequence eliminate narrative? Narrative is, after all, story-telling, not a database; and stories lead to closure – some narratologists believe that stories are structured by closure – which implies a linearity of temporal structure. The negative answer to this question can only be demonstrated practically, by making a work that proves the point. And this is what I have taken on as my general project as an artist. Through my work I want to say: ... *yes, we can have a narrative that is essentially interactive, that respects the necessity of closure for story-telling, and shifts the responsibility for its overall temporality from the maker to the viewer.*

Non-specific sequence is one instance of the more general notion of non-linearity. With non-linearity comes a dynamic between the viewer's time with the piece (which in any single session is, by definition, linear and continuous), and the space of the work, which is probably in some sense continuous. The viewer's experience will be of a narrative that in its representation of a fictional world is interrupted and affected by its viewers. To repeat – I have conceived my task as an artist as discovering or inventing depicted worlds that demand representation non-linearly – either because they are multi-faceted and must be looked at from many angles, or because the temporal flow is non-sequential.

In my work there is always a fixed database of material to be traversed in various ways determinable by a viewer, and this results in a temporally non-linear representation playing against the linear time of the viewer's experience. Because I am by temperament a filmmaker, my major interest is to create audiovisual data, then plot pathways through it. The viewer accesses the material along my pathways, which can be quite variable because multiple elements can be brought into play at any moment – e.g. all kinds of audio, including music, sound effects and voices, treated as independent malleable entities, separate from visual material; images, which can be combined in the space of the screen, or follow one another, played slow or fast or frozen; and text, that can at any moment be superimposed over images. This is a very rich palette, and can lead to a broad range of expressive possibilities. There is a section in SONATA, for example, where Tolstoy's anti-hero wife-killer Podsnyshev returns home from a trip to find his wife playing *The Kreutzer Sonata* with the violinist he suspects is her lover. Podsnyshev listens in the next room while he goes about his routine tasks – correspondence, bills, his diary, exercises. But the emotion of the music has such an intense effect on his mental state that he eventually bursts into the music room and stabs his wife to death. The scene is played so that a viewer can see either the calm, focused performance of the musicians or the frenzied activity of the husband.

In the recent version of SONATA the physical setup is a frame through which viewers look at a projected image. If the viewer points a finger through this frame, it interrupts a grid of infrared beams, and it is this pointing that provides the interface for the piece. In the music/murder scene, the viewer can determine what percentage of each room is seen on screen. Wherever a viewer points, the image is divided with a soft edge, on one side of which can be seen the activity in the music room, on the other the crazed jealous husband, pacing distractedly in his study. Pointing to the upper left of the screen jumps the action forward to the moment when the husband roars into the room and stabs his pianist-wife to death. Both the music-playing and Podsnyshev's activities continue, irrespective of what is shown on screen, but the composition of the image (in crude terms, what percentage of each scene is on screen) is determined by the viewer. In this instance, I have provided image materials for this dramatic scene, but the montage (i.e. what is seen at any moment) is determined by the viewer. Narrative time is always moving forward, and a viewer is always aware of the imminent closure, which he or she can activate with a single gesture. The tension between the activity in the two spaces portrayed, and the fact that the more you see of one room the less you see of the other, motivates the viewer to constantly change the scene arrangement, and kindles a sense of tension similar to that attributed to the protagonist. This is a kind of expression that can only be accomplished by means of interactivity, which connects the viewer with the jealous rage felt by the protagonist in a way that is not possible within the confines of traditional cinema.

For SONATA I provide all the audiovisual materials, and plot a network of potential montage paths through them. Viewers navigate through the piece along these montage paths. However, it is important to understand that there is always a sense of continuity as the image changes, achieved by the same kinds of technique that are used in film editing. My system of equipment allows me to treat sound and image as separate elements, so that sound can change while video continues, or (more commonly) vice versa.

The sound (music or dialogue) often continues while the image changes because of viewer input, giving a sense of fluidity to the experience and continuity to the narrative. Relying exclusively on random access does not imply that one must move through a piece in clunky quickstep.

Aesthetics of interactive works

Certainly there is a type of interactive work that depends exclusively on random access – usually with unpleasant results. The viewer of such a work is invited to make a choice from a menu of possibilities. The machine then delivers that material to the screen – it might be video, audio, text, or image files. Ken Feingold has compared this kind of interactivity to a candy machine. You put in your money, press a button, and the machine spits out the chocolate bar of your choice. The question is whether this model even deserves the designation 'interactive'. Feingold parodies this kind of work in his recent CD piece, *JCJ-Junkman* produced for the ArtIntact series of the ZKM Karlsruhe.[3] As we move further toward applications that have some expressive potential, we find that we need increasingly to use the power of the machine either to transform materials coded digitally or to combine materials in real time.

SONATA uses an analogue video switcher/mixer device to combine video materials, because at this time analogue methods are still cheaper and more efficient than digital. In this case, effects that are easily accomplished for stills by the use of a digital image editor like Photoshop, can be better achieved for video in real time by a controlled manipulation of the video signal. Whether the effects require electronic manipulation of binary coded data or of variable waveforms is irrelevant – the point is that manipulation of the image in real time is necessary to achieve the effect. The line between travel through a database and transformation of an image-set has been partially erased. And here comes the digital again. For in interactivity, the concept of digitization allows the possibility of the formation of new materials by a user.

This is a very different concept of interactivity – it gives the viewer tools or an environment in which to work, an environment which generates materials according to rules described in advance by the maker. Now we are not exploring an already existent dataspace, where the paths through the material and the nature of the data are the fundamental aesthetic issue – no, here we are in a world in which the user, in collaboration with the maker, creates something that the maker may not have predicted (though if it is based on algorithms or formulae, it is at least mathematically, if not intuitively, predictable). Now we have an idea of an artist making a pencil that can only draw in a certain way – what a future draughtsman will draw with

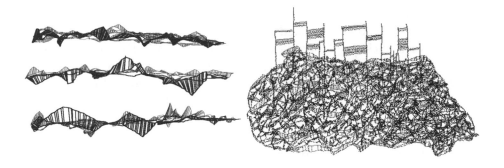

that pencil is unpredictable, though it is contained in the mathematical possibilities of the pencil. The virtual reality artist describes the rules of a navigable depicted space: how people will move through it is not known by the artist in advance. Consider the funny and original Bar Code Hotel, developed by Perry Hoberman between 1992 and 1994 at the Banff Center. His objects (teddy bears, paper clips, cheese wedges, bread loaves) move around the virtual space, under the control of the bar code wands of the users in the room. The artist's work is to plot the objects' behaviours, define the limits of the space, determine what happens when they collide, etc, etc, so that all possibilities are accounted for. Then exactly what happens within the space is unrestricted, algorithmically determined but quite unpredictable.[4]

The electronic artist John F. Simon Jr. has created several works that are paradigmatic in this respect, in that they enable the user to operate and create images , working within a space algorithmically defined by the artist. One of his projects is a set of digital brushes that can be used as tools for making images on a computer. The brushes are complex and fantastic, allowing the production of drawings with relatively few strokes of the stylus or mouse. The software is a delight to use, and the user quickly and easily produces interesting images. The odd thing is that in using one of these brushes one almost always seems to make a drawing that resembles one of John Simon's. In this way the project, apparently to provide a set of tools, in fact enables the artist who made the tools to practice his craft, generating his own images using the hands (and computers) of other people. It is as if Simon has made a machine to increase his output. Of course the question of authorship may be raised, especially if value or copyright gets attached to the work, but that is a separate issue. The project has a familiar ring to it, like a fairy tale in which a device that apparently does something for its finder in fact works in the interest of the person who misplaced it.[5]

Incidentally, I have suggested elsewhere that the most popular multimedia software package, Macromedia Director, is similar in this respect: it brings a conception of interactivity or 'multimedia' into every project it is used for. It is a conception of interactivity, centered around 'buttons' and a notion of 'choice' that I find deeply problematic. Advanced users of the software, of course, trick it, or bend it at least, into doing what they want it to do: but novice users repeat the same structure again and again. The difference is that in Simon's case, the brushes are conceived as limited tools to make a certain kind of drawing by making a certain kind of mark (he refers to Paul Klee on drawing and the nature of the line), while Macromedia Director is marketed as an all-purpose creative tool.

The Poetics of the Open Work

I find in Simon's project many parallels with the music works by Berio, Stockhausen, Pousseur, and Boulez, as described by Umberto Eco in his trailblazing essay 'The Poetics of the Open Work'. Each of these works has the form of a set of instructions that leaves open a number of factors usually considered essential to musical composition – the sequence of musical elements, for example, or the pitch or tempo or rhythm of notes played within the clearly defined framework. In the works described by Eco, it is the performer of the music that responds to the score and determines the form of the piece – in the work by John Simon, it is the user of the brushes that determines the final picture. In both cases the limits are clearly defined so that the authorship of the work is never in doubt, though performer in the case of the composers, and user in Simon's case, have much more control over the actual output than is usually the case in the production of art. Naturally there are exceptions and degrees of this, with John Cage in his most radical moments at one end of the scale, and jazz as a musical form which depends on improvisation at the other end.

> If a musical pattern no longer necessarily determines the immediately following one, if there is no tonal basis which allows the listener to infer the next steps in the arrangement of the musical discourse from what has physically preceded them, this is just part of a general breakdown in the concept of causation. [...] Multi-valued logics are now gaining currency, and these are quite capable of incorporating indeterminacy as a valid stepping-stone in the cognitive process. [...] From Mallarmé's *Livre* to the musical compositions we have considered, there is a tendency to see every execution of

the work of art as divorced from its ultimate definition. Every performance explains the composition, but does not exhaust it. Every performance makes the work an actuality, but is itself only complementary to all the other performances of the work. In short, we can say that every performance offers us a complete and satisfying version of the work, but at the same time makes it incomplete for us, because it cannot simultaneously give all the other artistic solutions which the work may admit.[...]

The possibilities which the work's openness makes available always work within a given field of relations. As in the Einsteinian universe, in the 'work in movement' we may well deny that there is a single prescribed point of view. But this does not mean complete chaos in its internal relations. What it does imply is an organizing rule which governs these relations. Therefore, to sum up, we can say that the 'work in movement' is the possibility of numerous different personal interventions, but it is not an amorphous invitation to indiscriminate participation. The invitation offers the performer the opportunity for an oriented insertion into something which always remains the world intended by the author.

If one replaces the terms 'performer' with 'viewer' in the above passage, Eco's ideas about the place of the author can easily be reapplied to interactive works, and his general ideas are a useful way to contextualize interactivity within a larger cultural framework.

I have described interactive works of two kinds: the first based on the possibility of random access to material in a database, the second on digitization which leads to the computer's transformation of materials in real time. The larger question is: what aesthetic ends can be achieved by interactively exploring a database of material, using the potential offered by Random Access to cinematic materials? What does interactivity give us that we did not have before?

Eco's answer is to describe a world-view underlying the need to develop works of this kind. A less general perspective might suggest that we can portray an aspect of experience that has been missing from our representations, a depiction of the simultaneity of experience. Into the representation of events we can now incorporate our responses and the fact that, in everyday experience, our responses bring about change in what we are responding to. We are, after all, active participants on the world's stage (most of the time). Interactivity has the potential to depict humanness as an active condition.

Electronic Cinema – On the Way to the Digital

Kay Hoffmann

Electronic cinema seems close to becoming a reality. During the last few years, digitalization has already become an important part of post-production. Bridges have been built between the photographic world of film and the electronic world of video and the computer, two worlds that have stood in opposition to each other like enemy brothers for decades. The problem of transmission of motion pictures via satellite in a high resolution mode is also being solved. Standing in the way of the realization of an electronic cinema has been, most of all, the lack of an adequate and effective method of projecting video signals on a large screen. Such high definition and proficient video beamers have been available in the USA as well as in Europe for some time, and are beginning to come close to the quality of projected film. Usually, one can only tell that the images are electronically generated in that they are so sharply focused. The English film commentator John Chittock goes even further: 'Improvements in the quality of video projection have now reached a point where the results on a cinema-size screen can be indistinguishable from 35mm film. Video projection systems have generally relied upon the use of three cathode ray tubes (red, green and blue) as their light and image source, but new systems have been developed which are no longer limited in their light output by the use of television tubes; in particular, a completely new technology employing microscopic mirrors is now yielding screen brightnesses to rival conventional film projection.'[1]

The disadvantage of these superbeamers is the cost, ranging up to $300,000, but they can be used to transmit and project film in several cinemas simultaneously. The advantages are primarily economic because distributors can save on the high costs of making prints and the inconvenience of transportation. After all, there is something anachronistic about the fact that in the USA, several thousand prints of the same film are still being packed in cans and shipped all over the continent, a realization that also struck George Lucas. He is optimistic that digitization will change the entire film industry: 'Digital technology is the same revolution as adding sound to pictures and the same revolution as adding color to pictures. Nothing more and nothing less.'[2] One the other hand, Lucas is realistic enough to understand that Hollywood is downright conservative when it comes to technological innovation and that technological development lags five years behind. 'Currently, the greatest use of digital technology is not at the big studios but at specialized production houses like Pixar, Digital Domain and Industrial Light and Magic, a unit of Mr. Lucas' privately held Lucas Digital.'[3]

The idea of an 'electronic cinema' is in fact hardly new, appearing again and again since the end of the 1920s during the experimental phase of television. But its realization has always seemed difficult, and in 1955, it was too early for the American historian of technology, Albert Abramson (CBS Hollywood) to be predicting the death of celluloid: 'The cinema has entered the electronic age. The electronic motion picture is a reality. Motion picture production is changing from a mechanical process to an electric one. The film camera is being replaced by the electronic television camera. Motion picture film is being superseded by magnetic tape. Even the motion picture projector is giving way to the large screen electronic reproducer.'[4] Ampex had just presented a two-inch video machine, a huge, stationary piece of equipment with the magnetic tape recording the images on open reels like audio tape. Tapes able to record ninety minutes weighed ten kilograms (22 pounds). Encased video cassettes were a development which was not introduced until the 1970s.[5] Besides the technical problems, filmmakers had several other reservations; as at most other times, Hollywood remained conservative, adopting an attitude of wait-and-see. Television and film had always perceived each other as bitter competitors and in the process of developing an electronic cinema each side would bide its time.[6]

Then at the Academy Awards Ceremony in 1979, Francis Ford Coppola heralded the coming electronic cinema: 'We're on the eve of something that's going to make the Industrial Revolution look like a small out-of-town tryout. I can see a communications revolution that's about movies and art and music and digital electronics and satellites, but above all, human talent – and it's going to make the masters of the cinema, from whom we've inherited this business, believe things that they would have thought impossible.'[7]

Coppola saw the computer as an opportunity for optimizing the organization of film shoots which would make production more cost efficient, shifting the balance of power toward filmmakers to exert more control over their films and away from the studios, holding the director to ransom with the enormous budgets. Coppola's concept put the computer at the center of production, from writing the first exposé to costing, all the way through the final phases of production. The computer was to centralize and manage all the information relating to the film. The exposé would be developed into a screenplay which would then be expanded with the first sketches, photos of locations or footage from screen tests and rehearsals – filmmaking as a step-by-step evolutionary process. As scenes were filmed, they would be scanned in. This way, it would be possible, for example, for the composer to begin planning the music far earlier. The electronication of production was to make it possible for a director in Hollywood to direct his teams at shoots around the world via satellite. Coppola's film, ONE FROM THE HEART (1982)[8] was to have been the prototype of this innovative movie-making. But at a cost of over thirty million dollars, the production was neither cost efficient nor particularly successful at the box office, taking only one million dollars worldwide. The dream of an electronic cinema had fallen flat once again. Only at the end of the 1980s, after several interesting short films and particularly impressive special effects scenes created with the computer, did interest in such ideas revive.

A similar goal of freeing film production from its industrial production and allowing the director more hands-on control was pursued by George Lucas with STAR WARS. Lucas is one of the *wunderkind* or movie-brat directors of Hollywood in the 1970s who went on to specialize in technical innovation with his company, which today focuses on digitization: 'Instead of making film into a sequential assembly-line process where one person does one thing, takes it, and turns it over to the next person, I'm turning it more into the process of a painter or sculptor. You work on it for a bit, then you stand back and look at it and add some more onto it, then stand back and look at it and add some more. You basically end up layering the whole thing. Filmmaking by layering means you write, and direct, and edit all at once. It's much more like what you do when you write a story.'[9] Such positions are astonishingly reminiscent of auteur cinema but are more commonly associated with the democratization and individual control of new media.

One must keep in mind that Coppola's concept had been powerfully influenced by the medium of video. Although this technology already had a long history going back to at least the 1940s, it would not become interesting other than for professional use in television until the 1970s. Hopes were raised that here was finally a visual medium over which one had individual control and which could be put to democratic use. In the 1970s, there were several euphoric concepts related to a 'television from below', intended to broadcast what was suppressed or could not be seen on official television. At least in Europe, the goal was to create a counter-cultural public and to use video in order to politicize the general public. Brecht's radio concept of the 1920s, the idea that the opposition between the broadcaster and the receiver should be dissolved, seemed possible with video. The simple man in the street was to be given a voice. Such ideas now seem naive, since it was soon becoming clear that people were dependent on the technology that came from the entertainment industry. In retrospect, the alternative video

54) 'Pile them high and sell them cheap' might be the motto of this video-sculpture by Nam Jun Paik, whose ironic commentaries have accompanied the (r)evolution of both television and video for the last three decades.

55) *Cinema has always eyed its rival with suspicion, laughing it off in the 1950s (in musicals like* IT'S ALWAYS FAIR WEATHER*), or unmasking its venality, corruption and manipulations, as in* BROADCAST NEWS *(1987), one of the comparatively rare number of feature films dealing with television.*

groups now appear to have served the industry, testing semi-professional equipment and opening up a market for the new technology. In this respect, their influence on making new forms of television and video presentable as a production technology for professional broadcasters cannot be underestimated. Of all the various video technologies in the 1970s, VHS, the worst of them in terms of quality, was to win out, backed by the Japanese company JVC/Matsushita and defeating its rivals Sony and Philips. Attempts at the end of the 1970s to replace VHS with video disks as the optimal image storage system also failed. However, since the early 1980s, when the major studios gave up their initial hesitation and began to exploit the potential of movies on tape, video has become, despite all its potential, a mere storage medium of pure entertainment product, effortlessly finding its place in the chain of film exploitation between the run in the cinema and the television broadcast. In the theatre outlets, selection has been skewed in such a way that, further down the line in all three media, the blockbuster principle reigns: a few large-budget films such as FORREST GUMP (1993), INDEPENDENCE DAY (1995), or THE LOST WORLD (1997), have become so dominant in the market that, thanks to huge advertising budgets and clever marketing techniques, there is little space for anything else. In Europe, American films maintain a 70% to 80% market share. At the same time, these marketing efforts have long since reached beyond the 'classic' media, so that the action heroes and branded goods are also present in the form of CD-ROMs, as video games or on the Internet, just as they are in theme parks and amusement arcades around the world. This multimedia exchangeability is made easier by digitization, but its not its primary cause.

The feature film is the determining factor in the movie and video business. On television, although it also plays an important role, the astronomic rise in the cost of broadcast rights in recent years has given a boost to nationally oriented and home-produced series, which are taking on an ever greater role for domestic European television. A formal comparison of these three audiovisual media shows that video, the latest among them, occupies a strangely vacillating position between cinema and television. It has barely managed to develop its own unique qualities, besides its ability to record programming and act as convenient storage medium.

Television/Video	Cinema
Small screen	Large screen
Superficiality per image	Information rich
Bad sound (usually)	Optimal sound (usually)
Electronically generated image	Photographic image on film
Electronic signal flow	Image by image
Equipment radiates light	Light is projected through film
View into light	View with light
Use in private space	Use in public space
Program delivery only	Also a social experience
Normal room lighting	Darker room
Secondary, requires little concentration	Primary, all senses involved
Dissipation (usual)	Deepening (usual)
Shows everything smaller	Shows everything larger
Set-up costs for equipment, fees (in Europe) and/or video rental	Price of ticket only

Television	Cinema/Video
Presence in everyday life	Escape from everyday life
Continuous programming	A single experience
Not dependent on number of viewers	Dependent on number of viewers and/or rentals
More national/regional	More international
Oriented to the moment	Not current
Wide range of programming, (information, education, culture and entertainment)	Primarily entertainment
Reality; issues	Fiction; stories
Distance; rational	Identification; emotional
Close-ups, zooms, movement	Establishing shots, tracking shots
Oriented to faces	Oriented to the body
Series	Individual stories
Ahistorical	Historical
Indirect pricing per viewer, (Advertising, cable, etc.)	Direct pricing per viewer
Reasonable monthly fee	High cost per view
No previous knowledge necessary, 'automatic' delivery	Knowledge necessary for selection
Whole society as audience	Targeted audiences

Cinema's qualities as compared to those of television and video have to do
with its character as a public event. After a crisis in cinema in the 1970s and
early 1980s, when many theater owners feared competition from video and
expected losses similar to those suffered when television was introduced,
cinema in the last few years has experienced a genuine renaissance. Both the
number of tickets sold and the amounts invested in these sacred halls have
risen. Part of this development, of course, are the multiplexes that have
sprung up around the world, which, for all their pluses and minuses, have
led to a revitalization of the cinema and reactivated public interest. At the
same time, they have also led to a further polarization of the market in
which a few blockbusters with a high number of prints take the larger por-
tion of the income while smaller and mid-range films and companies are increasingly squeezed out.

On the other hand, the IMAX format, for example, is flourishing. It makes
a unique visual experience possible in that the projected image is three
times as large as the 70mm format and ten times as large as the 35mm image.
This is possible because the large-format image is rotated from its standard
configuration, that is to say horizontally versus vertically, in relation to the
direction of the film. Recently, IMAX has introduced a wide variety of systems, including 3D. The films have, for the most part, been nature and educational films, but occasionally, feature films have been produced as well.
Special theaters with huge screens have been built for the IMAX system, usually located in museums or in leisure or amusement parks, and especially in
the last few years, the founding company has expanded dramatically. Here,
the unique experience is what counts, and even for relatively short informa-
tional films of half or three quarters of an hour, the audiences have been
flocking in. By the summer of 1997, there were more than 150 IMAX theaters
in 22 countries and 50 more are to be opened in the coming years. In 1996
alone, 60 million spectators watched an IMAX film; 500 million since the
founding of the company in 1970. What the example of IMAX clearly shows
is that cinemas with an extraordinary programme can exist in the market if
they can make the projected film a special event.

Since 1995 the German director Edgar Reitz (of HEIMAT fame) has been
head of the European Institute for Cinema in Karlsruhe which deals explicitly with the future of cinema:

> At present, a structural change is occurring which can be compared with the moment
> in which television changed the living and entertainment habits of people so drasti-
> cally. This is the age of digitization. It entails a certain kind of inflationary multiplica-
> tion of all electronic media found in the home. Our living rooms are being
> transformed into literal battlefields of commercial struggles for the time people have.

The meaning of entering into one's own four walls will change into something entirely new. We will not be coming from the outer world and stepping into our own private lives; rather, we will be meeting the world at home. It will be in our living rooms that we first find out what is happening in the world, whose contemporaries we are, what the world in which we live actually is. Things are strangely turning round. Once we used to seek shelter and freedom in the private sphere, now we will soon be seeking shelter outside of our apartments. The world in which stories are told to us, in which the world is newly-invented and not simply factually represented, this world is suddenly outside. We think that the current revolution of cinema is part of this.[10]

Reitz is convinced that in the future, even though movies will be shot on 35mm or 70mm film, the days of making physical copies to be shipped off are numbered. Cinema has only one chance as a 'public event' if it is able to offer an alternative to the media-jammed living rooms. At the moment, it is still an open question as to whether the electronic cinema will truly take place, since, as was noted at the beginning, a large amount of investment is required and much depends on the strategy of the majors, who will decide which and how many films they are willing to distribute electronically. One possible route of entry would naturally be for many theaters to show, along with films, live broadcasts from television, for example, soccer games or car races or elections. In this area, there have already been a few first attempts, but often with technically obsolete equipment. An important question remains whether an electronic cinema would lead to a further concentration on best-sellers and blockbusters, or if it could open niche markets for smaller movies. Taking into consideration the high rate of investment, one cannot be all that optimistic about the cultural variety which many advocates of electronic cinema expect.

Besides the changes in film delivery and cinema exhibition, digitization will in any case lead to new formal qualities. The first successful examples already exist. But attempts at dissolving linear narrative structure and arriving at entirely new content via interactivity – a commonly misused term – have so far not been very successful as a public medium, even as one wonders if interactivity actually has anything to do with cinema. George Lucas, who has also been involved in developing games, sees two entirely different kinds of objects: 'There's games, and there's movies. Movies are storytelling; you tell somebody a story. A game is interactive; you participate in some kind of an event with a lot of other people or with yourself, or with a machine. Those are two different things, and they've been around forever. Games have been here since the Greeks, and so has storytelling.'[11]

The Assault of Computer-generated Worlds on the Rest of Time[1]

Challenges and Opportunities for Documentary Filmmaking in Virtual Reality

Martin Emele

Everyone says that new worlds are opening up everywhere: welcome to cyberspace,[2] a space full of promise, even for documentary filmmakers, especially for documentary filmmakers. Whatever the changes in the mass media in the light of 'virtual reality'[3] and 'nonlinear' forms of communication eventually amount to, these radical developments give us an opportunity to reassess the definitions and categories we have often taken for granted.

As we know, heated debates are currently raging amongst professional documentary filmmakers about the 'reality' of images.[4] Doubts were voiced early, long before the advent of virtual worlds. In contrast to analogue media, for example photo-montage, in digital media manipulative changes can be made without leaving traces which makes the concept of an 'original' suddenly obsolete. As Joachim Paech claims: 'The electronic images are only imitations of the ontologically-based photographic reproduction process of film. This means they have lost the trace which leads from the objects to their developed image in photography and film. The view of the world does not need the objects themselves anymore; it needs the world only as a pretext or energy field for the electronic production of images. The traces of the real world are thereby annihilated.'[5]

While I can see Paech's anxiety, I regard his implict belief in the possible authenticity of a representation as false. In the context of documentary, the film image has always been a construction. In the end it is irrelevant whether the disappearance of the original copy in the digital world means that the changes can no longer be proved, and that it is, by definition, no longer a copy. Notwithstanding the anxious objections of the critics, it is irrelevant that images no longer relate to a model and therefore cannot be taken as sources of originality or truth. Every representation of a real object (whether in painting, photography, topography, three-dimensional reconstruction or in simple verbal description) is characterised by various degrees of changes in the type and amount of sensory data. No object composed of atoms can be reconstituted in its entirety by any medium. The Star Trek 'beamer', the only thing that could really change paradigms, does not yet exist. What has always been the case with the written or spoken word applies today to the digital image, and has applied in the past to the analogue image; the most one can say is that it was wrongly classified when it was put in the 'real life' category. Therefore, we must simply apply 'ars bene dicendi', a good portrayal in the virtual world means working 'well' technically and communicating 'good' ideas: nothing more, nothing less. The modern digital scissors differ from the real scissors of the past simply by their cutting accuracy, but they do not represent a quantitative leap. This said, the belief in an adequate representation of reality (on the part of both the maker and the recipient) is nonetheless still very relevant for mass media communication. I shall return to this point later.

(Virtual) Reality in Documentaries

Horst Bredekamp expresses the matter provocatively: 'There is nothing wrong with the manipulation of images [...] except the expectation that they should be "true".'[6] To use a graphic example: if we could agree on the fact that Geoff Hurst's shot during the 1966 World Cup Final between Germany and England was not behind the goal line (and we should agree, all English football fans please forgive me) – if, in other words, we could agree that the "Wembley Goal" was not a real goal, it would be legitimate to digitally manipulate the image of the ball in the existing film footage and to destroy the original.[7] But let me turn to a more fruitful and less emotionally charged area, in order to clarify the problem of 'documentary and virtual reality': documentation in the field of archaeology.

Archaeology I: The Development of Simulations

According to the film magazine *Premiere*, if the chariot race in BEN HUR were to be shot again today, the set would not be built by 1000 carpenters but by a small team of computer experts: 'Rome wasn't built in a data bank – but soon it will be.'[8] Computers not only make history, they also visualise it. It is instructive to look briefly at the infancy of computer-generated visualisation in the specific field of major TV documentaries; it can help us put in perspective the excitement over what is allegedly 'new'. The object of our scrutiny is the legendary city of Troy.[9]

In 1986 a BBC production made use of the then current tools of television graphics in an attempt to create an image of the vanished city with the help of coloured drawings.[10] They were based on Peter Conolly's children's book drawings,[11] which were animated, using zoom and pan.

In 1989 a simple model, built out of plywood, glue and cardboard, represented the city of Troy in a local German state TV channel programme.[12] Yet a higher level of technology had already been reached: thanks to an endoscope or 'finger' camera, an attempt to recreate the feeling of space was made. The time lapse error produced by this endoscope camera was included in the programme; TV has always been tolerant of mistakes in new technology. The rest of the programme was produced on High-Band SP. Of course, the technical resources of television at that time were way behind Hollywood special effects. Even so, a brief look at the development of production techniques on television is relevant.

As early as 1990, an exemplary production by the Zweite Deutsche Fernsehen (ZDF) proudly showed the first computer animation of the lost city of Troy. These early animations were characterised by simple surfaces, straight lines and strong colours. The images clearly implied that the Hellenic aristocracy of the year 1200 BC lived in shoe boxes or garages. I would hazard a guess that today, students from any design school, however small, could create these kinds of images in one afternoon. At that time, even with sponsorship, a large proportion of the production budget was used for the latest computer animation technology.[13] The expensive and time-consuming little miracle was shown at length, often in stills, because the computer capacity did not yet allow for today's rapid flights and random perspective changes.

It appears we have not yet found an appropriate aesthetic in the area of computer animation. It seems unavoidable that with the development of new technology there will be an initial phase when the technology will dictate the constraints and capabilities of its application. The next step should be the use of this technology by creative people who have successfully wrested the monopoly of understanding the new technology from the technicians. The pace of technological development has so far prevented advances in this next phase.

I have no intention of pleading the case of the good, old, long and long-winded documentary. In the light of most of the virtual worlds presented nowadays in documentaries, one wonders why film has developed a language at all over the past 100 years. Shot and countershot, full shot and close-up are all part of narrative techniques intuitively understood by viewers. In computer animation, it sometimes seems as if these film techniques had not yet been invented. Unfortunately, in my experience, many of the mostly young computer animators appear incompetent, if not illiterate when it comes to film language. They often come from fields like graphics or architecture and start out with no basic knowledge of film form or film narrative.

But bad aesthetics are not as great a problem as the supposed truth content of these artificially-produced images. Interestingly enough, the Troy reconstructions – the drawings, model and computer animation – are all
based on the same source material, i.e. sketches made by an archaeologist in
the 1960s. The viewers' belief that the world of the past really looked like
this is meant to be heightened by the medium used to recreate it – in this
case: from pencil sketches and cardboard models to computer animation.
The higher the technological level used for the reconstruction, the stronger
the belief in its authenticity. Surprisingly, this applies both to the audience
and the creators, and even more paradoxically, scientists, too, fall for the
magic of a near-perfect visualisation of images of the past, and are suscepti-
ble to the belief in the seeming infallibility of the computer. This is only logical in the light of the commentary from the above example of the first
primitive 3-D construction: 'The computer has reconstructed King Priam's
citadel for us'.[14] The 'deus ex machina' has become a welcome replacement
for historical depth. Of course, the computer does not reconstruct anything.
Where exactly is the 'citadel' in which 'King Priam', who is primarily an invention of Homer's, is supposed to have lived? The apparently objective,
neutral computer is used as a substitute for the 'expert authority', so often
quoted and misquoted by the mass media. The computer becomes an ideal-
ised and idealising machine for the one-dimensional television world. At
this point, computers represent 'infinite potential', they embody 'objective'
values, and simultaneously have an almost magical aura, changing history
by their natural yet artificially embedded 'virtual reality', making us forget
what a precarious illusion the belief in an actual image of the past finally is.
Homer's listeners of the spoken story were more aware than the tv viewer
today of one important thing, namely that imagination of the past is always
a projection. When it comes to technologically produced representations,
many people do not seem to have realised this yet.

The belief in the authenticity of the invented computer images is, however, only one of the problems with computer animation. The more is visualised, the more space has to be filled with images. If, for example,
archaeologists only know about part of a vanished city, they can either
show blank space for the rest of it or invent houses. Both options are dubi-
ous. Often only a tiny proportion of the material which is needed to reconstruct a picture of a settlement is available. To build a whole city out of this
would be the same as reconstructing a 1000-piece puzzle from only one
piece.[15] Surfaces have to be invented where only the structure of a wall is
known. Roofs are usually entirely fabricated. To take one example: in the reconstructed rooms of the central Anatolian city of Çatal Höyük – a simulation I am working on at the Staatliche Hochschule für Gestaltung in

Karlsruhe – the head of the accompanying excavation wanted more living elements. He wanted pigs running around. We could have reconstructed the size and weight of the pigs from bones found at the site, but the idea stalled over the question of whether to have pink pigs or wild, black pigs. We didn't know the pigs' skin colour, and didn't want to restrict the viewers' imagination.

In fact, the question of colour is often not taken into account. This means that the development in colour representation has lagged behind. Computer reality faces exactly the same problem as painters faced earlier. Only a limited number of colours are available (the number is estimated at 32768 colours, the amount that the monitor and the programme are capable of generating and displaying). But this is nothing new for the makers of analogue films. The colour of their world was always dependent on the temperature of light, on filters and on white balance. For a red tone, Kodak film stock was used, and for a green tone, Fuji stock.

Archaeology II: Documentation as Projection

If the world of the monitor becomes too concrete, we no longer see other possibilities. We know that there is, above all, a correspondence between the images we don't see and those we imagine. In many instances digital visualisation forces an 'on' image where an 'off-screen' suggestion could be much more effective. Permanent computer animation input also leads to the fading of historic time and place. The actual feeling of an archaeology film, the historical dimension, disappears. A few years ago filmmakers were still faced with a big problem when they stood on an empty field where a city was supposed to have once existed. In those distant times sound and image collages were used. Paintings and stories tried to make clear that this was the site of something 'past'. Today the scene flickers in greater or lesser perfection over the screen, the past is with us again thanks to video stanzas. History becomes concrete, real, no longer bound by time and space. This is the real attack of a computer-generated world on the rest of time.

The attempt to visualise the past reveals the limits of material objects or, rather, the limits of the depiction of material objects, especially in the area of archaeology. To return to the subject of Troy: nothing but dust and dry stones, meaningless except for a particular group's belief in its history which is indeed authenticated by the stones. Whether the wall surrounding Troy is drawn, photographed, or digitalised, whether it is real or felt through a cyberspace glove, only true knowledge can fill in the gaps left by our limited sensory perception. It is the level of technology that determines the degree to which the producer can interpret the dense past. Notably, the two extremes – hand drawing and virtual reality – are usually regarded as providing a complete interpretation, while the analogue and digital steps, although selective, actually yield a higher percentage of peripheral information and include more of the total context without, however, being more objective.[16] 'Cyberspace can be seen as a new manifestation of Kant's instruction to understand the world as a projection of our consciousness. Metaphors not only apply to the represented world, but also provide valid criteria for differentiating between various levels of reality which reveal themselves to our senses in varying degrees and in different ways.'[17] Virtual reality is thus not a new media reality but instead offers a new opportunity to understand the medium. The new technology enables us to redefine the place of the medium in the symbolic order of society.

The British archaeologist Ian Hodder is attempting to incorporate this kind of knowledge in his daily work. According to him, the seemingly fixed departure point of every archeological interpretation, i.e. the material relics, is in fact influenced by the method of the dig and even created by it. In other words, the excavator finds what he expects to find. In Hodder's words: 'Interpretation occurs at the trowel's edge.'[18] In the end it is a question of interpretation whether an artefact 'exists' or not:

> Micro-artefacts may only be recovered because of full water screening of 'floor' contexts. The same artefact from a 'fill' would have less chance of recovery and might simply 'not exist'. Thus the objective existence of an artefact as 'data' depends on the interpretation that has been made prior to and during excavation.[19]

Archaeology III: CHAMP

Ian Hodder is head of the excavation at the Central Anatolian site of Çatal Höyük, a neolithic hill settlement in the heights of Konya, 250 km south-east of Ankara. Çatal Höyük is regarded as the oldest and largest neolithic town which has yet been discovered. The population numbered several thousand. Çatal Höyük has excited great interest, mainly due to the discovery of art objects worked with a file in sophisticated living quarters. It was also the first settlement to trade with distant regions. Examples of the earliest metalwork and evidence of large animal farming have been found there. The quality of the art objects, as well as the obvious importance of women in the community, are further factors which give the excavation site an international reputation. CHAMP – the Çatal Höyük Achaeology and Multimedia Project – is an interdisciplinary project run jointly by the University of Cambridge and the Staatliche Hochschule für Gestaltung in Karlsruhe (HfG). Its origin and future state could be described as follows: The HfG's director, Heinrich Klotz first realized his concept of visualising historic architectural ensembles using scale models at the German Museum of Architecture in

Frankfurt, the sister institution of the HfG. At his suggestion, the Zentrum für Kunst und Medientechnologie Karlsruhe (ZKM) began in 1992 to produce the first three-dimensional computer animations of Çatal Höyük. CHAMP was then developed by the film department at the HfG, headed by Lothar Spree. In 1995 the Karlsruhe team began the first complete documentation of the excavation and analysis at the archaeological site of Çatal Höyük, with a number of students taking turns to collect the audiovisual information at the dig throughout the excavation.

Visualization is one of the most important, but also one of the most problematic aspects in the production of modern knowledge. One of the tasks of the documentation team is the day-by-day recording of the work done and the progress made at Çatal Höyük. Members have to be on the alert at all times, recording on request or selecting scenes from the daily work routine which might be of interest to scientists or a wider public. However, any other events that might turn out to be important have also to be recorded. Group discussion in the trenches and individual accounts of excavation progress and laboratory work are taped on video to assess the course of excavation and special problems or questions as they arise. Interviews with the various scientists given at various stages of their work and research are also recorded. In this way, team members can point to any information they consider relevant, debates can be captured and illustration provided. In the on-site laboratory these videos are digitised, edited into short clips and stored on the database with attached key-words. The database can thus be used to retrieve not only field descriptions, Autocad drawings, artefact locations and diary information for any particular unit, but also to keep on video the unit, its discoveries and interpretations. The editing process is of course selective, but the visual documentation always comprises more 'peripheral' information than texts and includes more of the surrounding context within which team members are working and interpretations made.

The aim of CHAMP is to link video and 'virtual' computer reconstructions with archaeological data for the first time in an integrated database which will enhance scientific understanding of archaeological sites, as well as offering a representation of our cultural heritage to a wider audience, while developing new forms of long-term documentation in the new media and the 'virtual museum'. The multifunctional CHAMP database should provide a general resource of reusable digitised content. The database for the wider public will work on the basis of three-dimensional reconstructions. It will be possible to 'walk around' the virtual site. Links are provided from particular objects or people to other levels, for example to the biography of the site excavator. Information is also given about the history of the site, construction details and the history of the excavation. In the virtual room one can not only move around in three dimensions but also change from one time zone to another. In this respect, it is a four-dimensional database. The observer can change his or her position and the period of viewing at any time. The user can pick up objects at the place they were originally found, turn them over and examine them for details. Access is also given to all data which was collected on this find, for example forms, descriptions, videos, discussions, scientific lectures. The CHAMP database should be usable in various media (Internet, CD, realtime machine) and starting from various degrees of knowledge. Internet users can call up information on the excavation.[20] In one particular section, all the scientific data is accessible, so that project assistants throughout the world can work directly with the computer in Cambridge. In the discussion room of the virtual museum of the ZKM – also on the World Wide Web – it will be possible in the near future to chat with other virtual visitors or to join an online lecture about Çatal Höyük.

So much for the description of our aims and the results we have obtained on the project. Yet as Ian Hodder rightly says: 'Simply to introduce new technologies is clearly insufficient [...]. The technologies perhaps provide an opportunity rather than a solution.'[21]

Documentation in Virtual Reality

The aim of CHAMP is a multi-media database with the largest possible access for the public as well as the largest possible amount of reflexivity, contextuality, interactivity and multivocality. In four words: *documentation in virtual reality*. Even if this multimedial nonlinear documentation has not yet fully matured in practice, the possibilities as well as the problems are already apparent. On the one hand, there is Ian Hodder's requirement to fully and comprehensively record digging progress and decision process in the group on video. The permanent video documentation, daily digitalisation, editing and incorporating into the video database have 'become very central to our methodology. Not only do the videos allow later critique and evaluation of the construction of data on site, but they also lead to a greater information flow about interpretation (as people listen to each other live or on playback in the laboratory) and a greater readiness to submit one's own assumptions to scrutiny. As members of the team pointed out, the ever-present eye of the camera means that thought processes are much more out in the open.'[22]

As well as the head of the excavation's comment on the epistemological processes, implying that they may be affected by the presence of the medium, such a comprehensive record is both the basis and the precondition for every nonlinear audiovisual documentation which deserves the name.

But the 'ever-present eye of the camera' does not only conjure up the Orwellian nightmare, it also produces practical problems. The price for the reflexivity and the desired multivocality is the dilemma of selection – the traditional job of the documentary filmmaker – as well as the problem of how to deal with the multiplicity of reality (and the levels of reality), leading to a constant expansion of variants and an exponential rise in 'data'. Inevitably, this makes excessive demands on the students who are doing the recording work at the site, as well as on the processing possibilities. Not only do they have to do the audiovisual recording, they also have to feed the scientific data into the computers at the site house. Even on an uneventful day, an eight-hour shift at the excavation site requires a multiple processing time in order to distil some levels and time excerpts of this 'reality' and make them available in the multimedia database.

Supposing it were possible to create such a multi-layered data or data file, how could the information be made available to the user? In the realm of nonlinear multimedia documentation there exists the ideal of a relatively 'neutral', 'self-learning' database, assuming an equal neutrality concerning the intentions of the authors.[23] Let us take as an example the thousands of digital or digitised photos of each stage. In the established tradition they are labelled by the 'original' authors with subjectively chosen and inevitably limited key-words, such as 'animal bones' or 'Area 15A'. A 'neutral' database can make do with relatively few key-words to start with – content, possible links and information about the data are initially chosen by the original creator; the database, however, can then learn from every user who has looked through the photos – for the sake of argument, let's say – filed under the title 'Sunset'. It might be possible to offer the various user groups different key-words or, via a neuron net or 'Fuzzy Logic Guide', to find an agreed compromise between the author's key-words and the user's key-words. The more variety there is in the user's key-words as compared to the author's, the more the balance, however, shifts in favour of the former. If a user copies the defined images into a file, this file can be given a key-word which can then be fed into the database during the copying of an object. In this way, a 'Sunset' group could be put together. This kind of group or 'trace' can later be made available to other users. It would possibly be very subjective or, from various points of view, even 'wrong' – but what does 'wrong' mean in the context of multivocality?

A possible change in reception must be taken into account between the audience of the traditional documentary film and the user of the multimedia database. The didactic narrative impetus of the documentary film assumes that the viewer is almost uneducated, and that his interest must be awakened. For a nonlinear database, however, the user must be relatively

56) *Traditionally, scale models served to reconstruct buildings of perished cultures such as the legendary city of Troy. Today's computer-simulated total environments may be preferred by television producers, but do they give the viewer an improved experience?*

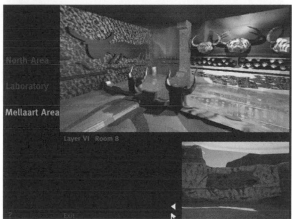

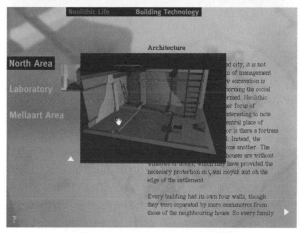

57), 58), 59) Sites and simulations are combined in order to bring the excavations of the neolithic settlements of Catal Höyük to a wider public. Huge databases are assembled, to be accessed and discussed over the Internet. The aim is to get archaeologists, scientists, historians and an interested lay audience together, all of them becoming visitors in a virtual museum.

competent and educated. This potential user must not only have experience with computers, but also a certain level of knowledge of archaeology. In order to interact with the multimedia database it might be necessary to offer the user explanations and tools which facilitate access. This kind of user-instruction functions differently from the classical documentary film, but has the same implications regarding didacticism and suspense. The less knowledge we assume on the part of the potential multimedia recipient, the greater the authorial instruction must be. Nevertheless, it is an absolute must to create a documentation which permanently clarifies its construction : 'The protected observation point outside actual events, which gives us certainty of escape, no longer exists. The time of the detached view of life is over.'[24] Just as in a real museum, the nonlinear documentation in a virtual museum must make possible – and indeed stimulate – the combination of objects. 'From the comparison and the juxtaposition of objects conversations, contradictions and revelatory exchanges can emerge, and from relativism and friction, sparks of meaning can fly.'[25]

For many people the 'virtual world' seems like a way out, the depiction of an object-related three (four) dimensional environment. According to Hodder: 'The intention at Çatal Höyük is also to use virtual reality to provide a non-specialist 'front-end' to the database. Users will be able to 'fly' into the site, into individual buildings, 'click' on paintings or artefacts and so move gradually, if desired, into all the scientific information available in the database.'[26] This kind of organisation would fulfill the claim some theoreticians make of a 'spatialisation' of narrative.[27] Hodder has great expectations for this type of virtuality: 'Potentially, users will be able to move through the site, exploring information, and coming to their own decisions about the 'data'. For example, one of the problems we have at Çatal Höyük is in deciding whether a building is in some sense a 'house'. Rather than accepting our conclusions on this, the data will be available, as far as that is possible, so that users can come to their own conclusions about the definition of a 'house' at Çatal Höyük.'[28]

However, we must be able to ask how far spatial information differs in its structure from the arrangement of a museum before the arrival of virtuality. In the classical educational and preservation rooms of a museum there has always been access to rooms housing various themes. The possibility of 'intuitive' information seeking (entering or not entering various rooms) or 'penetrating deeper into the material' (studying the object or simply reading the caption) has always existed. There was also the opportunity to research in archives and magazines. The old museum is in some of these aspects even superior. As Eckhard Siepmann put it, 'Not only is the object present in its famous authenticity and material form – the sense impression of the "real" room through which the participant moves freely and apprehends through his "body in motion" is also decisive.'[29]

The atomic museum offers possibilities of slowness and reflection through activation of all the senses in a real room, a store for authentic objects in a new context. Only the real artefact is a preservation of human work in material-object form. On the other hand, in the virtual museum there are much wider and more easily accessible work and search possibilities for each visitor. Lifting the object out of the everyday context no longer means taking it out of a glass case,[30] i.e. the declaration of it as a museum piece, but through digitalisation, by putting it into an artificial (and incomplete) everyday context, a virtual room. Yet even this virtual room may allow its visitors free subjective movement and may even activate some, if not all, of the senses. Perhaps it will also lead to the reconstruction of subjectivity which, as we know, enhances perception and stimulates reflection.[31] Who knows, there may even be a 'virtual authenticity' in the secondary world?

With the spatial tendency we always come up against the effect, mentioned earlier in the historical retrospect, of cementing the images of the past, even if it is now only virtual cement. According to Hodder, virtual reality has already proved itself very important 'in providing a deeper understanding of what it could have been like to move around within and between the buildings at the site'.[32] Yet there is a definite danger that we obtain too restricted an image of the past world through virtual reality. Individual excavators have started complaining that they no longer see what is really at the site but already have the computer reconstruction in mind. Yet, if we wanted to offer variations to the design of the rooms (is the two-level room really the only such model or are there two separate layers, one on top of the other?), we would soon find ourselves in a five-dimensional documentation. This would be difficult to use.

Virtual Reality and Documentation

A definite advantage of virtual nonlinear documentation is – whether internet-based or as location-based entertainment – its potential as an event. Television documentaries do not have this status any more, for many reasons, whilst in museums and at exhibitions this potential still exists. The single broadcast is only rarely discussion material for the potential viewer the following day. Programmes are too numerous and varied and the likelihood of a repeat is almost certain. Events on the Internet get talked about and must be consciously chosen. Is there a competent public for this nonlinear documentation which has been feasible for a long time? Is there a corresponding forum? This is also an area for future exploration, and relevant research into acceptance has only just begun.[33]

The competent recipient of the nonlinear documentation would have to be 'eye trained' in the use of icons[34] in order to understand the many layers which fold over one another in the multimedia world. The real and the mediated mingle and penetrate one another on many different levels. Let us take as an example the micro-artefacts from the floating horizon in Çatal Höyük. They are real and authentic objects, yet we can only experience them as signs, invisible except under the electron microscope. Another example: In the Ankara museum we placed a sculpture entitled 'Mother Goddess', a real artefact, on a rotating pedestal and filmed it. The 'real' footage served my computer colleague Burkhard Detzler as a model for a vectoral three-dimensional grid over which the surface from the film was 'pasted'. The finished object in the database represents all possible data, but can also be inserted into a classical film sequence in every position with every movement and form of lighting. If we pan between the glass cases and realise at the editing computer that in the case of the 'Mother Goddess' there is a bad reflection, the computer object can be made to replace the real film object perfectly. An obsidian mirror from Çatal Höyük which has been created in the same way can be turned on the screen by using the mouse. Combined with an integrated camera above the computer screen and an intelligent programme (which specialists still have to write for us) the face of the current user appears as a reflection in the mirror in 'realtime'. This is of course only a feeble replacement for actually feeling the real mirror and seeing the real reflection, but it is still an enticing possibility.

In the light of the 'renewability' of reality in audiovisual documentation, there is a fresh demand for theoreticians and makers to think about appropriate conceptual categories. Genre frontiers have become questionable. We must redefine the boundaries of terms such as 'documentary', 'data', 'simulation' and 'information'. We must define terms such as 'infotainment' and 'info-adventure' more exactly. Consequently, the trust in the material structure and authenticity of the exhibition object must be destabilised. We must reflect on the increasing virtualisation of the world and the hegemonial demands of immaterial signs: 'Since immateriality has begun to define everyday life more and more, our relationship to materiality is changing. Virtual mould is growing unavoidably and irrepressibly over the surface of objects.'[35]

Documentation in virtual reality also means a widening of the context. Future documentary producers must bring together awareness and preparation for an interactivity in the sense that the files on offer (the data and the images) can be questioned and seen from various perspectives. Makers and users must be aware of the central role of interpretation in the whole process of the construction of reality. Widening, but also specifying the context also means guarding against a tendency to individualisation and fragmentation through the current globalisation of the 'information society'. For this, Hodder has coined the phrase 'glocalising'.

The abundance of presentation of virtual reality representations can result in different developments. On the one hand many different virtual museums could be created by different user-groups. This would deprive the author (as well as the researcher and scientist) of power over a part of his work. He invents the playing field and, at the most, the rules of the game. The previous mid-field star becomes the referee. This model requires an active, searching user; the barrier between work and free time, between creativity and consumerism disappears. On the other hand, a passive recipient who listens in boredom to the virtual – linear – narrative may also exist. The question 'What does the future user want?' would lead us far into the field of speculation and demands extensive research. In any case, the reality of the virtual museum dominating in the Cyberspace of the future will reflect the societies which produce it.[36]

Other forms of documentation in virtual reality can be envisaged, though it is not clear whether we should call them experiments or games. Stephen Hudson, a postgraduate student of Colin Shell's research unit in Cambridge, is modelling a definition of communication structures which may have had a strong role in the development of the human race from hunters and gatherers to farmers. His programme might help us achieve a deeper understanding of this process. A new possibility for CHAMP: hundreds of avatars moving around in the virtual Çatal Höyük, representations of the former inhabitants, according to the numbers and gender balance estimated for that time. They are programmed with the estimated communication structure and with possible roles to play. How would this artificial society react? Would developments take place or would we only witness meaningless stuttering? Virtual worlds of human history – music of the future.

Selected Bibliography

Albert Abramson, *Electronic Motion Pictures. A History of the Television Camera*, Berkeley, Los Angeles: University of California Press, 1955.

Hubertus von Amelunxen, Stefan Iglhaut, Florian Rötzer, Alexis Cassel (eds.), *Fotografie nach der Fotografie*, Munich: Verlag der Kunst, 1996.

Hubertus von Amelunxen, Andrei Ujica (eds.), *Television/Revolution. Das Ultimatum des Bildes. Rumänien im Dezember 1989*, Marburg: Jonas Verlag, 1990.

Gary H. Andersen, *Video-Editing and Post-Production: A Professional Guide*, White Plains: Knowledge Industry Publications, 1993 (3rd ed.).

Ien Ang, *Living Room Wars: Rethinking Media Audiences for a Postmodern World*, London: Routledge, 1996.

Bruce A. Austin (ed.), *Current Research in Film: Audiences, Economics, and Law*, Norwood: Ablex Publishing Corporation, 1985.

Christopher W. Baker, *Computer Illusion in Film & TV*, Indianapolis: Alpha Books, 1994.

Thomas F. Baldwin, *Convergence. Integrating Media, Information & Communication*, Thousand Oaks: Sage Publications, 1996.

Tino Balio (ed.), *The American Film Industry*, Madison: The University of Wisconsin Press, 1976.

Raymond Bellour, *Passage de l'image*, Paris: Centre Georges Pompidou, 1990.

Raymond Bellour, Ann-Marie Duguet (eds.), *Vidéo*, Paris: Le Seuil, 1988.

Raymond Bellour, Colin MacCabe (eds.), *Jean-Luc Godard: Son + Image*, New York MOMA, 1992.

Walter Benjamin, 'The Work of Art in the Age of Mechanical Reproduction', in *Illuminations* (edited by Hannah Arendt), New York: Schocken, 1969.

John Berger, *Ways of Seeing*, Harmondsworth: Penguin, 1972.

John Berger, *About Looking*, New York: Pantheon, 1980.

Christa Blümlinger (ed.), *Sprung im Spiegel. Filmisches Wahrnehmen zwischen Fiktion und Wirklichkeit*, Wien: Sonderzahl, 1990.

Leo Bogart, *The Age of Television. A Study of Viewing Habits and the Impact of Television on American Life*, New York (3rd ed.), 1972.

Jay David Bolter, *Writing Space: The Computer, Hypertext and the History of Writing*, Hillsdale, NJ: Lawrence Erlbaum Associates, 1991.

Norbert Bolz, *Eine kurze Geschichte des Scheins*, Munich: Wilhelm Fink Verlag, 1992 (2nd ed.).

Norbert Bolz, *Am Ende der Gutenberg-Galaxis. Die neuen Kommunikations-verhältnisse*, Munich: Wilhelm Fink Verlag, 1993.

Stewart Brand, *The Media Lab. Inventing the Future at MIT*, New York: Viking, 1987.

John T. Caldwell, *Televisuality: Style, Crisis and Authority in American Television*, Rutgers University Press, New Brunswick, 1995.

Dominic Case, *Film Technology in Post Production*, Jordan Hill: Focal Press, 1997.

C. W. Ceram, *Archaeology of the Cinema*, New York: Harcourt, Brace & World, n.d.

Benjamin M. Compaine (ed.), *Issues in New Information Technology*, Norwood: Ablex Pub. Corp., 1988.

Benjamin M. Compaine, *Understanding New Media. Trends and Issues in Electronic Distribution of Information*, Cambridge: Ballinger, 1984.

Peter Conrad, *Television. The Medium and its Manners*, Boston, London, Henley: Routledge & Kegan Paul, 1982.

Jonathan Crary, *Techniques of the Observer*, Cambridge, Mass.: MIT Press, 1992.

George Cromstock, Steven Chaffee, Natan Katzman, Maxwell McCombs, Donald Roberts, *Television and Human Behavior*, New York: Columbia University Press, 1978.

David Crowley, David Mitchell, *Communication Theory Today*, Cambridge: Polity Press, 1994.

Sean Cubitt, *Videography. Video Media as Art and Culture*, Houndsmill, Basingstoke, London: Macmillian Education, 1993.

Daniel J. Czitrom, *Media and the American Mind. From Morse to McLuhan*, Chapel Hill: University of North Carolina Press, 1982.

Peter D'Agostino, *Transmissions: Theory and Practice of a New Television Aesthetics*, New York: Tanam Press, 1985.

Daniel Dayan and Elihu Katz, *Media Events. The Live Broadcasting of History*, Cambridge, Mass.: Harvard University Press, 1994.

Ben De Leeuw, *Digital Cinematography*, Boston: AP Professionals, 1997.

Carmine R. De Sarlo, *TV Commercial Film Editing: Professional Motion Picture Pre- and Post-Production, including Animation, Rotoscoping, and Video Tape*, Jefferson: McFarland, 1985.

Mark Dery, *Escape Velocity*, New York: Grove Press, 1996.

Marshall Deutelbaum (ed.), *Image on the Art and Evolution of the Film*, New York: Dover Publications, 1979.

Howard F. Didsbury, Jr. (ed.), *Communications and the Future. Prospects, Promises, and Problems*, Bethesda: World Future Society, 1982.

Timothy Druckrey, Geoffrey Batchen et al., *Metamorphosis, Photography in the Electronic Age*, New York: Aperture, 1994.

Timothy Druckrey (ed.), *Electronic Culture*, New York: Aperture, 1996.

Robert Edmonds, *The Sights and Sounds of Cinema and Television. How the Aesthetic Experience Influences Our Feelings*, New York: Teachers College Press, 1982.

John Ellis, *Visible Fictions. Cinema : Televison : Video*, London, Boston, Melbourne, Henley: Routledge & Kegan Paul, 1982 (rev. edition: 1993).

John Ellis, 'Speed, Film and Television: Media Moving Apart', in John Hill and Martin McLoone (eds.), *Big Picture, Small Screen: The Relations Between Cinema and Television*, University of Luton Press/John Libbey, 1996.

Thomas Elsaesser, Jean-François Lyotard, Edgar Reitz, *Der zweite Atem des Kinos*, Frankfurt: Verlag der Autoren, 1996.

Martin Esslin, *The Age of Television*, San Francisco: W. H. Freeman and Company, 1982.

Roger F. Fidler, *Mediamorphosis: Understanding New Media*, Thousand Oaks: Pine Forge Press, 1997.

Karl Gerbel, Peter Weibel (eds.), *Mythos Information. Welcome to the Wired World*. @rs electronica 95, Wien, New York: Springer Verlag, 1995.

Gregor T. Goethals, *The TV Ritual – Worship at the Video Altar*, Boston: Beacon Press, 1981.

Rose K. Goldsen, *The Show and Tell Machine. How Television Works and Works You Over*, New York: Delta Books, 1977.

David A. Gordon, *Controversies in Media Ethics*, White Plains, 1996.

Jostein Gripsrud, *The Dynasty Years: Hollywood Television and Critical Media Studies*, London: Routledge, 1995.

Debra Grodin, Thomas Lindlof, *Constructing the Self in a Mediated World*, Thousand Oaks: Sage Publications, 1996.

Lynne S. Gross, *Electronic Moviemaking*, Belmont: Wadsworth Pub., 1997 (3rd ed.).

Thomas H. Guback, *The International Film Industry. Western Europe and America since 1945*, Bloomington, London: Indiana University Press, 1969.

Hans Ulrich Gumbrecht, K. Ludwig Pfeiffer (eds.), *Materialität der Kommunikation*, Frankfurt: Suhrkamp, 1988.

John Halas, *Graphics in Motion*, Boston: Focal Press, 1981.

Doug Hall, Sally Jo Feifer (eds.), *Illuminating Video*, New York: Aperture, 1989.

Peter Christian Hall (ed.), *Fernsehen im Überfluß. Programme im digitalen Medienzeitalter*, Mainz: ZDF, 1996.

John G. Hanhardt (ed.), *Videoculture. A Critical Investigation*, Layton: Peregine Smith Books in association with Visual Studies Workshop Press, 1986.

Philip Hayward, Tana Wollen (eds.), *New Technologies of the Screen*, London: BFI Publishing, 1993.

John Hill, Martin McLoone (eds.), *Big Picture, Small Screen. The Relations Between Film And Television*, Luton: University of Luton Press, 1996.

William E. Hines, *Operating Cinematography for Film and Video: A Professional and Practical Guide*, Los Angeles: Ed-Ventures Films/Books, 1997.

Winston William Hodge, *Interactive Television. A Comprehensive Guide for Multimedia Technologies*, New York: McGraw-Hill, 1996.

Kay Hoffmann, *Am Ende Video – Video am Ende? Aspekte der Elektronisierung der Spielfilmproduktion*, Berlin: edition sigma, 1990.

Kay Hoffmann (ed.), *Trau – Schau – Wem. Digitalisierung und dokumentarische Form*, Konstanz: UVK Medien, 1997.

Alain Jaubert, *Fotos, die lügen. Politik mit gefälschten Bildern*, Frankfurt: Athenäum Verlag, 1989.

Jacques Kermabon and Kumar Shalami (eds.), *Cinema and Television*, London: Sangam, 1991.

John J. Larish, *Understanding Electronic Photography*, Blue Ridge Summit: TAB Books, 1990.

Bruno Latour, *Aramis or the Love of Technology*, Cambridge: Harvard University Press, 1996.

Teresa de Lauretis, Stephen Heath (eds.), *The Cinematic Apparatus*, New York: St. Martin's Press, 1985.

Stephen Last, *Beyond the Horizon. Communications Technologies: Past, Present and Future*, Luton: University of Luton Press, 1997.

Wolfgang Leister, Heinrich Müller, Achim Stößer, *Fotorealistische Computeranimation*, Berlin, Heidelberg: Springer Verlag, 1991.

Martin Lister (ed.), *The Photographic Image in Digital Culture*, New York: Routledge, 1995.

John R. MacArthur, *Second Front. Censorship and Propaganda in the Gulf War*, New York: Hill and Wang, 1992.

Brian McKernan (ed.), *The Age of Videography: Twenty Years that Changed the Way We See Ourselves*, New York: Miller Freeman, 1996.

Carolyn Marvin, *When Old Technologies Were New*, Oxford: Oxford University Press, 1988.

Patricia Mellencamp, *Logics of Television*, London and Bloomington: BFI Publishing and Indiana University Press, 1990.

Ned Miller (ed.), *The Post-Broadcasting Age. New Technologies, New Communities*, London 1996.

William J. Mitchell, *The Reconfigured Eye. Visual Truth in the Post-Photographic Era*, Cambridge, Mass.: MIT Press, 1994.

James Monaco, *Media Culture. Televison, Radio, Records, Books, Magazines, Newspapers, Movies*, New York: Delta Book, 1978.

James Monaco, *American Film Now. The People, The Power, The Money, The Movies*. New York: Oxford University Press, 1979.

Mike Morrison, *The Magic of Interactive Entertainment*, Indianapolis: Sams Pub., 1994.

Mary Anne Moser (ed.), *Immersed in Technology: Art and Virtual Environments*, Cambridge, Mass.: MIT Press, 1996.

Hamid Mowlana, *Global Communications in Transition*, Thousand Oaks: Sage Publication, 1996.

Steve Neale, *Cinema and Technology: Image, Sound, Colour*, Bloomington: Indiana University Press, 1985.

Bill Nichols, *Representing Reality: Issues and Concepts in Documentary*, Bloomington: Indiana University Press, 1991.

Bill Nichols, *Blurred Boundaries: Questions of Meaning in Contemporary Culture*, Bloomington: Indiana University Press, 1994.

Eli M. Noam, Alex J. Wolfson (eds.), *Globalism and Localism in Telecommunications*, New York: Elsevier, 1997.

Eli M. Noam, Joel C. Millonzi (eds.), *The International Market in Film and Television Programs*, Norwood: Ablex Pub. Corp., 1993.

Eli M. Noam, *Video Media Competition. Regulation, Economics, Technology*, New York: Columbia University Press, 1985.

Thomas A. Ohanian, *Digital Nonlinear Editing: New Approaches to Editing Film and Video*, Boston: Focal Press, 1993.

Richard Patterson, Dana White (eds.), *Electronic Production Techniques. An American Cinematographer Reprint*. Hollywood: American Cinematographer, 1984.

Patrice Petro (ed.), *Fugitive Images: From Photography to Video*, Bloomington: Indiana University Press, 1995.

Carl R. Plantinga, *Rhetoric and Representation in Nonfiction Film*, Cambridge, New York: Cambridge University Press, 1997.

Edgar Reitz, *Bilder in Bewegung. Essays. Gespräche zum Kino*, Reinbek: Rowohlt, 1995.

Michael Renov (ed.), *Theorizing Documentary*, New York: Routledge, 1993.

Howard Rheingold, *Virtual Reality*, New York: Summit, 1991.

Robert A. Rosenstone, *Visions of the Past. The Challenge of Film to our Idea of History*, Cambridge: Harvard University Press, 1995.

Florian Rötzer (ed.), *Digitaler Schein. Ästhetik der elektronischen Medien*, Frankfurt: Suhrkamp, 1991.

Florian Rötzer, Peter Weibel (eds.), *Strategien des Scheins. Kunst Computer Medien*, Munich: Klaus Boer, 1991.

Florian Rötzer (ed.), *Telepolis, Die Zeitschrift der Netzkultur, Hollywood Goes Digital. Neue Medien und neues Kino*, Mannheim: Bollmann, 1997.

Barry Salt, *Film Style and Technology*, London: Starword, 1992 (2nd ed.).

Gerhard Schumm, *Der Film verliert sein Handwerk. Montagetechnik und Filmsprache auf dem Weg zur elektronischen Postproduction*, Münster: MakS Publikationen, 1979.

Gerhard Schumm, Hans J. Wulff (eds.), *Film und Psychologie. Wahrnehmung, Kognition, Rezeption*, Münster: MakS Publikationen, 1990.

Roger Silverstone, *Television and Everyday Life*, London: Routledge, 1994.

Ralph Lee Smith, *The Wired Nation, Cable TV: The Electronic Communications Highway*, New York, Evanston, San Francisco, London: Harper Colophon Books, 1972.

Thomas G. Smith, *Industrial Light & Magic. The Art of Special Effects*, New York: Ballantine Books, 1986.

Society of Motion Picture and Television Engineers Technical Conference (ed.), *Film and Video Synergies: Creation to Delivery: Proceedings*, White Plains: SMPTE, 1996.

Society of Motion Picture and Television Engineers 75th Anniversary Collection, *Milestones in Motion Picture and Television Technology*, White Plains: SMPTE, 1991.

Society of Motion Picture and Television Engineers (ed.), *Video Picture of the Future. High Definition Television, Television Graphics and Special Effects, Video Tape Formats, Microcomputers*, Scardsdale, 1983.

Nadia Magnenat Thalmann, Daniel Thalmann, *Synthetics Actors in Computer-Generated 3D Films*. Berlin, Heidelberg a.o.: Springer Verlag, 1990.

John B. Thompson, *The Media and Modernity. A Social Theory of the Media*, Stanford: Stanford University Press, 1995.

Michael Tobias (ed.), *The Search for Reality: the Art of Documentary Filmmaking*, Studio City: Michael Wiese Productions, 1997.

Mark Cotta Vaz, Patricia Rose Duignan, *Industrial Light & Magic: Into the Digital Realm*, New York: Ballantine Books, 1996.

Paul Virilio, *War and Cinema: The Logic of Perception*, London: Verso, 1988.

Harald L. Vogel, *Entertainment Industry Economics. A Guide for Financial Analysis*, Cambridge, London, New York a.o.: Cambridge University Press, 1986.

Matthias Wähner, *Mann ohne Eigenschaften. Man Without Qualities*. Munich: Münchner Stadtmuseum, 1994.

Charles Warren (ed.), *Beyond Document: Essays on Nonfiction Film*, Hanover: University Press of New England, 1996.

Janet Wasko, *Movies and Money. Financing the American Film Industry*, Norwood: Ablex Publishing Corporation, 1982.

Paul Watzlawick, Peter Krieg (eds.), *Das Auge des Betrachters. Beiträge zum Konstruktivismus*, Munich, Zürich: Piper Verlag, 1991.

Paul Watzlawick, *Wie wirklich ist die Wirklichkeit? Wahn Täuschung Verstehen*, Munich: Piper Verlag, 1978.

Kraft Wetzel (ed.), *Neue Medien contra Filmkultur?*, Berlin: Volker Spiess, 1987.

David Manning White, Richard Averson (eds.), *Sight, Sound and Society. Motion Pictures and Television in America*, Boston, 1968.

George E. Whitehouse, *Understanding the New Technologies of the Mass Media*, Englewood Cliffs: Prentice-Hall, 1986.

Christopher Williams (ed.), *Cinema: the Beginnings and the Future*, London: University of Westminster Press, 1996.

Raymond Williams, *Television. Technology and Cultural Form*, New York, 1975.

Brian Winston, *Claiming the Real. The Documentary Film Revisited*, London: BFI Publishing, 1995.

Brian Winston, *Technologies of Seeing. Photography, Cinematography and Television*. London: BFI Publishing, 1996.

Gene Youngblood, *Expanded Cinema*, New York: Dutton, 1970.

Siegfried Zielinski, *Zur Geschichte des Video-Recorders*, Berlin: Volker Spiess, 1986.

Siegfried Zielinski, *Audiovisionen. Kino und Fernsehen als Zwischenspiele in der Geschichte*, Reinbek: Rowohlt, 1989.

List of Contributors

The Editors

Thomas Elsaesser is Professor of Film and TV Studies at the University of Amsterdam and General Editor of Film Culture in Transition. Among his publications are *New German Cinema* (1989), *Early Cinema: Space Frame Narrative* (1990), *A Second Life* (1996) and *Fassbinder's Germany* (1996).

Kay Hoffmann holds a PhD from the University of Marburg and is Academic Director and Author at the Haus des Dokumentarfilms Stuttgart. For this publication the EIKK has commissioned him to be editor. Furthermore he works as a filmjournalist and organises film- and TV-Festivals. His books as author and editor include *Am Ende Video – Video am Ende* (1990) and *Natur und ihre filmische Auflösung* (1994), *Zeichen der Zeit* (1996) and *Trau-Schau-Wem* (1997).

The Authors

Mick Eaton studied social anthropology and mass-communication, before turning to directing plays and films. He has published a number of key articles on television in such journals as *Screen*. Part of the 1980s he spent in Australia, before returning to England to devote himself full-time to writing screenplays for television, docu-dramas and feature films. Among his credits are *Fellow Traveller* (about the McCarthy era) and *Why Lockerby?* (the investigation into the Pan Am disaster). Other feature films of his are in production.

Martin Emele is a lecturer and senior researcher at the Hochschule für Gestaltung, Karlsruhe. He is in charge of the audio-visual archive and interactive presentation of CHAMP, an archaeological project described in his contribution. He works also as permanent staff member at the 'European Institute of Cinema Karlsruhe' (EIKK).

John Ellis is currently Professor at Bournemouth University. After teaching at the University of Kent, he founded his own production company Large Door in 1982, which produces programmes devoted to the media, such as the series *Visions*, a 32-part series on Western and non-Western cinema. Besides being an independent producer, he is the author of *Visible Fictions* (1982/1993), a standard work for film and television studies.

Stan Lapinski is an author and independent screenwriter living in Amsterdam. A former editor of *Skrien*, he has written a number of libretti and screenplays, as well as curating a retrospective at the Nederlands Filmmuseum.

Lev Manovich holds a PhD from the University of Rochester. He is a theorist and artist working in new media, who has been involved in computer cinema since 1984 as an animator, programmer, researcher and educator. He has published over a dozen articles on the theory and history of computer animation, computer imaging, virtual spaces, multimedia, digital cinema and media archaeology. Currently, he is preparing for publication a book on the social and cultural origins of computer media and its connection to the 1920s European avant-garde entitled *The Engineering of Vision from Constructivism to Virtual Reality*. He is on the faculty of the University of California, San Diego, Visual Arts Department.

Edgar Reitz is a producer and filmmmaker living in Munich. A founder-member of the New German Cinema, his films as director include *Mahlzeiten* (1966), *Die Reise nach Wien* (1973), *Stunde Null* (1976), *Heimat* (1984), *Die Zweite Heimat* (1992). Since its founding in 1995 he is director and chairman of the 'European Institute of Cinema Karlruhe' (EIKK).

Joyce Roodnat works as a journalist and is one of the leading art critics of the *NRC Handelsblad*.

Conrad Schoeffter is of Swiss origin and works as an independent producer and media-consultant. After studying film directing and production in the United States, he set up in 1983 a production company and consultancy firm called Hollywood Inc, dividing his time betwen Basel and Los Angeles. In 1990 he conducted the scenario workshop of IDFA, the International Documentary Festival in Amsterdam.

Pierre Sorlin is professor of sociology and audiovisual media at the Sorbonne, Paris, and a director at the Institute of Contemporary History in Bologna. He is the author of numerous books and essays on film history, media sociology and culture, as well as documentaries on topics of cinema and history. His most recent publications include *European Cinemas, European Societies, 1939-1990* (1990), *Esthétique de l'audiovisuel* (1992), and *Mass Media and Society* (1994).

Ed Tan trained as a psychologist and film theorist, gaining his doctorate in 1991. After working at the Department of Theatre Studies of the University of Amsterdam and co-founding the Department of Film and Television

Studies, he was in 1995 appointed Professor of Word and Image Studies at the Vrije Universiteit, Amsterdam. Working also as a researcher at the University of Utrecht, he is the author of *Film as Emotion Machine* (1995).

René van Uffelen is a journalist and author working in Amsterdam. He regularly writes for *Skrien*, of which he is a contributing editor.

Brian Winston is Head of the School of Communications, Design and Media at the University of Westminster, London. His previous posts include Director of the Centre of Journalism Studies at the University of Cardiff and Dean of the School of Communication at Pennsylvania State University. Among his many publications are *Misunderstanding Media* (1986) and *Claiming the Real* (1994).

Grahame Weinbren is an avant-garde filmmaker living in New York, who has been developing an interactive cinema since 1981. His three installation pieces *The Erl King* (1983-1986), made in collaboration with Roberta Friedman, *Sonata* (1991/3) and *March* (1995 & 1997) have been exhibited internationally. His writings have been published in *Millenium Film Journal*, *Leonardo*, *Kunstforum*, *Trafic*, and other journals.

Vito Zagarrio is a filmmaker, lecturer and author specializing in cinema/tv relations. He lives in Rome and is director of the Ancona film festival, organizing retrospectives devoted to the film industry and television. Among the books he has edited are *La televisione verso Hollywood* (1986) and *La televisione presenta... la produzione della* RAI *1965-1975* (1990).

Siegfried Zielinski is Professor of Media Arts and Founding Rector of the Kunsthochschule für Medien, Cologne. His previous academic positions include appointments in Berlin and Salzburg. He is a prolific author and lecturer, and among his many publications are *Zur Geschichte des Video-Recorders* (1986) and *Audiovisionen* (1989).

List of Illustrations

31/32 Production stills CRASH 2030 (1994), Hessischer Rundfunk Frankfurt, Haus des Dokumentarfilms Stuttgart.

33/34 Postcards BABYLON 2 (1993), Dschoint Venture Zürich, Haus des Dokumentarfilms Stuttgart.

35 Production still TELEVISION FEVER (1963), Süddeutscher Rundfunk, Haus des Dokumentarfilms.

36 Postcard, Hoffmann Collection.

37 Courtesy of the Cinemathek Haags Filmhuis, The Hague.

38 Still from BATTLESHIP POTEMKIN, Stiftung Deutsche Kinemathek, Berlin.

39 Still from VIDEOGRAM OF A REVOLUTION (1993), Harun Farocki, Haus des Dokumentarfilms.

40 Postcard THE NIBELUNGEN (1924), Hoffmann Collection.

41 Promotion still JURASSIC PARK (1993), UIP, Hoffmann Collection.

42 Streetscene Stuttgart, Photo Kay Hoffmann.

43 Promotion photo Cinedom in Cologne, Hoffmann Collection.

44 Phone card Jeanne Moreau, Edith Kleibel Berlin.

45 Promotion still SEL Alcatel, Stuttgart.

46 - 53 Courtesy of Grahame Weinbren.

54 Video-sculpture „V-pyramid" (1982) by Nam June Paik, Haus des Dokumentarfilms.

55 Promotion still BROADCAST NEWS (1987), Fox, Hoffmann Collection.

56 Model of Troy by Süddeutscher Rundfunk, Hochschule für Gestaltung Karlsruhe.

57, 58, 59 Production stills simulation Catal Höyük, Hochschule für Gestaltung Karlsruhe.

Publication Data

Lev Manovich, 'To Lie and to Act: Cinema and Telepresence', first published in German in *Ars Electronica*, Linz, 1995.

Lev Manovich, 'Towards An Archaeology of the Computer Screen', first published in German in *Kunstforum International*, 132 (November – January 1996): 124-135; and (in English and in Russian) in *NewMediaLogia*. Moscow, Soros Center for the Contemporary Art, 1996.

Edgar Reitz, 'Speed is the Mother of Cinema', first published in German in Thomas Elsaesser, Francois Lyotard, Edgar Reitz (eds.), *Der zweite Atem des Kino* (Frankfurt: Verlag der Autoren, 1996).

Joyce Roodnat, 'On the Big Screen every Doctor gets a Starring Role' first published in Dutch in *NRC Handelsblad* 3/12/1994.

Grahame Weinbren, 'Random Access Rules', first published in German in *Telepolis* (Munich: Heise Verlag, 1996).

Notes

Notes to 2: Cinema Futures: Convergence, Divergence, Difference

1 The world's stock-exchanges, the movement of currencies and commodities, of labour and services, or the manufacture of weapons and the technologies of warfare would have been as decisively altered even without digital sound and images. Which is not to say, that warfare and cinema or global trading and television do not have profound aspects in common. See Paul Virilio, *War and Cinema: The Logics of Perception*, London: Verso, 1988 or Pat Mellencamp, (ed.), *Logics of Television*, Bloomington: Indiana University Press, 1990.

2 André Bazin, 'Ontology of the Photographic Image', in *What is Cinema*, Berkeley and Los Angeles: University of California Press, 1967, p. 14. See also in the same volume, his essay 'The Myth of Total Cinema', pp. 17-22.

3 The conference was organized by Rien Hagen and GertJan Kuiper, of the Cinematheek Haags Filmhuis, The Hague, which made available the contributions by Mick Eaton, John Ellis, Joyce Roodnat, Pierre Sorlin, Conrad Schoeffter, Ed Tan, Vito Zagarrio, Brian Winston.

4 'Late Capitalism' is a notion first made popular by Ernest Mandel. It is used by Fredric Jameson, who refers to it as the 'untranscendable horizon' of our contemporary thinking in 'Postmodernism, or The Cultural Logic of Late Capitalism', originally in *New Left Review* no. 146, July-August 1984, pp. 53-92.

5 See Wilhelm Roth, 'Video alternativ' in Kraft Wetzel (ed.), *Neue Medien gegen Filmkultur?* Berlin: Volker Spiess, 1987, pp. 21-221. For an example of an earlier manifesto about an alternative public sphere for the cinema, see Gideon Bachmann, 'Typologie der Mächtigen und Ohnmächtigen im Filmgeschäft', *Jahrbuch Film*, 1968.

6 The phrase was coined by Alexander Kluge.

7 Kevin Kelly and Paula Parisi, 'Beyond STAR WARS what's next for George Lucas', in *Wired*, February 1997, p. 164.

8 See among others, Laurent Manoni *Le grand art de l'ombre et de la lumière*, Paris: Nathan, 1994; Charles Musser, *Before the Nickelodeon*, Berkeley and Los Angeles: University of California Press, 1991; Siegfried Zielinski, *Zur Geschichte des Videorecorders*, Berlin: Volker Spiess, 1986.

9 Anne Marie Dugay, *Jean-Christophe Averty*, Paris: Dis Voir, 1991. Similar pioneers existed elsewhere in Europe. In Germany, the work of Michael Leckebusch and others is being rediscovered by journals such as *Weltwunder der Kinematographie* (edited by Joachim Polzer). See also Otto Gmelin, *Philosophie des Fernsehens*, Baden-Baden, 1967.

10 See, for instance, Doug Hall and Sally Jo Fifer (eds.), *Illuminating Video: An Essential Guide to Video Art*, New York: Aperture, 1987, and Gary Schwartz (ed.), *The Luminous Image*, Amsterdam: Stedelijk Museum, 1984.

11 The news of the re-styling of Barbie Doll late in 1997 was announced by Mattell, its brand-owner and manufacturer, as if it had developed a new anti-aircraft missile. I recall a Mattell employee in Southern California telling me about his visits to Israeli and South African arms manufacturers in the mid-1970s for the purposes of cross-licensing toy technology and weapon electronics.

12 Godard's *Histoire(s) du cinéma* is a kind of rewriting of film culture across his own films and video aesthetics. See Raymond Bellour and Colin MacCabe (eds.), *Jean-Luc Godard: Son + Image*, New York: Modern Museum of Art, 1992.

13 'Cinema and Television: Jean Renoir and Roberto Rossellini interviewed by André Bazin', *Sight and Sound*, June 1960.

14 In most European countries, the debate around cinema and television was vigorously conducted throughout the 1970s and 1980s. See, among the sharpest and most amusing contributions, Serge Daney, *Le Salaire du Zappeur*, Paris: Editions Ramsay, 1988, or among the most acrimonious, the debate in Germany around the 'amphibious film', summarized in Hans C. Blumenberg, 'Bildschirm contra Leinwand', *Die Zeit* 23 June 1978. Wim Wenders' film CHAMBRE 666, made at the Cannes Film Festival of 1982, interviews a dozen or so European film directors as to their (mostly negative) views about television.

15 If one adds the various governmental funding measures for film production, one comes to the following figures for 1993: in Germany, 85% of all the money invested in films comes from television and/or the State, in the Netherlands it is even as high as 94%, while in France it amounts to 51% and in Great Britain 33% (quoted in *Skrien*, Kain en Abel supplement, October, 1993, p. 25).

16 For the late 1980s, see Zielinski, in Kraft Wetzel (ed.), *Neue Medien contra Filmkultur?*, p. 84.

17 Serge Daney, *Ciné-Journal*, 1982, quoted in *Skrien*, Kain en Abel supplement, October 1993, p. 15.

18 See Walter Benjamin on the commodity in his *Charles Baudelaire: A Lyric Poet in the Era of High Capitalism*, London: New Left Books, 1973, esp. pp. 165-171 and Jean Baudrillard, *The Mirror of Production*, St Louis: Telos Press, 1975.

19 Commentators have coined the phrase of the 'television class-society', meaning that audiences will be segmented (and served) according to their income, which is to say, their value to advertisers, the paymasters of commercial television. See Kraft Wetzel (ed.), *Neue Medien contra Filmkultur*, p. 66, and several essays in Nick Browne (ed.), *American Television*, Langhorne, PA: Harwood, 1993.

20 This applies mainly to Hollywood, and has been attributed to new marketing concepts like the blockbuster, and to new technologies like digital special effects. But as the following will try to show, such determinism foreshortens the argument, especially now that it seems the European cinema – notably from Britain and Germany – is finding new audiences at home (a spate of comedies in Germany) and abroad (in the case of Britain, hugely successful films like FOUR WEDDINGS AND A FUNERAL, TRAINSPOTTING and THE FULL MONTY).

21 Bertolt Brecht, 'Radiotheorie: der Rundfunk als Kommunikationsapparat', *Gesammelte Werke*, Band 18 Schriften zur Literatur und Kunst, Frankfurt: Suhrkamp, 1973, pp. 120, 127.

Notes to 3: Towards an Archaeology of the Computer Screen

1 Earlier versions of this essay were presented at the 'Generated Nature' symposium (Rotterdam, November 1994) and the 'NewMediaLogia' symposium (Moscow, November 1994). I am grateful to the participants of both symposia as well as to the students in my 'Visual Theory' seminar for their many very useful comments and suggestions.

2 The degree to which a frame that acts as a boundary between the two spaces is emphasized seems to be proportional to the degree of identification expected from the viewer. Thus, in cinema, where the identification is most intense, the frame as a separate object does not exist at all – the screen simply ends at its boundaries – while both in painting and in television the framing is much more pronounced.

3 Here I agree with the parallel suggested by Anatoly Prokhorov between window interface and montage in cinema.

4 For these origins, see, for instance, C.W. Ceram, *Archeology of the Cinema*, New York: Harcourt, Brace & World, Inc., 1965.

5 Beaumont Newhall, *Airborne Camera*, New York: Hastings House, Publishers, 1969.

6 This is more than a conceptual similarity. In the late 1920s John L. Baird invented 'phonovision', the first method for the recording and the playing back of a television signal. The signal was recorded on Edison's phonograph record by a process very similar to making an audio recording. Baird named his recording machine 'phonoscope'. Albert Abramson, *Electronic Motion Pictures*, University of California Press, 1955, pp. 41-42.

7 *Echoes of War*, Boston: WGBH Boston, n.d., videotape.

8 Ibid.

9 Ibid.

10 On SAGE, see Paul Edwards, 'The Closed World. Systems discourse, military policy and post-World War II U.S. historical consciousness', in *Cyborg Worlds: The Military Information Society*, eds. Les Levidow and Kevin Robins, London: Free Association Books, 1989; Howard Rheingold, *Virtual Reality*, New York: Simon & Schuster, Inc., 1991, pp. 68-93.

11 Edwards, p. 142.

12 'Retrospectives II: The Early Years in Computer Graphics at MIT, Lincoln Lab, and Harvard', in *SIGGRAPH '89 Panel Proceedings*, New York: The Association for Computing Machinery, 1989, pp. 22-24.

13 Ibid., pp. 42-54.

14 I will address important later developments such as bitmapped display and window interface in a future article.

15 Rheingold, p. 105.

16 Quoted in Rheingold, p. 104.

17 Roland Barthes, 'Diderot, Brecht, Eisenstein', in *Image-Music-Text*, ed. Stephen Heath, New York: Farrar, Straus and Giroux, 1977, pp. 69-70.

18 Ibid.

19 As summarized by Martin Jay, 'Scopic Regimes of Modernity', in *Vision and Visuality*, ed. Hal Foster, Seattle: Bay Press, 1988, p. 7.

20 Quoted in Jay, p. 7.

21 Ibid, p. 8.

22 Quoted in Jay, p. 9.

23 For a survey of perspectival instruments, see Martin Kemp, *The Science of Art*, New Haven: Yale University Press, 1990, pp. 167-220.

24 Ibid., pp. 171-172.

25 Ibid., p. 200.

26 Ibid.

27 Anesthesiology emerges approximately at the same time.

28 Walter Benjamin, 'The Work of Art in the Age of Mechanical Reproduction', in *Illuminations*, ed. Hannah Arendt, New York: Schocken Books, 1969, p. 238.

29 Anne Friedberg, *Window Shopping: Cinema and the Postmodern*, Berkeley: University of California Press, 1993, p. 2.

30 See, for instance, David Bordwell, Janet Steiger and Kristin Thompson, *The Classical Hollywood Cinema*, New York: Columbia University Press, 1985.

31 Quoted in Friedberg, p. 215.

32 Ibid., p. 214.

33 Friedberg, p. 134. She refers to Jean-Louis Baudry, 'The Apparatus: Metapsychological Approaches to the Impression of Reality in the Cinema', in *Narrative, Apparatus, Ideology*, ed. Philip Rosen, New York: Columbia University Press, 1986, and Charles Musser, *The Emergence of Cinema: The American Screen to 1907*, New York: Charles Scribner and Sons, 1990.

34 Quoted in Baudry, p. 303.

35 Friedberg, p. 28.

36 A typical VR system adds other ways of moving around, for instance, the ability to move forward in a single direction by simply pressing a button on a joystick. However, to change the direction the user still has to change the position of his/her body.

37 Rheingold, p. 104.

38 Ibid., p. 105.

39 Ibid., p. 109.

40 Marta Braun, *Picturing Time: The Work of Etienne-Jules Marey (1830-1904)*, Chicago: The University of Chicago Press, 1992, pp. 34-35.

41 Rheingold, pp. 201-209.

42 Quoted in Reingold, p. 201.

43 Here I disagree with Friedberg who writes, 'Phantasmagorias, panoramas, dioramas
    – devices that concealed their machinery – were dependent on the relative immobil-
    ity of their spectators.', Friedberg, p. 23.

Notes to 4: Louis Lumière – the Cinema's First Virtualist?

1   *Le Cinéma: Vers son deuxième siècle,* conference held at the Odéon, Paris, 20 March
    1995.

2   Press handout of Douchet's lecture, in English, p.1.

3   ibid.

4   See William Uricchio, 'Cinema als omweg?', *Skrien*, 199, 1995, pp. 54-57.

5   See, for instance, Michael Punt, 'The elephant, the spaceman and the white cockatoo',
    in M.Lister (ed.), *Photography in the Age of Digital Culture*, London: Routledge, 1995,
    pp. 51-77.

6   The fact that there is – at least in Europe – a broad agreement to assign to the Lumière
    Brothers the honour of having 'invented' what we now call the cinema must not
    eclipse the achievements and memory of the two dozen or so other pioneers, show-
    men, inventors and scientists who in 1895 were working either on similar machines
    or specific problems crucial to the reproduction of motion on life-size images. For a
    substantive and recent account, see Laurent Manoni, *Le grand art de la lumiere et de
    l'ombre: archéologie du cinema*, Paris: Nathan, 1994.

7   See William Uricchio, loc. cit.

8   Although the formula 'the disease of which it pretends to be the cure' is credited to
    Karl Kraus a propos of psychoanalysis, it might be said to be constitutive of capital-
    ism: what Marxists from George Lukacs to Fredric Jameson call the 'reification' pro-
    cess, and in which, according to these scholars, the cinema is deeply implicated. See
    Fredric Jameson, 'The Invention of Italy', in *Signatures of the Visible*, New York: Rout-
    ledge, 1992, pp. 187-232.

9   See Noel Burch, 'A Parenthesis on Film History', in *To The Distant Observer*, London:
    Scolar Press, 1979, pp. 61-66, where he speaks of the 'Edisonian imaginary' and also
    his 'Charles Baudelaire versus Dr Frankenstein' in *Afterimage*, no 8/9, Spring 1981,
    pp. 4-21.

10 Locating Louis Lumiere within the scientific community to which he first presented
    the *cinématographe* suggests that while the machine was recognized as groundbreak-
    ing, it was by no means perceived as novel. See the report published in *La Nature*, 31
    August – 7 September 1895, about the July 1895 presentation, which quotes the report
    of M. A. Gay, but begins by informing its readers of how the *cinématographe* belongs to
    the history of photography, representing 'a new system of chronophotography', it-
    self defined as 'a tool for fixing fugitive events – phenomena too fast, too slow, too
    small, too big to be perceived with the human eye, in order to be able to study them at
    leisure and with reflection ('étudier longuement et méditer').' In a letter to Georges
    Demeny, Louis Lumière describes one of his films as 'a chronophotographic series of
    eight hundred prints'.

11 *La Poste*, January 12, 1896.

12 Tom Gunning, 'An Aesthetics of Astonishment: Early Film and the (In)credulous Spectator', *Art & Text*, no 34, Spring 1989, pp. 31-45.

13 Marshall Deutelbaum, in 'Structural Patterning in the Lumière Films', first published in *Wide Angle*, vol. 3 no. 1, 1979, pp. 28-37.

14 Marshall Deutelbaum calls them 'operational processes', Deutelbaum, p.31.

15 Deutelbaum, pp. 30, 32.

16 See also the discussion of the frame by Andre Bazin, in 'Peinture et cinéma', *Qu'est-ce que le cinéma?*, vol. 1, Paris: Le Cerf, 1959, p. 188 and a more recent thematization of Louis Lumiére and painting by Jacques Aumont in *L'oeil interminable*, Paris: Seguier, 1989.

17 This raises questions of reception, of the 'frames' existing for the audience in the conditions of performance and presentation. See André Gardies, *L'espace du cinéma*, Paris: Méridiens-Kliencksieck, 1993.

18 Here, history has a way of repeating itself. Lev Manovich (in 'Digital Cinema') has pointed out how QuickTime movies on the internet or motion video on interactive CD-ROMs utilize the form of the loop, pioneered by Edison (http:www.ix.de/tp). My suggestion is that the echoes in Lumière indicate its importance for thinking about cinematic 'continuity' in general.

19 See Norman Bryson, *Vision and Painting: the Logic of the Gaze*, London: Routledge, 1983 and Jonathan Crary, *Techniques of the Observer*, Cambridge, Mass.: MIT Press, 1992.

20 For instance, Gilles Deleuze, in his *Cinema I: L'Image mouvement*, Paris: Seuil, 1984 reads German Expressionist cinema across just such a matrix.

21 The stereoscope features prominently in Jonathan Crary's *Techniques of the Observer*, MIT Press, 1992. But see also the reprint of Oliver Wendell Holmes, 'The Stereoscope and the Stereographe'[1859], in Alan Trachtenberg (ed.), *Classical Essays in Photography*, New Haven, Island Books 1980.

22 There is an impressive collection of stereoscopic views on show in the Institut Lumière in Lyon, and the Rijksmuseum in Amsterdam holds a most magnificent – and rarely shown – set of stereo views from the Paris World Fair of 1896, as well as from the Amsterdam World Fair, eight years later, in 1904.

23 This is the position taken by Noel Burch, *Life to Those Shadows*, Berkeley and Los Angeles: University of California Press, 1990.

24 One of the longest obituaries to appear on the death of Auguste Lumière was in a medical journal, praising his work in designing measuring devices for fitting artificial limbs to war veterans. Referred to in Lisa Cartwright, *Screening the Body: Tracing Medicine's Visual Culture*, Minneapolis: University of Minnesota Press, 1995, p. 1.

25 It may be interesting to recall that stereoscopy, as a device for three-dimensional vision, only gives the illusion of such vision thanks to the computational processes in the brain: the stereoscope produces a cognitive effect, in other words, rather than reproducing a perceptual fact. See Albrecht Hoffmann, *Das Stereoskop*, Munich: Deutsches Museum, 1990, p. 9.

26 The journalist's phrase is quoted in Martin Loiperdinger and Harald Pulch's television film *Lumière* (1995).

27 Stereoscopy, rather than having fizzled out as a nineteenth century entertainment, superseded by the cinema, is to this day crucial in space research and weather reports, and in the form of photo-grammetry remains an essential tool for topographical measuring and surveyance work. This may provide a none too distant line connecting, after all, the *cinématographe* considered as an improved system of chrono-photography with the first Lumière films considered as stereoscopic cognitivist exercises. Taking successive images, and converting their temporal distance into a spatial distance in order to reconstruct volume, mass and contours would seem an activity that allows one to understand why the Lumières might have been interested in sonar probes capable of measuring the topography of different terrains – an aural stereoscopy if you like. Albrecht Hoffmann, *Das Stereoskop*, Munich: Deutsches Museum, 1990, pp. 32-37.

28 Even Auguste Lumière's interest in artificial limbs can be linked to the stereoscope. It seems that since the days that Oliver Wendell Holmes applied stereoscopy to the design of the replacement limbs fitted to American Civil War veterans, doctors have continued to use stereoscopic measurements in order to calculate and thereby optimize the motor-coordination of patients obliged to wear prosthetics. See K.W. Wolf-Czapek, *Angewandte Photographie in Wissenschaft und Technik*, Berlin, 1911.

Notes to 6: *Fin de Siècle* of Television

1 This paper was written at the beginning of the 1990s. Some of the artefacts and media systems mentioned have in the meantime become antiques, while others did not even exist in the ever-expanding global audiovisual department store.

2 For a closer examination of this structural change, see S. Zielinski, 'Zur Technikgeschichte des BRD-Fernsehens', in Knut Hicketier (ed.), *Geschichte des Fernsehens in der Bundesrepublik Deutschland*, vol 1 (Munich: Fink, 1993), pp. 135-170.

3 During the 1990s, the CD-rom took over mainly this function, especially for children and youth culture in general, accompanied by closed-circuit and internet computer games.

4 Raymond Williams, 'Mobile Privatisierung', in *Das Argument*, vol 26, March/April 1984, p. 260 ff.

5 At the National Research Institute of Television and Broadcasting in Moscow, where intensive tests are being run on all the current technical concepts, including the Soviet one, a very interesting experiment was carried out a short while ago: with a series of Sony appliances arranged in the 'Diorama' design of the RAI, test persons were confronted with various objects, both as real images and HiVision images. An arrangement of mirrors made it impossible for the test persons to identify the source of the images. The impressive result was that in the majority of cases the test persons held the HiVision images for the real ones (see *World Broadcast News*, October 1989, p.16).

6 This title in German is a play on words: 'Kluges Fernsehen' also means 'intelligent television'.

7   Alexander Kluge/Oskar Negt, *Öffentlichkeit und Erfahrung*, Frankfurt: Suhrkamp, 1972, p. 220 ff.

8   Gabor Body: 'Was ist Video?', in Veruschka Body and Gabor Body (eds.), *Axis – Auf der elektronischen Bühne Europa*, Cologne: DuMont, 1986, p. 90.

9   Alexander Kluge, *Geschichte und Eigensinn*, Frankfurt: Zweitausendeins, 1981.

Notes to 13: 'I See, if I Believe it' – Documentary and the Digital

1   Wolfgang Timpe, 'Wir sind Opfer. Günther Jauch hat die gefälschten Beiträge des Michael Born gesehen, geprüft und gesendet – schuldig aber sollen andere sein,' *Die Woche*, 25.10.1996.

2   Kogawa Tesuo, 'Towards a Reality of "Reference": The Image and the Era of Virtual Reality,' *Documentary Box*, No. 8 (1995), p. 1.

3   Alain Jaubert, *Fotos, die lügen. Politik mit gefälschten Bildern*, Frankfurt: Athenäum Verlag, 1989.

4   William J. Mitchell, *The Reconfigured Eye. Visual Truth in the Post-Photographic Era*. Cambridge, Mass.: MIT Press, 1994, p. 4.

5   Kay Hoffmann, interview with Jeff Apple in the 1995 film *Trau-Schau-Wem: Vertrauen im Zeitalter der Digitalisierung*.

6   Brian Winston, *Claiming the Real. The Documentary Film revisited*. London: BFI Publishing, 1995, p. 253.

7   See Kay Hoffmann (ed.), *Trau-Schau-Wem. Digitalisierung und dokumentarische Form*. Konstanz: UVK Medien, 1997.

8   Martin Schlappner, 'Moving Stories', *DOX. Documentary Film Quarterly*. Winter 1995, p. 12.

9   Kay Hoffmann, *Zeichen der Zeit. Zur Geschichte der Stuttgarter Schule*, München: TR-Verlagsunion, 1996.

Notes to 14: Theatrical and Television Documantary

1   See John Ellis' essay in this volume.

2   Brian Winston, *Claiming the Real*, London: BFI Publishing, 1995, pp. 127-158.

3   Josef Maria Eder, *History of Photography*, trans. Edward Epstean, New York: Dover, 1972, p. 239.

4   Ian Hacking, 'Was There a Probabilistic Revolution 1800 -1930', in Lorenz Kruger et al. (eds.), *The Probabilistic Revolution, Volume 1: Ideas in History*, Cambridge, Massachusetts: MIT Press, 1987, p. 45.

5   Robert Colls & Philip Dodd, 'Representing the Nation: British Documentary Film 1930 – 1945', *Screen*, vol. 21, no. 1, Spring 1985, p. 22.

6   John Grierson, *Grierson on Documentary*, Forsyth Hardy (ed.), London: Faber, 1979, p. 50.

7   Stephen Jones, *The British Labour Movement and Film 1918-1939*, London: Routledge and Kegan Paul, 1987, p. 23.

8   Nicholas Pronay, 'John Grierson and the Documentary – 60 Years On', *Historical Journal of Film, Radio and Television*, vol. 9, no. 3, 1989, p. 235.

9   Paddy Scannel (1986), 'The Stuff of Radio' in John Corner (ed.) *Documentary and the Mass Media*, London: Edward Arnold, 1986, pp. 7-14.

10   *Ibid.*, p. 14.

11   Margaret Dickinson & Sarah Street *Cinema and the State: The Film Industry and the British Government 1927 – 1984*, London: BFI Publishing, 1985, p. 8.

12   Norman Swallow (1982), 'Rotha and Television' in Paul Marris (ed.), *BFI Dossier 16: Paul Rotha*, London: BFI Publishing, 1982, pp. 86-9.

13   John Corner, 'Documentary Voices', in John Corner (ed.), *Popular Television in Britain*, London: BFI Publishing, 1991, p. 44.

14   Colin Seymour-Ure, *The British Press and Broadcasting*, Oxford: Blackwell, 1992, p. 338: *BBC Handbook 1960*, London: BBC, p. 226: *BBC Handbook 1966*, London: BBC, p. 42: *BBC Handbook 1976*, London: BBC, p. 118: *BBC Handbook 1986*, London: BBC, p. 148, Auguston Preta et al., *The Quest for Quality: Survey on Television Scheduling Worldwide*, Rome: RAI, General Secretariat of Prix Italia, June, 1986, p. 48.

15   A 1996 RAI study revealed that public service broadcasters (e.g. NOS, CBC and RAI itself) typically devoted about ten per cent of output to documentary (Auguston Preta et al., *The Quest for Quality*, 1996, pp. 16, 37, 41).

16   Colin Seymour-Ure, *The British Press*, p. 138; William Phillips, 'The Fourfront {sic} of Programming?', *Television*, vol.31, no.7, November/December, 1994, p. 27.

17   Brian Winston, *Technologies of Seeing: Photography, Cinematography and Television*, London: BFI Publishing, 1996, pp. 75-80.

18   Interview conducted 28 July 1997, London.

19   Charles Hammond Jr., *The Image Decade: Television Documentary 1965-1975*, New York: Hastings House, 1981, p. 250.

20   Christopher Russell et al., *The Veronis, Suhler and Associates Communication Industry Forecast*, New York: VSA, 1996, p. 138.

Notes to 16: From Butterflies and Bees to ROGER AND ME

1   Exceptions that confirm the rule are the recently made MICROCOSMOS by Marie Perennou and Claude Nuridsany, PEOPLE OF THE FOREST and THE LEOPARD SON by Hugo van Lawick. These nature documentaries did make it onto the cinema screen.

2   This does not mean that reality should be fictionalised, but does require a filmmaker who has the talent to interpret such stories from reality and possesses a good feeling for storytelling.

3   Consider the irony: 'I made LE CHAGRIN because I was asked to. I would rather have made a musical with Fred Astaire and become famous.'

4   For a description of Clarke's work one can refer to: David Thomson, 'Walkers in the World: Alan Clarke', in *Film Comment*, May/June, 1993.

5   Until well into the 1980s, the satirical television-duo Van Kooten en De Bie could cause large groups of Dutchmen to dig up non-existent hidden treasures or to vote for fictional political parties.

6   Some filmmakers are well aware of this, which is illustrated by the increase of the so called fake-documentary over the last years. Both the International Documentary Festival Amsterdam (Idfa) and the Film Festival Rotterdam, which leans more towards the feature film, show films such as EINSTEIN'S BRAIN, LAP ROUGE by Lodewijk Crijns and FORGOTTEN SILVER by Peter Jackson. Once again, the choice of subject-matter is safe. For more about the fake-documentary see: Gert-Jan Zuilhof, 'Fake', in the *Catalogus Film Festival Rotterdam 1997* and Patricia Pisters, 'Het plezier van bedrog', in *Skrien*, February/March, 1997.

7   See above, Joyce Roodnat, 'On the Big Screen, Every Doctor Has a Starring Role'.

8   When LAP ROUGE appeared on television (in 'Het uur van de wolf', NPS, 15 September 1997), it was introduced with the word 'charlatan', but without explicictly mentioning that the entire film was staged. Possibly, it was not thought necessary because the press had already extensively covered the film. The film follows a tradition on Dutch television of portraying the eccentric in documentary style (e.g. SHOWROOM, PARA-DIJSVOGELS).

Notes to 17: To Lie and to Act: Cinema and Telepresence

1   On presentational system of early cinema, see Charles Musser, *The Emergence of Cinema: The American Screen to 1907*, Berkeley: University of California Press, 1990, p. 3.

2   Paul Johnson, *The Birth of The Modern: World Society 1815-1830*, London: Orion House, 1992, p. 156.

3   Dziga Vertov, 'Kinoki. Perevorot' (Kinoki. A revolution): *LEF* 3, 1923, p. 140.

4   Brenda Laurel, quoted in Rebecca Coyle, 'The Genesis of Virtual Reality', in *Future Visions: New Technologies of the Screen*, edited by Philip Hayward and Tana Wollen, London: British Film Institute, 1993, p. 162.

5   Scott Fisher, 'Visual Interface Environments', in *The Art of Human-Computer Interface Design*, edited by Brenda Laurel, Reading, Mass.: Addison-Wesley Publishing Company, Inc., 1990, p. 430. (Emphasis LM).

6   Fisher defines telepresence as 'a technology which would allow remotely situated operators to receive enough sensory feedback to feel like they are really at a remote location and are able to do diffirent kinds of tasks.' Fisher, p. 427.

7   Bruno Latour, 'Visualization and Cognition: Thinking with Eyes and Hands', *Knowledge and Society: Studies in the sociology of culture past and present* 6 (1986), pp. 1-40.

8   Latour, p. 22.

9   Latour, p. 8.

Notes to 18: Digital Cinema: Delivery, Event, Time

1   See, for instance, Kevin Robbins, 'The Virtual Unconscious in Postphotography', in Tim Druckrey (ed.), *Electronic Culture*, New York: Aperture 1996, pp. 154-163.

2   This has been one of the major conceptual problems of so-called 'screen theory' as well as the 'ontology' of André Bazin it was meant to deconstruct. See the introductions in Phil Rosen (ed.), *Narrative, Apparatus, Ideology*, New York: Columbia University Press, 1985.

3   See also Erkki Huhtamo, 'Time Machines in the Gallery: An Archaeological Approach in Media Art' in Mary Anne Moser (ed.), *Immersed in Technology: Art and Visual Environments*, Cambridge, Mass.: MIT Press, 1996.

4   Despite mature technical solutions, there are doubts if feature films will soon be beamed into theatres. See Kay Hoffmann's essay printed below.

5   The video market is the through-put system, which supplements the cinema's function as the poster-billboard. The video cassette as best-seller has, like the big theatrical release, a relatively short shelf-life and thus in principle needs fewer specialized outlets: if every news-stand or department store can sell the top ten of the month, there is less need for videotheques, would be the conventional argument.

6   '[The production] boom is not in television. It is in theatrical feature films. A feature gets promoted by its theatrical distributor and reviewed in the press. To the cable industry, that is the value of your film: the hoopla that surrounds it. They could not care less about your *chef d'oeuvre* as such. What they buy is the audience awareness of it.' Conrad Schoeffter, above.

7   Companies like Disney or Industrial Light & Magic fund extensive in-house research-and-development units, staffed with the best brains from the MIT media lab.

8   'The cinema of the future will be a simulated roller coaster ride. Go see *Star Tours* at Disneyland. That is the prototype. The cinema auditorium of the future will be a modified flight simulator. You will literally fasten your seat belt for the ultimate flight of fancy. That's why you're seeing alliances forming between the motion picture and aircraft industries.' Conrad Schoeffter, above.

9   See the interview with George Lucas in *Wired*, February 1997, p. 164.

10 '[Real-live action films with actors] may become merely the default values of the system cinema, in the future, all kinds of other options are possible, so that both narrative and live action may seem to be options rather than constitutive features of cinema.' Lev Manovich, 'Digital Cinema' (http://www.jupiter/ucsd.edu/~manovich).

11 'Cinema emerged out of the same impulse which engendered naturalism, court stenography and wax museums. Cinema is the art of the index; it is an attempt to make art out of a footprint.' Lev Manovich, 'Digital Cinema'.

12 'Born from animation, cinema pushed animation to its boundary, only to become one particular case of animation in the end. [...] The same applies for the relationship between production and post-production.' Lev Manovich, 'Digital Cinema'.

13 For an interesting account of this 'expressive' mode in contemporary television, see John T. Caldwell, *Televisuality: Style, Crisis and Authority in American Television*, New Brunswick: Rutgers University Press, 1995.

14 Kevin Kelly and Paula Parisi, Beyond STAR WARS, what's next for George Lucas, *Wired*, February 1997, p. 163.

15 'As a media technology, cinema's role was to capture and to store visible reality. The difficulty of modifying images once they were recorded was exactly what gave cinema its value as a document, assuring its authenticity.' Lev Manovich, 'Digital Cinema'.

16 'The literal interpretation of cinema as a roller coaster ride is brought to the fore whenever a new technology comes along. A new technology comes along whenever television becomes too big. There was a roller coaster ride in THIS IS CINERAMA. One of the first films in Sensurround was called ROLLER COASTER. One of the first IMAX films featured roller coaster and similar rides.' Conrad Schoeffter above.

17 But see Siegfried Zielinski's essay in this volume, significantly predicting even the 'fin de siècle' of television.

18 See, among many possible sources, William J. Mitchell, *City of Bits*, Cambridge, Mass.: MIT Press, 1995.

19 See the studies by Dave Morley, *Family Television*, London: Comedia, 1987, and Ien Ang, *Living Room Wars*, London: Routledge, 1994.

20 See Jane Feuer, 'The Concept of Live Television – Ontology as Ideology', in E.Ann Kaplan (ed.) *Regarding Television*, Los Angeles: American Film Institute, 1983, pp. 12-22, and Fredric Jameson, 'Reading without Interpretation: postmodernism and the video text' in Colin MacCabe et.al. (eds.) *The linguistics of writing*, Manchester: Manchester University Press, 1987, pp. 199-223.

21 Thomas Elsaesser, 'TV through the Looking-Glass', in N. Browne (ed.), *American Television*, Langhorne, PA: Harwood, 1993, 97-120.

22 The concept of segmented flow was introduced by John Ellis, *Visible Fictions*, London: Routledge, 1983.

23 'Television's greatest prowess is its ability to be there – both on the scene and in your living room (hence the most catastrophic of technical catastrophes is the loss of signal.' Mary Ann Doane, 'Information, Crisis, Catastrophe', in Patricia Mellencamp, *Logics of Television*, London and Bloomington: BFI Publishing and Indiana University Press, 1990, p. 238.

24 For an extensive discussion of media-events, see Daniel Dayan and Elihu Katz, *Media Events*, Cambridge: Harvard University Press, 1994.

25 Unlike a true Mexican stand-off, however, this one played relatively briefly, since David Kuresh, his headquarters and his followers were soon consumed by flames or choked in the smoke. What one remembers are the wind-blown, undulating images, taken with a static camera, extremely long focal lens and held for what seemed like hours, reminiscent at once of a film by Andy Warhol and a Bill Viola video-piece.

26 Mary Ann Doane, in Mellencamp, pp. 227-228.

27 Television 'transforms record into actuality or immediacy', Mary Ann Doane, in Mellencamp, p. 228.

28 See Thomas Elsaesser, 'One Train May be Hiding Another', in *The Lowlands: Yearbook of Dutch and Flemish Studies*, Rekkem: Stichting Ons Erfdeel, 1996.

29 For more detailed information about the history of exhibition practice, see Charles Musser, *The Emergence of cinema I: The American Screen to 1907* (New York: Scribners, 1991) and Douglas Gomery, *Shared Pleasures: A History of Movie Presentation in the United States*, Madison: University of Wisconsin Press, 1992.

30 Among (German) art cinema directors, Edgar Reitz has always pleaded for the event-status of the cinema. See his paper in Kraft Wetzel (ed.), *Neue Medien gegen Filmkultur?*, Berlin: Volker Spiess, 1987, p. 140.

31 'Gespräch mit Edgar Reitz', *Telepolis* no. 2, June 1997, p. 71.

32 John Ellis, above.

33 'Interview with Gianni Amelio' in Kraft Wetzel (ed.), *Neue Medien contra Filmkultur?*, Berlin: Volker Spiess, 1987, p. 33.

34 Isabelle Raynaud, 'Multi-Media Interactive', lecture given in Amsterdam, 7 June 1996.

35 For a more detailed discussion, see Jay David Bolter, *Writing Space: The Computer, Hypertext, and the History of Writing*, Hillsdale, NJ: Lawrence Erlbaum Associates, 1991.

36 See Andy Cameron, 'Simulations', *WWW.Hypermedia Research Centre*, p.4

37 The book, of course, has always known random access of a fairly extensive kind: pagination, chapter headings provide sophisticated navigational tools, as does size, allowing one to skip and assess at a glance how far one is from the end.

38 See Lev Manovich, 'To Lie and to Act: Cinema and Telepresence', above.

39 See his essay below, as well as Grahame Weinbren, 'Interactive Cinema', *New Observations* no. 70, New York, 1989, and also 'In the Ocean of Streams of Story' in *Millennium Film Journal* no. 28, Spring 1995.

40 Andy Cameron, 'Simulations', *WWW.Hypermedia Research Centre* (n.d.) p. 4.

41 Walter Benjamin, 'The Work of Art in the Age of Mechanical Reproduction', in *Illuminations* (edited by Hannah Arendt), New York: Schocken, 1969, pp. 222-223.

Notes to 19: The Television Screen: from Spoil-sport to Game-maker

1   The following information comes from Julian Hochberg,'Representation of motion and space in video and cinematic displays', in K.R. Boff, L. Kaufman, J.P. Thomas (eds.), *Handbook of Perception and Human Performance, vol I: Sensory processes and perception*, New York: Wiley, 1986,, pp. 22/1-22/64.

2   The following is from Negroponte, in *Scientific American*, September 1991, pp. 76-83.

3   Conway has proven that his cellular automaton 'Life' is 'undecidable'. It is impossible to make out whether the patterns generated are endlessly varied or ultimately repeat themselves.

4   J. Horgan, 'The Death of Proof', in *Scientific American*, October 1993, pp. 75-82.

Notes to 20: Random Access Rules

1   Grahame Weinbren, 'In The Ocean of Streams of Story', *Millenium Film Journal* no 28, Spring 1995 ('Interactivities').

2   Sigmund Freud, 'From the History of an Infantile Neurosis' in *The Wolf Man by The Wolf Man*, New York: Basic Books, 1971, p. 173.

3   An abbreviated version on the web at: http://www2.sva.edu/ken/jcj1.html.

4   Bar Code Hotel is represented on the web at: http://www.portola.com/people/perry/BarCodeHotel/index.html.

5   For more examples of Simon's work there are three drawings at http://www.users.interport.net/~gering/jfsjr.html and four drawings at http://www.plexus.org/simon.html. These sites also contain links to other projects by the artist.

6   Umberto Eco, 'The Poetics of the Open Work', from *The Open Work* pp. 15, 19, reprinted in Umberto Eco, *The Open Work*, tr. Anna Concogni, Cambridge Massachussetts: Harvard University Press: 1989.

Notes to 21: Electronic Cinema: On the Way to the Digital

1   John Chittcock, 'Back to the Future: the Cinema's Lessons of History', in Christopher Williams (ed.), *Cinema: the Beginnings and the Future*, London: University of Westminister Press, 1996, p. 224.

2   Kevin Kelly and Paula Parisi, 'Beyond STAR WARS, what's next for George Lucas', *Wired*, February 1997, p. 165.

3   James Sterngold, 'Digital Studios: It's the Economy, Stupid – George Lucas Sees Technology as a Wondrous Tool and a Cost-Cutter', *The New York Times*, 25 December 1995.

4   Albert Abramson, *Electronic Motion Picture, A History of the Television Camera*, Berkeley/Los Angeles: University of California Press, 1955, p. 1.

5   For a more detailed account, see Siegfried Zielinski, *Zur Geschichte des Videorecorders*, Berlin: Spiess Verlag 1986.

6   See Kay Hoffmann, *Am Ende Video – Video am Ende? Aspekte der Elektronisierung der Spielfilmproduktion*, Berlin: Edition sigma 1990.

7   'Mating Film with Video for ONE FROM THE HEART', *American Cinematographer*, 1/1982, p. 22.

8   'Coppola's Electronic Cinema System', *American Cinematographer*, 8/1982, pp. 777-781.

9   Kevin Kelly and Paula Parisi, 'Beyond STARWARS, what's next for George Lucas', *Wired*, February 1997, pp. 162-165.

10   Kay Hoffmann, 'Keine Konserve: Edgar Reitz zur Zukunft des Kinos', *KulturNews*, 1/1997, p. 14.

11   Kevin Kelly and Paula Parisi, 'Beyond STARWARS, what's next for George Lucas', *Wired*, February 1997, p. 212.

Notes to 22: The Assault of Computer-generated Worlds on the Rest of Time

1   The title is a reference to the film by Alexander Kluge THE ATTACK OF CONTEMPORARY REALITY ON THE REST OF TIME (1985).

2   It is widely accepted that the term 'Cyberspace' was coined in 1984 by the sci-fi author William Gibson in his novel *Neuromancer* ('Cyberspace. A consensual hallucination experienced daily by billions of legitimate operators, in every nation, by children being taught mathematical concepts... A graphic representation of data abstracted from the banks of every computer in the human system. Unthinkable complexity. Lines of light arranged in the nonspace of the mind, clusters and constellations of data...'' – William Gibson (William Gibson: *Neuromancer*; New York 1984, p. 51)). 'Present incarnation: the 'Internet'. Also known as: the 'Net', the 'Web', the 'Matrix'." (WWW: Mark/Space Anachron City Library: Cyberspace;) in the narrow sense 'Cyberspace' could be almost identical to 'virtual reality'. For Virtual reality (VR – also known as 'artificial reality', 'virtual worlds', 'virtualities'." (WWW: Mark/Space Anachron City Library: Virtual reality)) I suggest the following definition: a reality not made up of atoms but of bits (For the definition of 'bit' compare: Ein Bit – das unbekannte Wesen; in Nicholas Negroponte: *Total Digital. Die Welt zwischen 1 und 0 oder die Zukunft der Kommunikation*, Munich, 1995, pp. 22-26). VR refers to the playful or artistic forms, rather than the narrative development, and is based on multi-dimensional spaces. The term 'Cyberspace' is often used for the entire computer network with all its game possibilities, also in WWW:Mark/Space Anachron City Library. Here VR is described as 'a visual form of cyberspace'.

3   'Used today in architecture, engineering and design, tomorrow in mass market entertainment, surrogate travel, virtual surgery and cybersex, by the next century VR will have transformed our lives' (in Virtual Reality, 1991; quoted from WWW:Mark/ Space Anachron City Library: Virtual Reality)

4   Among the many publications, cf e.g. 'Archaeologische Simulation zwischen lineare Medien und virtuellem Museum'; in Kay Hoffmann (ed.), *Trau-Schau-Wem. Digitalisierung und dokumentarische Form*, Konstanz: WK Medien, 1997.

5   Joachim Paech: 'Der Schatten auf dem Bild, Vom filmischen zum elektronischen "Schreiben mit Licht" oder "L'image menacé par l'écriture et sauvé par l'image même"'; Michael Wentzel, Herta Wolf in: *Der Entzug der Bilder. Visuelle Realitäten;.* Munich 1984, pp. 213-233, p. 231.

6   Horst Bredekamp: 'Politische Theorien des Cyberspace'; in: *Die Frage nach dem Kunstwerk unter den heutigen Bildern*; Hans Belting, Siegfried Gohr (eds.), Stuttgart 1996, pp. 31-50, p. 44.

7   To avoid great excitement: in the light of my later exposition it would be correct to offer several versions of reality, i.e., goal and non-goal, and then to destroy the so-called original.

8   Lauren Goldstein, 'The black lot', *Premiere*, January 1996, p. 91.

9   See Martin Emele, *Neue und Alte Mythen in den deutschen Medien – Troia und Schliemann* (forthcoming).

10   Bill Lyons/Michael Wood, *In Search of the Trojan War*, BBC 1986.

11   Peter Conolly, *The Legend of Odysseus*, Oxford: OUP, 1986.

12   Süddeutsche Rundfunk Stuttgart TV programme, 'Abenteuer Wissenschaft', Südwest 3, aired 4.12.1989.

13 Eberhard Thiem, Helga Lippert, Arno Peik: Terra X – Rätsel alter Weltkulturen, Kreuzfahrt mit Odysseus, Teil 1: Von Troja zur Insel des Windes; ZDF, 23.12.90, 7.30pm, 45 mins, Editor: Thomas Morgott-Carqueville, scientific consultant: Dr. Armin Wolf, producer: Gottfried Kirchner.

14 Thiem/Lippert/Peik: Kreuzfahrt 1; at 9 mins, 30 secs.

15 See Kay Hoffmann, 'Funde im Netz. Archäologie zum Anklicken – eine multimediale Spurensuche', *Antike Welt* 2/97, pp. 135-139, p. 135.

16 For the 'classical' documentary filmmaker it is a decisive experience when people who otherwise always deal with fixed conditions of rooms and objects are suddenly expected to make rooms and objects out of the (in this case black) void. Even an invisible sky has to be present, to allow reflections on the objects.

17 Horst Bredekamp: 'Politische Theorien des Cyberspace'; in: Hans Belting, Siegfried Gohr (eds.), *Die Frage nach dem Kunstwerk unter den heutigen Bildern*, Stuttgart 1996, pp. 31-50, p. 45.

18 Hodder, Interview with the author, 1997.

19 Hodder, Loc. cit.

20 See http://catal.arch.cam.ac.uk//catal/catal.html and http://www.hfg-karlsruhe.de/projects/vam/index.html

21 Hodder, loc. cit.

22 Hodder, loc. cit.

23 I am grateful to Jörg Berdeux at the Karlsruhe University for explanation and inspiration.

24 Eckhard Siepmann, 'Subjektivität und Museum'. Opening lecture at the Bundeskongress des Verbands der Museumpädagogen in Berlin, 19.10.1994; manuscript p. 14.

25 Gottfried Korff, 'Paradigmwechsel im Museum?', in *Ohne Titel. Sichern unter... Unbeständige Ausstellung der Bestände des Werkbund-Archivs*; ed. by Werkbund -Archiv, Berlin 1995, pp. 22-32, p. 27. Korff is referring to real objects.

26 Hodder, loc. cit.

27 See Yvonne Spielmann, 'Bausteine zu einer Theorie intermedialer Bildgestaltung', in: *Die Frage nach dem Kunstwerk unter den heutigen Bildern*; ed. by Hans Belting and Siegfried Gohr, Stuttgart 1996, pp. 139-162, p. 148; and Fredric Jameson, 'Postmoderne und Utopie', in *Postmoderne – globale Differenz*; ed. by Robert Weinemann and Hans Ulrich Gumbrecht, Frankfurt 1991, pp. 73-109.

28 Hodder, loc. cit.

29 Eckhard Siepmann. 'CD-ROM: Lumpensammler im Datenraum', in *Ohne Titel. Sichern unter... Unbeständige Ausstellung der Bestände des Werkbund-Archivs*; ed. by Werbund-Archiv, Berlin 1995, pp. 72-79, p. 75.

30 Korff, loc. cit.

31 Eckhard Siepmann, 'Subjektivität und Museum'. Opening lecture at the Bundeskongress des Verbands der Museumpädagogen in Berlin, 19.10.94; manuscript p. 5.

32 Hodder, loc. cit.

33 See the questionnaire included in *Antike Welt* no 2/1997.

34 Horst Bredekamp, 'Politische Theorien des Cyberspace', in *Die Frage nach dem Kunstwerk unter den heutigen Bildern*; ed. by Hans Belting and Siegfried Gohr, Stuttgart 1996, pp. 31-50, p. 45.

35 Eckhard Siepmann. 'CD-ROM: Lumpensammler im Datenraum', in *Ohne Titel. Sichern unter... Unbeständige Ausstellung der Bestände des Werkbund-Archivs*; ed. by Werbund-Archiv, Berlin 1995, pp. 72-79, p. 77.

36 With reference to the (distorted) images of this mirror, I am rather pessimistic. Science fiction novels have considered this for some time. High culture and education cannot be expected here, according to them. The manifestation of the new virtual world is the cyberclown AWGY; Auggie, hero of the novel "Die Stunde des Clowns", who develops radical ideas. Everything which the subject thinks up must have an effect in reality on the subject. Accordingly, Auggie, an imaginary figure created by various users, develops its own consciousness, which is a collective consciousness and which has an effect on each of its users and creators. The new technology therefore gives us the chance of again ruminating over the possibility that a fantasy figure, as a concrete mythical being out of a book, film and now out of the net, is a real threat to everyday life. Where previously Dracula, the Golem, and the machine man seemed possibilities, there is now the virtual, not even atomic, clown, who is all the more threatening. (Cf Cole Perriman: *Terminal Games*, New York 1994).

Index